Situational Prevention of Organised Crimes

Crime Science Series

Series editor: Gloria Laycock

Published titles

Superhighway Robbery: Preventing e-commerce crime, by Graeme R. Newman and Ronald V. Clarke

Crime Reduction and Problem-oriented Policing, edited by Karen Bullock and Nick Tilley

Crime Science: New approaches to preventing and detecting crime, edited by Melissa J. Smith and Nick Tilley

Problem-oriented Policing and Partnerships: Implementing an evidence-based approach to crime reduction, by Karen Bullock, Rosie Erol and Nick Tilley

Preventing Child Sexual Abuse: Evidence, policy and practice, by Stephen Smallbone, William L. Marshall and Richard Wortley

Environmental Criminology and Crime Analysis, edited by Richard Wortley and Lorraine Mazerolle

Raising the Bar: Preventing aggression in and around bars, pubs and clubs, by Kathryn Graham and Ross Homel

Situational Prevention of Organised Crimes
Edited by Karen Bullock, Ronald V. Clarke and Nick Tilley

Situational Prevention of Organised Crimes

Edited by
Karen Bullock, Ronald V. Clarke
and Nick Tilley

LONDON AND NEW YORK

First published by Willan Publishing 2010
This edition published by Routledge 2012
2 Park Square, Milton Park, Abingdon, Oxon OX14 4RN
711 Third Avenue, New York, NY 10017

Routledge is an imprint of the Taylor & Francis Group, an informa business

© The editors and contributors 2010

All rights reserved; no part of this publication may be reproduced, stored in a retrieval system, or transmitted in any form or by any means, electronic, mechanical, photocopying, recording or otherwise without the prior written permission of the Publishers or a licence permitting copying in the UK issued by the Copyright Licensing Agency Ltd, Saffron House, 6–10 Kirby Street, London EC1N 8TS.

ISBN 978-1-84392-772-3 hardback
ISBN 978-0-415-62803-7 paperback

British Library Cataloguing-in-Publication Data

A catalogue record for this book is available from the British Library

Project managed by Deer Park Productions, Tavistock, Devon
Typeset by TW Typesetting, Plymouth, Devon

Contents

Abbreviations	*vii*
Figures and tables	*viii*
Notes on contributors	*ix*
Foreword by Gloria Laycock	*xv*
Preface Karen Bullock, Ronald V. Clarke and Nick Tilley	*xvii*
1 Introduction Karen Bullock, Ronald V. Clarke and Nick Tilley	1
2 Situational crime prevention and cross-border crime Edward R. Kleemans, Melvin R.J. Soudijn and Anton W. Weenink	17
3 Preventing organised crime: the case of contraband cigarettes Klaus von Lampe	35
4 Sex trafficking: a target for situational crime prevention? James O. Finckenauer and Ko-lin Chin	58
5 Situational prevention of organised timber theft and related corruption Adam Graycar and Marcus Felson	81
6 Situational organised crime prevention in Amsterdam: the administrative approach Hans Nelen	93
7 Mortgage fraud and facilitating circumstances Barbra van Gestel	111
8 Infiltration of the public construction industry by Italian organised crime Ernesto U. Savona	130
9 Situational prevention against unlawful influence from organised crime Lars Korsell and Johanna Skinnari	151

10 Organised crime and crime scripts: prospects for disruption   172
    Graham Hancock and Gloria Laycock

11 Policing mobile criminality: towards a situational crime
    prevention approach to organised crime   193
    Stuart Kirby and Sue Penna

Index   213

Abbreviations

ACPO	Association of Chief Police Officers
ALPR	Automatic Licence Plate Recognition
AML Regulations	Anti Money Laundering Regulations
BCS	British Crime Survey
BIBOB Act	Public Administration Probity Screening Act (in the Netherlands)
BKA	Bundeskriminalamt (German Federal Crime Intelligence Office)
Brå	Brottsförebyggande rådet (Swedish National Council for Crime Prevention)
CITES	Convention on International Trade in Endangered Species of Wild Flora and Fauna
CPIA	Criminal Procedures and Investigation Act (1996)
EPSRC	Engineering and Physical Sciences Research Council
FATF	Financial Action Task Force
FIU	Financial Intelligence Unit (in the Netherlands)
HMRC	Her Majesty's Revenue and Customs
HSE	Health and Safety Executive
ICE	Immigration and Customs Enforcement (in the USA)
IOM	International Organisation for Migration
MCA	Marine Coastguard Agency
NGO	Non-governmental organisation
NIJ	National Institute of Justice, US Department of Justice
NIM	National Intelligence Model
NCIS	National Criminal Intelligence Service
OCG	Organised crime group
RIEC	Regional Intelligence and Expertise Centre (in the Netherlands)
RILO	Regional Intelligence Liaison Office for Western Europe
SAR	Suspicious activity report
SBA	Bureau for Screening and Auditing (in the Netherlands)
SCP	Situational crime prevention
SCPO	Serious Crime Prevention Order
SIO	Senior investigating officer
SOCA	Serious Organised Crime Agency
SOCPA	Serious Organised Crime and Police Act 2005
SOCU	Serious and Organised Crime Unit
TIR	Transport International Routier
UNODC	United Nations Office on Drugs and Crime
WODC	Research and Documentation Centre (in the Netherlands)

Figures and tables

Figures

10.1 Representation of the constituent parts of organised crime — 177

Tables

1.1	Twenty-five techniques of situational prevention	3
1.2	Two models of organised crime	7
1.3	Facilitating conditions that enable theft of cars for export	8
1.4	Step-by-step modus operandi for trafficking in stolen cars	9
6.1	Intervention techniques within the framework of the Van Traa Project	99
6.2	Intervention techniques within the framework of the SBA Bureau	103
6.3	Intervention techniques within the framework of the Integrity Bureau	106
9.1	Preventive methods against unlawful influence from organised crime	167
10.1	Robbery script	173
10.2	Breakdown of prepay mobile phone use for operations A, B and H	180
10.3	The integrated organised crime script	186

Notes on contributors

Karen Bullock is a lecturer in criminology at the University of Surrey. She holds a PhD from the University of London and spent almost 10 years as a researcher at the UK Home Office. Her research interests lie primarily in crime reduction, policing and interventions with offenders.

Ko-lin Chin is Professor, School of Criminal Justice at Rutgers University, Newark, New Jersey. He is author of *Chinese Subculture and Criminality: Non-traditional Crime Groups in America* (Greenwood Press 1990), *Chinatown Gangs: Extortion, Enterprise and Ethnicity* (Oxford University Press 1996), *Smuggled Chinese: Clandestine Immigration to the United States* (Temple University Press 1999), *Heijin: Organized Crime, Business, and Politics in Taiwan* (M.E. Sharpe 2003), *The Golden Triangle: Inside Southeast Asia's Drug Trade* (Cornell University Press 2009) and co-editor of *Handbook of Organized Crime in the United States* (Greenwood Press 1994). Currently, he is conducting a research project on sex trafficking in Asia and the US with Professor James O. Finckenauer.

Ronald V. Clarke is University Professor at the School of Criminal Justice, Rutgers University. Trained as a psychologist, he holds a PhD from the University of London. Dr Clarke was employed for 15 years in the British Government's criminology research department, where he had a significant role in the development of situational crime prevention and the British Crime Survey. He is founding editor of *Crime Prevention Studies* and is author or joint author of more than 220 publications, including, *The Reasoning Criminal* (Springer-Verlag 1986), *Situational Crime Prevention: Successful Case Studies* (Harrow and Heston 1997), *Become a Problem Solving Crime Analyst* (Jill Dando Institute 2003) and *Outsmarting the Terrorists* (Praeger 2006).

Marcus Felson is Professor of Criminal Justice at Rutgers University. He is author of *Crime and Nature* (SAGE Publications 2006) and *Crime and Everyday Life* (SAGE Publications, fourth edition, 2010). He originated the routine activity approach to crime rate analysis, and is currently studying the co-offending process. A graduate of the University of Chicago, he received his PhD from the University of Michigan. Professor Felson works on very down-to-earth theories with very tangible applications. Professor Felson has been a guest lecturer in many nations throughout the world.

He has given talks on crime to applied mathematicians at several universities, including UCLA, Rutgers, and at the Centro di Ricerca Matematica Ennio De Giorgi Scuola Normale Superiore, Pisa, Italy.

James O. Finckenauer is Professor II (Distinguished Professor) at the Rutgers University School of Criminal Justice in Newark, NJ. From 1998–2002, he was Director of the International Center at the National Institute of Justice of the US Department of Justice, while on academic leave. Dr Finckenauer's research and teaching interests include international and comparative criminal justice, transnational organised crime, and criminal justice policy, planning and evaluation. He is the author, co-author or co-editor of nine books – including his most recent one on the Mafia – as well as numerous articles, chapters and reports.

Barbra van Gestel is researcher at the Research and Documentation Centre (WODC), Dutch Ministry of Justice. She has published on the interplay between media and law enforcement, crime in the housing sector and on policy to combat human trafficking.

Adam Graycar is Professor in the Research School of Social Sciences at the Australian National University in Canberra. Previous posts have included: Dean of the School of Criminal Justice at Rutgers University; Director of the Rutgers Institute on Corruption Studies; Head of the Cabinet Office, Government of South Australia; and Director of the Australian Institute of Criminology.

Graham Hancock is a senior manager in the UK Serious Organised Crime Agency (SOCA). Previously he was an officer with Essex Police and spent time on the National Crime Squad during which time he led on investigations into organised crime (primarily drug, people and firearms trafficking). He has also spent time at the Home Office looking at joint working initiatives on reducing the supply of firearms into and within the UK. He has an MSc in Crime Science from University College London.

Stuart Kirby completed a 30-year career with the Lancashire Constabulary in 2007. His final post, as Detective Chief Superintendent in command of the specialist Crime and Operations Division, had responsibility for the investigation of terrorism, homicide and organised crime. During his career he commanded many overt and covert policing operations and was also deployed as a hostage negotiator. He was also twice recipient of the UK Problem Oriented Policing award. Since leaving the police force he has become a lecturer in Criminology at Lancaster University where he has maintained an academic interest in offender behaviour, policing and the investigation of serious crime.

Notes on contributors

Edward R. Kleemans is Professor at the Faculty of Law of Vrije Universiteit, Amsterdam (Serious and Organised Crime and Criminal Justice) and Head of the Crime, Law Enforcement and Sanctions Research Division of the Research and Documentation Centre (WODC), Dutch Ministry of Justice. He coordinates the Organised Crime Monitor, which published reports to Parliament in 1998, 2002 and 2007. He has published on organised crime, drugs, drug trafficking, human smuggling and human trafficking, frequent offenders, urban crime patterns, rational choice theories, theoretical developments, criminal careers, developmental and life-course criminology, and repeat victimisation. He has been co-editor of the *Dutch Journal of Criminology* since 2000.

Lars Korsell is a lawyer, doctor in criminology and head of a research unit at the Swedish National Council for Crime Prevention in Stockholm. His main fields of research are economic and organised crime. He has also used situational crime prevention in several works on, for example, methods to prevent economic crime, preventing cheats and fiddles and the structure of corruption in Sweden.

Klaus von Lampe is assistant professor at John Jay College of Criminal Justice, Department of Law, Police Science and Criminal Justice Administration, in New York. He is originally from Germany where he has practised law as an attorney and worked as a researcher at Freie Universität Berlin. His research interests include the conceptual history and theory of organised crime, the empirical manifestations of organised crime in the form of cigarette smuggling, drug trafficking and underworld power structures, and strategic analysis in the area of organised crime. Dr von Lampe is the author, co-author and co-editor of numerous journal articles and books on crime, crime control and crime analysis. He is editor-in-chief of the journal *Trends in Organized Crime* and associate editor of *Crime, Law and Social Change*.

Gloria Laycock graduated in psychology from University College London in 1968 and completed her PhD at UCL in 1975. She worked in the Home Office for over 30 years of which almost 20 were spent on research and development in the policing and crime prevention fields. She has extensive research experience in the UK and has acted as a consultant on policing and crime prevention in North America, Australia, New Zealand, Israel, South Africa and Europe. She is currently an advisor to HEUNI, a UN-affiliated crime prevention organisation based in Helsinki. She is currently Head of the UCL Department of Security and Crime Science, Director of the UCL Jill Dando Institute of Security and Crime Science and Director of the new £7 million Engineering and Physical Sciences Research Council (EPSRC)-funded Doctoral Training Centre in Security Science at UCL. She was awarded an OBE in the Queen's Birthday Honours 2008 for services to crime policy.

Hans Nelen is professor of criminology of the faculty of law at Maastricht University, the Netherlands. Between 1986 and the beginning of 2001 he was employed as a senior researcher and research supervisor at the Research and Documentation Centre of the Ministry of Justice in the Netherlands (WODC), mainly involved in drug, fraud, organised crime, corporate crime and police research. Between 2001 and 2006 he was associate professor and senior researcher at the Institute of Criminology of the Vrije Universiteit, Amsterdam. During the last decade Nelen has published several books and articles on a variety of criminological subjects, i.e. corruption and fraud, dilemmas facing lawyers and notaries, the administrative approach to organised crime, the proceeds-of-crime approach, drugs, evaluation of legislation, and evaluation of law enforcement activities.

Sue Penna is Senior Lecturer in Applied Social Science at Lancaster University. Her research interests are in the fields of policy as a technology of governance; organised crime; the interface between social welfare and criminal justice; and theories of social change. She is the author of *Theorising Welfare. Enlightenment and Modern Society* (Sage, with Martin O'Brien) and co-editor of *Theorising Modernity* (Pearson).

Ernesto U. Savona has been Professor of Criminology at the Università Cattolica del Sacro Cuore in Milan since 2003. He is also Director of TRANSCRIME, a Joint Research Centre of the Università degli Studi di Trento and the Università Cattolica del Sacro Cuore. Professor Savona's research activity has centred on the analysis of crime statistics, law and social change, effectiveness of legislation, organised/economic crime and criminal justice systems, crime and economics and corruption. He has recently concentrated his research on developing a methodology to measure the impact of legislation. Professor Savona was nominated President of the European Society of Criminology for the years 2003/2004 and has been consultant to the United Nations, Council of Europe, the European Union and various national governments. In 2003 he was appointed Editor-in-Chief of the *European Journal on Criminal Policy and Research*, an international refereed journal published by Springer, and is on the editorial board of the *Journal Sociologia del Diritto*.

Johanna Skinnari is a researcher at the Swedish National Council for Crime Prevention in Stockholm. Her main fields of research are organised crime and unlawful influence, for example the financial management of organised drug crime, illicit money in Swedish casinos, the exertion of unlawful influence on public servants and police encounters with organised crime.

Notes on contributors

Melvin R.J. Soudijn is Senior Researcher at the National Crime Squad of the Netherlands Police Agency. He has published on Chinese human smuggling, organised crime, art crime, and drug trafficking. His current research is primarily focused on money laundering.

Nick Tilley is a professor in the Department of Security and Crime Science at University College London. He is interested in theoretically informed applied social science, especially as this relates to the prevention of crime and disorder. He has published a dozen books and more than 150 reports, chapters and journal articles, mostly relating to policing, crime reduction and programme evaluation methodology.

Anton W. Weenink is Senior Researcher at the National Crime Squad of the Netherlands Police Agency. He has published on Russian reform, East European organised crime, the arms trade, terrorism, and crime in the Caribbean.

Foreword

Gloria Laycock

Countering organised crime is one of the major challenges of the twenty-first century. As globalisation develops and the world becomes more interconnected the opportunities for crime grow commensurately. Situational crime prevention (SCP) is an approach to crime control based on the notion that a major driver for crime is opportunity. It is, therefore, perhaps a little surprising that it has not been much in evidence in the academic literature on the control of organised crime despite the considerable literature demonstrating its success in preventing a wide variety of other types of offending such as burglary, theft, car crime and many aspects of violence including terrorism (see issues of *Crime Prevention Studies* edited by Ron Clarke for numerous examples, and specifically Clarke and Newman 2006 on counter-terrorism).

As many crime scientists will know, SCP calls for the systematic analysis of the crime problem, an identification of the facilitating opportunity structures and the introduction of measures to block, reduce or remove the opportunities which enable the offending to take place. A careful evaluation of the effects might lead to some modification of the response or to a real reduction in the presenting offending. This is known as action research.

One of the advantages of this approach is that it opens up a much richer range of crime control techniques than the usual law enforcement response of detection and conviction. SCP stresses the importance of preventing or disrupting the offending, not simply responding to it through the criminal justice system. And there is far more to it than the traditional target hardening with which it is so closely associated. It includes, for example, increasing perceived risk which can be introduced not only at the level of the individual but also directed at groups or associations of offenders. Kennedy's (2008) groundbreaking work in this area illustrates the potential power of the approach in reducing gun crime and controlling open drug markets, both of which are variously linked to organised criminal activities.

Why then has there been relatively little application to the challenges of tackling organised criminal activities of what looks like a promising set of techniques? Perhaps one of the major reasons is that the activities associated with the offending itself are complex and may run over a prolonged period involving a number of individuals who may or may not be connected in any permanent sense. Knowledge about the offending process is hard to come by; it may be partial and the interests of the law enforcement agencies are primarily detection/conviction focused rather than being targeted at the more comprehensive understanding of the whole crime process itself. In other words it is difficult, time-consuming and calls for rather different skills than those normally held by policing agencies.

Despite the difficulties there are encouraging signs that the attention of some academics is now turning to ways in which the more systematic application of this approach to organised crime might develop. This book pulls together work from a number of these academics who have experience of both organised crime and situational crime prevention. The contributions illustrate the potential of the approach, although most authors would probably agree that there remains much more work to do if the systematic application of situational techniques is to become anywhere near standard practice for the law enforcement agencies concerned with the control of these offences.

Gloria Laycock
Series Editor
UCL Jill Dando Institute of Security and Crime Science

References

Clarke, R. and Newman, G. (2006) *Outsmarting the Terrorists*. Westport CT: Praeger Security International.
Kennedy, D. (2008) *Deterrence and Crime Prevention*. London: Routledge.

Preface

This book brings together revised versions of invited papers first presented at a conference on Situational Crime Prevention and Organised Crime that was held at Cumberland Lodge in Great Windsor Park on 23–25 March 2009. The attendees included Jyoti Belur, Karen Bullock, Ronald Clarke, Jim Finckenauer, Adam Graycar, Graham Hancock, Stuart Kirby, Edward Kleemans, Lars Korsell, Gloria Laycock, Mangai Natarajan, Hans Nelen, Ernesto Savona, Johanna Skinnari, Nick Tilley, Henk Van de Bunt and Klaus von Lampe.

The only paper included in this collection that was not presented at the Cumberland Lodge meeting is that by Stuart Kirby and Sue Penna. All papers presented at the meeting were critically discussed at some length and were then revised in light of the remarks made. Following this the revised versions were submitted to the editors, who sent them out for refereeing. Referees' and editors' suggestions were then fed back to the authors, who went on to produce the versions that appear here. Kirby and Penna's paper was refereed in the same way as the others. Following a modest amount of moral pressure and bullying the contributors and referees kept pretty well to the deadlines set for them. We appreciate the efforts of all involved in helping bring this project to its conclusion.

Most of the refereeing was undertaken by those at the meeting, although we are grateful also to Cris Coxon, Paul Ekblom, Niall Hamilton-Smith, Johannes Knutsson, Simon Mackenzie and Graeme Newman for commenting on some of the papers.

The meeting was funded and organised by UCL's Jill Dando Institute of Crime Science, with support from Rutgers University, New Jersey. We thank Gloria Laycock and Adam Graycar for arranging this funding. Thanks are also due to the excellent administrative work of the UCL staff and for the magnificent hospitality provided at Cumberland Lodge.

Karen Bullock
Ronald V. Clarke
Nick Tilley

Chapter 1

Introduction

Karen Bullock, Ronald V. Clarke and Nick Tilley

This collection examines the scope for tackling organised crimes through situational techniques and some of the opportunities and challenges this entails. This introduction begins by describing the core ideas drawn upon in the chapters that follow for those readers who may not be familiar with what is meant by 'situational crime prevention' and by 'organised crime'. It also outlines what we believe is needed in the study of organised crime for the purpose of devising situational interventions.

What is situational crime prevention?

Situational crime prevention focuses on crimes rather than criminals. It targets the near causes of crime events, primarily the availability of opportunities founded in routine activities, rather than the distant causes of offenders' criminality such as poverty or inequality. It tries to identify practical ways in which opportunities for the commission of crimes may be reduced or their harms minimised. The focus of situational crime prevention is on specific offences rather than on crime in general. Undertaking situational crime prevention involves the analysis of subsets of offences with common opportunity structures with a view to homing in on modifiable conditions that enable or encourage the crime. The methods used are those of action research. That is, specific crimes are taken, the opportunity structures enabling them are identified, interventions are put in place to try to close the opportunity and the effects are then assessed to check whether or not the strategy has worked. If it has not, some other element in the opportunity structure may be sought to see whether the crime can be reduced by attending to it.

Situational crime prevention is underpinned by 'rational choice' theory. This contends that offenders' behaviour is purposive, is orientated to obtaining utilities of some sort, and that real and perceived changes in risk, effort and reward can affect decisions. It further draws on 'routine activities theory'. That is the idea that changes in everyday life alter the supply, distribution and movement of suitable targets for crime, capable guardians, and likely offenders. Further it is informed by 'crime pattern theory'. This takes the view that the spatial distribution of crime is a function of the everyday patterns of work, play and residence that bring potential offenders into contact with crime targets where the risks of being caught and recognised are relatively low. The processes involved in delivering situational crime prevention additionally have much in common with problem-oriented policing. Reflecting the action model described above, problem-oriented policing is concerned with detailed analysis of recurring crime problems, the identification of features of that problem at which preventative action may be targeted and a commitment to evaluation of any interventions.

Situational crime prevention and its cognate theories contrast with other criminological approaches to explaining and controlling crime. These have focused overwhelmingly on offenders and groups of offenders. They have been concerned more with the drivers of criminality than with the nature of the crimes themselves. The dispositions of individuals and groups to commit crime are of chief interest. Policies and practices in turn have attended to the factors which have been assumed to lead a person to become involved in crime in the first place or lead those already involved to desist from their criminal ways. The underlying assumption has often been that unless criminal dispositions are dealt with effectively overall crime levels will not be reduced and if the opportunity for one crime is removed, another will take its place through processes of 'displacement'.

Elaboration of the theories of situational crime prevention goes back some 30 years. The practice of situational prevention of crime and predation, however, is ubiquitous: it is found in all places, at all times and amongst the animal as well as human populations. Processes of evolution have led to the survival of those who are adequately protected against predators. Over the past 30 years many techniques of situational crime prevention have been elaborated and these fall under five main headings: reduction in reward; increase in difficulty; increase in effort; reduction in provocation; and removal of excuses (see Table 1.1).

These techniques have been widely adopted. There have further been significant developments in methods of analysing crime problems that can help identify pinch-points for intervention (immediate features of the opportunity structure for crime that may be open to closure). An important development has been the 'crime script', which describes the essential steps involved in the crime (Cornish 1994). Once identified the crime script can help reveal those points where measures might plausibly be applied to optimise the preventive pay-off.

Table 1.1 Twenty-five techniques of situational prevention

Increase the effort	Increase the risks	Reduce the rewards	Reduce provocations	Remove excuses
1. Target harden • Steering column locks and ignition immobilisers • Anti-robbery screens • Tamper-proof packaging	6. Extend guardianship • Go out in group at night • Leave signs of occupancy • Carry mobile phone	11. Conceal targets • Off-street parking • Gender-neutral phone directories • Unmarked armoured trucks	16. Reduce frustrations and stress • Efficient lines • Polite service • Expanded seating • Soothing music/muted lights	21. Set rules • Rental agreements • Harassment codes • Hotel registration
2. Control access to facilities • Entry phones • Electronic card access • Baggage screening	7. Assist natural surveillance • Improved street lighting • Defensible space design • Support whistleblowers	12. Remove targets • Removable car radio • Women's shelters • Pre-paid cards for pay phones	17. Avoid disputes • Separate seating for rival soccer fans • Reduce crowding in bars • Fixed cab fares	22. Post instructions • 'No Parking' • 'Private Property' • 'Extinguish camp fires'
3. Screen exits • Ticket needed for exit • Export documents • Electronic merchandise tags	8. Reduce anonymity • Taxi driver IDs • 'How's my driving?' decals (transfers) • School uniforms	13. Identify property • Property marking • Vehicle licensing and parts marking • Cattle branding	18. Reduce temptation and arousal • Controls on violent pornography • Enforce good behaviour on soccer field • Prohibit racial slurs	23. Alert conscience • Roadside speed display boards • Signatures for customs declarations • 'Shoplifting is stealing'

Continued

Situational Prevention of Organised Crimes

Table 1.1 Continued

Increase the effort	Increase the risks	Reduce the rewards	Reduce provocations	Remove excuses
4. Deflect offenders • Street closures • Separate bathrooms for women • Disperse pubs	9. Use place managers • CCTV for double-decker buses • Two clerks for convenience stores • Reward vigilance	14. Disrupt markets • Monitor pawn shops • Controls on classified ads • License street vendors	19. Neutralise peer pressure • 'Idiots drink and drive' • 'It's OK to say No' • Disperse troublemakers at school	24. Assist compliance • Easy library checkout • Public lavatories • Litter receptacles
5. Control tools/weapons • 'Smart' guns • Restrict spray paint sales to juveniles • Toughened beer glasses	10. Strengthen formal surveillance • Red light cameras • Burglar alarms • Security guards	15. Deny benefits • Ink merchandise tags • Graffiti cleaning • Disable stolen mobile phones	20. Discourage imitation • Rapid repair of vandalism • V-chips in TVs • Censor details of *modus operandi*	25. Control drugs and alcohol • Breathalysers in bars • Server intervention programmes • Alcohol-free events

Sources: Clarke and Eck (2003); Cornish and Clarke (2003); Website: www.popcenter.org

We have seen the conduct of many empirical studies that illustrate the application of situational crime prevention to a wide range of offences. There have also been a large number of studies that have sought to discover whether or not the fears that displacement is an inevitable corollary of situational crime prevention are justified. The findings are clear. While there is sometimes displacement of crime it is rarely complete. Moreover, 'diffusion of benefits', where the preventive effects of situational crime prevention measures extend beyond their operational range, is also common (Guerette and Bowers 2009).

Situational crime prevention, reflecting the primary government policy interests in crime in most Western societies, has tended until recently to be applied most often to conventional high-volume crimes, such as shop theft, burglary, vehicle theft and domestic violence. There is, however, a growing literature on its wider application, for example to internet crime, child abuse, and terrorism (Clarke 2009). The case has been made that situational crime prevention has a role to play also in dealing with organised crime (Bouloukos, Farrell and Laycock 2003; Cornish and Clarke 2001; Ekblom 2000; Felson 2006; Natarajan and Clarke 2004; Van de Bunt and van der Schoot 2003; van der Schoot 2006). This volume extends that case and also includes studies providing a range of examples illustrating how situational crime prevention strategies may be developed in practice and what might be accomplished by their implementation. Before turning to a summary of the themes identified in this collection we consider debates about the nature of organised crime and how this has traditionally been understood and tackled.

What is organised crime?

Most definitions of organised crime have focused on the nature of criminal organisations. This requires that a distinction be made between what counts as organised crime and what does not. The commission of certain crimes is generally seen to involve a modicum of 'organisation'. International trafficking in people and drugs constitute good examples. In practice, however, distinguishing between crimes that are organised and those that are not has proven very tricky.

The popular image conjured up by 'organised crime' is that of the Mafia and the mob: large-scale, enduring, violent, and hierarchical groups involved in diverse criminal activities. Many of those with responsibilities for defining organised crime for the purposes of policy and practice, however, have adopted rather broader definitions. We illustrate with some examples.

For the European Union, to speak of organised crime requires that at least six out of a set of 11 characteristics need to be present, four of which must be those numbered 1, 3, 5 and 11 of the following list:

1. collaboration of more than two people;
2. each with own appointed tasks;
3. for a prolonged or indefinite period of time;
4. using some form of discipline or control;
5. suspected of the commission of serious criminal offences;
6. operating at an international level;
7. using violence or other means suitable for intimidation;
8. using commercial or businesslike structures;
9. engaged in money laundering;
10. exerting influence on politics, the media, public administration, judicial authorities or the economy;
11. determined by the pursuit of profit and/or power. (Elvins 2003: 34)

In the UK, the Serious Organised Crime Agency defines organised criminals as 'Those involved on a continuing basis, normally working with others, in committing crimes for substantial profit or gain, for which a person aged 21 or over on first conviction could expect to be imprisoned for three or more years' (SOCA 2006).

In Germany, the Bundeskriminalamt (BKA, the German Federal Crime Intelligence Office) defines organised crime as 'the planned violation of the law for profit or to acquire power, which offences are each, or together, of a major significance, and are carried out by more than two participants who co-operate within a division of labour for a long or undetermined timespan using: (a) commercial or commercial-like structures, or (b) violence or other means of intimidation, or (c) influence on politics, media, public administration, justice and legitimate economy' (van Duyne 1995).

Certain themes are clearly present in these official definitions: organised crime is serious crime, it has potentially international reach, it is conducted in groups and its motivation is power or profit. However, as official documentation tends to make clear, much organised offending is characterised by fluid networks and groups. Indeed, if the relatively broad definitions of organised crime used by the European Union, the British Serious Organised Crime Agency or the German Bundeskriminalamt described above are accepted it follows that much of what is treated as organised crime will not be committed by mafias but by small groups of criminal entrepreneurs.

Table 1.2 highlights the distinction between Mafia-like organised crime and that associated with networks of criminal entrepreneurs, which are often responsible for the kinds of crime covered by the EU, UK and German definitions.

Table 1.2 Two models of organised crime

Organised crime syndicates	Networks of criminal entrepreneurs
Few in number	Many
Large	Small
Regional/national	Local
Stable, enduring	Unstable, temporary
Outside normal society	Integrated in society
Structured	Loosely knit
Hierarchical	'Flat' organisation
Static membership	Fluid membership
Differentiated roles	Undifferentiated roles
Entrenched leadership	Changing leadership
Formal rules/regulations	Informal agreements
Criminal identity	Business identity
Full-time illegal operations	Part-time operations
Ties of loyalty	Business relationships
Use of violence	Avoidance of violence
Crime generalists	Crime specialists
Abundant resources	Limited resources
Sophisticated technology	Everyday technology
Seek opportunities	Respond to opportunities

Source: Adapted from Natarajan and Clarke (2004); Brown and Clarke (2004)

How does situational crime prevention see organised crime?

In seeking to apply situational crime prevention techniques definitions of organised crime do not matter much, because the organisation itself is not the main focus of attention. Reflecting the discussion above, the focus of activity should be on analysing crimes which are committed by those implicated in 'organised crime', however this is characterised, with the aim of specifying their methods. The purpose is to identify pinch-points that will effectively reduce opportunities, such that relatively sustained preventive effects are produced. The organisation of organised crime becomes much less interesting, although not entirely irrelevant. According to Levi (1998: 456) 'different forms of crime may require different levels of organization'. Indeed, considering the way a criminal organisation or a network of entrepreneurs operates (or needs to operate) may help identify preventive interventions using any of the options available from the broad repertoire of situational techniques. Situational measures that remove opportunities for sustaining the forms of organisation and networks that are necessary to commit those offences clearly, therefore, are one method for their prevention. This may comprise, for example, removing the facilitating conditions which allow offenders to launder money or obtain false documentation.

Cornish and Clarke (2002) describe a number of distinctive features that are typical of organised crimes:

- They involve a complex interplay of criminal actors, equipment, locations and activities.
- Offences tend to be repeated, using a particular *modus operandi*.
- They are committed by organised groups of offenders who provide the infrastructure, resources, skills and experience necessary to plan and carry them out.
- The longevity, continuity and complexity of organised groups vary from very temporary associations created for a particular project (McIntosh 1975), through those formed to commit a time-limited series of offences (Cressey's (1972) 'working groups'), to enduring organisations, or businesses, which invest in ongoing criminal activities.
- The level at which an organised group operates – transnational, national, regional and local (Hobbs 1998) – will be dictated in part by the nature and scope of the organised crimes in which it is or is becoming involved (Stelfox 1998).

Studying organised crimes for the purposes of situational crime prevention involves deconstructing this complexity, in order to identify the various opportunity structures that are used during their commission. The ultimate purpose of this analysis is to identify promising preventive pinch-points. The opportunity structures for any particular crime problem include both the immediate physical and social conditions needed for the offence and the wider social arrangements ('facilitating conditions') that make the crime possible.

Table 1.3 Facilitating conditions that enable theft of cars for export

---

Strong demand for low-cost stolen cars in developing countries
Millions of cars cross national borders daily
Vast numbers of unchecked containers are shipped daily from developed countries
Many different ports involved with varying security
Substantial legal trade between countries in used cars
Law enforcement activity seen to hinder free trade
Many countries cannot control illegal import of cars that have *not* been stolen
No international standard for vehicle documents and registration
Car registration procedures not properly enforced in some countries
Corruption widespread among officials in undeveloped countries
Vehicle theft not a high law enforcement priority
Immigration has brought many offenders to developed countries with contacts in their home countries

---

To illustrate, Table 1.3 sets out the facilitating conditions for the specific problem of theft of cars for export. These clearly constitute part of the opportunity structure. They describe a broad context that facilitates trafficking in stolen cars, although what is included differs from the immediate circumstances for the theft of a vehicle which may then be illegally exported. The particular opportunity structures that enable the theft of vehicles suitable for export will thus also have to be identified. Furthermore the stolen vehicles have to be transported from the locations where they are stolen to the destination where they are to be sold and, along the way, must have their illicit origins effectively disguised. Clearly many steps are involved in international trading in stolen vehicles and these are summarised in Table 1.4.

Table 1.4 Step-by-step modus operandi for trafficking in stolen cars

---

Preferred cars identified
Street criminals commissioned to find and steal the cars
Brought to secure location where identity may be changed
Stored until ready to transport across border
Loaded in sealed container onto ship, either whole or disassembled
Or simply driven across border
At destination handed over to local contact
Or collected at dock by such person
May be legally registered
May be sold on open market or to private buyer

The example of trafficking in stolen vehicles suggests that for complex organised crimes there will generally be suites of interconnected and interdependent crime scripts that allow the higher-order compound offence to take place. It is into these sub-scripts that the overall offence can usefully be deconstructed. Cornish and Clarke (2002) argue, thus, that the complex offences associated with organised crime may usefully be treated as including the following general features:

- a string of interlinked offence scripts, each component script having its own stages, casts, locations and activities;

- an extended 'master-script' that guides or, at least, makes sense of the whole process by nesting individual scripts within a larger purpose;

- division of labour so that commission of each of the component offences is carried out by subsets of the total cast; and

- one or more organisational structures appropriate to the nature of the specific crime under analysis.

There may sometimes be a 'Mr Big' pulling the strings of those involved in complex crimes as they act out their parts in the performance of the extended master-script. In other instances, as with the legitimate market, those involved in the different stages in the production of the crime may know or care little about one another. The importer of stolen cars, for example, may have little interest or involvement with those who steal the cars from the streets in a distant country and the scripts they follow. Parts of the master-script may, thus, be owned and orchestrated by different directors.

In summary, in relation to any given organised crime, problem analysis for situational crime prevention purposes will be helped by unpacking the sets of crime scripts involved. These will reveal the opportunity structures that enable the activities involved in the production of the organised crime to be identified and, from them, those which are most open to intervention.

How should organised crime be studied for situational crime prevention?

In principle conducting studies of organised crime problems for the purpose of developing situational crime prevention strategies and tactics should be as achievable as with burglary or shop theft. In practice such endeavours face a number of challenges.

So far few studies of specific organised crime problems have been undertaken. This is partly due to a shortage of personnel who are competent and interested in doing them. It is partly also to do with their intrinsic difficulty. While it is possible to undertake ethnographic studies on craft and project crimes, obtaining fieldwork access to study complex organised crimes, which depend upon concealment for their continuing success, is likely to be much more difficult. Mack put it well when he commented that 'Successful criminals are by definition inaccessible. The major skill they have in common, over and above their special expertise, is that of keeping out of sight' (Mack 1972: 50). In addition, conventional data sources used to unpick the nature of crimes for situational responses (such as police-recorded crime data and victimisation surveys) may be unsuitable for the detailed analysis of organised crime problems. This may result from a) under reporting and under recording of events and b) a lack of detail about the commission of these crimes contained in such sources of data. Alternative sources of data to facilitate studies of organised crime are available and may in practice have to be used. These include interrogation of police files and of police officers involved in the investigation of organised crime. Gaining access to police services to elicit such information, however, is often difficult. Furthermore, detailed record keeping is patchy.

Conducting case studies of crime problems and police and partner responses to them is time-consuming and technically difficult. While this might not matter much for research for its own sake, it does matter when that research is orientated to policy and practice. The problem is that we may end up suggesting solutions to yesterday's problems. Organised crime is dynamic. New opportunity structures emerge and old ones fade, for example as technology, administrative arrangements, migration patterns, transport provisions and political conditions change. Offenders adapt and innovate. This is particularly true for those who are involved in organised crime as a business, and this forms part of its complexity. Keeping up for preventive purposes means that we will need to devise ways of conducting analyses that are good enough to find preventive situational pinch-points in time to pre-empt emerging organised crime problems.

Given the importance of developing and refining analytic frameworks, there is nevertheless a case to be made for undertaking detailed studies of organised crime problems using traditional methods of research, even though these may ultimately have little direct policy relevance. For policy and practice purposes, however, it may well be more fruitful to use a mix of speedier research strategies and rapid appraisal techniques (Beebe 1995). Such 'quick-and-dirty' research should be able to outline the contours of organised crimes in enough detail to guide preventive approaches and interventions. Moreover specific intelligence-gathering exercises could also be undertaken, where required, in relation to particular crime commission issues. For example, in the case of trafficking in stolen vehicles intelligence might be collected on the procedures for the reregistration of cars in different countries which in turn may help shape preventative practices.

Methods for practical and relatively rapid analyses of organised crime problems with the aim of developing situational crime prevention techniques might include the following:

- analysing published studies from a script perspective;

- studying the police and prosecution case papers of known crimes (e.g. Natarajan and Belanger 1998; Natarajan 2006);

- interviewing experts in depth about script elements and linkages;

- studying the reports of undercover operations;

- interviewing those involved in the legal analogues of crime, such as the export of used cars or the running of legal internet video sites, in order to understand the means by which legal business is transacted and the loopholes available to offenders; and

- undertaking ethnographic research, where this is possible and can be done quickly.

Although there is a great deal of evidence showing its effectiveness for other types of offending, little is known specifically about the outcome effectiveness of situational crime prevention in relation to organised crime. In particular, the problem of displacement may be different for organised crime than for volume crime. While the rational choice assumptions behind situational crime prevention appear to be especially applicable to organised crime where calculations of cost, benefit and effort are liable to be made more carefully in relation to the criminal ventures chosen, equally it may be the case that if thwarted in one set of criminal activities alternatives will be more actively sought than is the case with many street criminals. Hence, situational measures may successfully prevent one form of organised crime (or otherwise disrupt the activities of a network) by increasing risk or effort or by reducing rewards, while at the same time prompting those affected actively to pursue alternatives. Equally some situational measures directed at preventing one form of crime (for example, those affecting money laundering) may produce diffusion of benefit effects in relation both to other forms of organised crime (for example, those generating the money by drug trafficking) and subsequently to street crime. However, so far we know little about the level, nature and rate of criminal adaptation specifically in relation to organised crime.

What next? A research and policy agenda

The research and policy agendas for situational crime prevention to be developed as a way of reducing organised crimes need to be closely aligned to one another, as the following makes clear.

There are strong theoretical and empirical arguments for policy and practice investments in situational crime prevention as a way of addressing organised crime problems. The studies drawn together in this volume illustrate what can be learned about organised crime and its prevention by adopting a situational approach. National and international bodies with responsibilities for organised crime would do well to divert some of their efforts to situational prevention rather than simply to enforcement. Indeed the traditional focus on the activities of individuals and groups together with the primary concern of many responsible agencies with enforcing the criminal law may be one reason why relatively little attention has so far been paid to the situational prevention of organised crime problems.

The Serious Organised Crime Agency (SOCA) in Britain does have harm reduction (rather than maximising numbers of arrests) as its explicit major aim and this would be well served by attempting systematically to analyse its specific priority problems with a view to finding accessible pinch-points. Adopting such an approach would involve a substantial investment of analytic effort into identifying the opportunity structures that are used as the crime scripts at work in the problems are played out, and then figuring out which may be closed or modified and in what ways. National and international agencies could facilitate such analyses of organised crime by improving record-keeping and widening access to researchers to help develop forms of analysis that can be conducted in-house relatively quickly to a standard that can inform the selection of preventive interventions in real time.

Three linked priorities exist for research. The first is to conduct action research of the sort commonly used in situational crime prevention. In particular, demonstration projects could be set up to explore the potential for situational crime prevention as a strategy to deal with forms of organised crime problems. The second priority, already noted, is that of developing record-keeping arrangements, data collection methods and analytic techniques that can be used routinely and that will yield findings that are capable of informing situational prevention strategies. The third priority is that of evaluating the outcomes of situational prevention of organised crime, attending in particular to the patterns of adaptation, displacement and diffusion of benefits that are produced. This will be technically challenging, but ultimately crucial for working out whether the situational approach can deliver significant net crime reduction benefits.

The contribution of this collection

The chapters brought together in this collection illustrate and extend the application of situational crime prevention to organised crime in a variety of different ways. In doing so they shed light on the nature of certain organised crime problems and demonstrate the opportunities – and risks – that the adoption of situational crime prevention techniques may present to those seeking to understand and tackle these problems.

- The collection explores the relevance of situational crime prevention to a wide range of crime types: timber theft (Graycar and Felson), people trafficking for sex work (Finckenauer and Chin) and for seasonal workers (Kirby and Penna), contraband cigarettes (von Lampe), mortgage fraud (van Gestel), corruption in public construction (Savona) and smuggling (Kleemans *et al.*). In each of these chapters the details of the specific offences are examined and the chapters show how situational preventive strategies could be (or have been) developed to address them.

- The use more broadly of crime scripts as a way of analysing organised crime and identifying potential pinch-points to prevent them is explored and illustrated in a number of the chapters (Hancock and Laycock; Savona; von Lampe).

- The framework of situational preventive techniques is applied to organised crime problems in various chapters (van Gestel; Graycar and Felson; Korsell and Skinnari; Nelen; von Lampe).

- The importance of understanding the facilitating conditions for specific organised crimes is brought out explicitly or implicitly in all the chapters. The global economic conditions which act as facilitators for certain organised crimes recur in various chapters (Finckenauer and Chin; Kirby and Penna; Kleemans *et al.*; von Lampe) although the conditions for some organised crime are primarily rooted in local conditions (van Gestel; Korsell and Skinnari; Nelen; Savona).

- The role of 'legitimate' actors in facilitating organised crime problems is highlighted in a number of chapters (van Gestel; Kleemans *et al.*; Nelen), as are mechanisms for raising awareness of such legitimate actors as a means of disrupting organised criminality.

- The chapters illustrate the variety of research techniques that can be applied in the situational analysis of organised crime. A number of chapters point to the difficulties of generating systematic information on organised crime problems. Data sources that are utilised include large-scale surveys (Finckenauer and Chin; Korsell and Skinnari); examination of case records (van Gestel; Hancock and Laycock; Kleemans *et al.*; von Lampe), in-depth face-to-face interviews with offenders, victims or officials (Finckenauer and Chin; Hancock and Laycock; von Lampe), interrogation of press archives (von Lampe) and synthesis of findings from previous studies (Graycar and Felson).

Overall, the promise of situational crime prevention as a way of tackling organised crime is made clear in this volume, although the chapters consistently highlight the complexity and plasticity of organised crime. This creates challenges for those responsible for developing strategies aimed at reducing these problems and illustrates the need for continued attention to understanding the way organised crime is manifested.

References

Beebe, J. (1995) 'Basic Concepts and Techniques of Rapid Appraisal', *Human Organization*, 54(1): 42–51.

Bouloukos, A.C., Farrell, G. and Laycock, G. (2003) *Transnational Organised Crime in Europe and North America: The Need for Situational Crime Prevention Efforts*. HEUNI. http://www.heuni.fi/uploads/0gyxd5c8.pdf

Brown, R. and Clarke, R.V. (2004) 'Police Intelligence and Theft of Vehicles for Export: Recent UK Experience', in M.G. Maxwell and R.V. Clarke (eds), *Understanding and Preventing Car Theft. Crime Prevention Studies*, volume 17. Monsey, NY: Criminal Justice Press.

Clarke, R. V. (2009) 'Situational Crime Prevention: Theoretical Background and Current Practice', in M.D. Krohn, A.J. Lizotte and G.P. Hall (eds), *Handbook on Crime and Deviance*. New York: Springer Science+Business Media.

Clarke, R.V. and Eck, J.E. (2003) *Become a Problem Solving Crime Analyst*. Cullompton, UK: Willan Publishing.

Cornish, D.B. (1994) 'The Procedural Analysis of Offending and its Relevance for Situational Prevention', in R.V. Clarke (ed.), *Crime Prevention Studies*, volume 3. Monsey, NY: Criminal Justice Press (accessible at www.popcenter.org).

Cornish, D.B. and Clarke, R.V. (2002) 'Analyzing Organised Crimes', in A.R. Piquero and S.G. Tibbetts (eds), *Rational Choice and Criminal Behaviour: Recent Research and Future Challenges*. Hamden: Garland Science.

Cornish, D.B. and Clarke, R.V. (2003) 'Opportunities, Precipitators and Criminal Decisions: A Reply to Wortley's Critique of Situational Crime Prevention', in M. Smith and D.B. Cornish (eds), *Theory for Situational Crime Prevention. Crime Prevention Studies*, volume 16. Monsey, NY: Criminal Justice Press (accessible at www.popcenter.org).

Cressey, D. (1972) *Criminal Organization: Its Elementary Forms*. New York: Harper and Row.

Ekblom, P. (2000) 'Preventing Organized Crime: A Conceptual Framework', Presentation at Europol workshop on Organized Crime, The Hague, May 2000 (available from p.ekblom@csm.arts.ac.uk).

Elvins, M. (2003) 'Europe's Response to Transnational Organised Crime', in A. Edwards and P. Gill (eds), *Transnational Organised Crime: perspectives on global security*. London: Routledge.

Felson, M. (2006) *The Ecosystem for Organized Crime*, HEUNI Paper No. 26. Helsinki: HEUNI (http://www.heuni.fi/uploads/2rreolo2h.pdf).

Guerette, R.T. and Bowers, K.J. (2009) 'Assessing the Extent of Crime Displacement and Diffusion of Benefits: A Review of Situational Crime Prevention Evaluations', *Criminology*, 47(4): 1331–1368.

Hobbs, D. (1998) 'Going Down the Local: The Local Context of Organised Crime', *The Howard Journal*, 37: 407–22.

Levi, M. (1998) 'Perspectives on Organised Crime: An Overview', *The Howard Journal*, 37 (4): 335–45.

McIntosh, M. (1975) *The Organisation of Crime*. London: Macmillan.

Mack, J.A. (1972) 'The Able Criminal', *British Journal of Criminology*, 12 (1): 44–4.

Natarajan, M. (2006) 'Understanding the Structure of a Large Heroin Distribution Network: A Quantitative Analysis of Qualitative Data', *Journal of Quantitative Criminology*, 22(2): 171–92

Natarajan, M. and Clarke, R.V. (2004) 'Understanding and Controlling Organised Crime: The Feasibility of a Situational Approach', Paper presented at the annual Environmental Criminology and Crime Analysis Seminar, Wellington, New Zealand, July (electronic copy available from rvgclarke@aol.com).

Natarajan, M. and Belanger, M. (1998) 'Varieties of Upper-Level Drug Dealing Organizations: A Typology of Cases Prosecuted in New York City', *Journal of Drug Issues*, 28(4): 1005–26.

Serious Organised Crime Agency (SOCA) (2006) *The United Kingdom Threat Assessment of Serious Organised Crime 2006/7*. London: SOCA.

Stelfox, P. (1998) 'Policing Lower-Levels of Organised Crime in England and Wales' *The Howard Journal*, 37(4): 393–406.

Van de Bunt, H. and van der Schoot, C. (2003) *Prevention of Organised Crime*. The Hague: WODC 215 (http://english.wodc.nl/onderzoeksdatabase/traceren-van-mogelijkheden-voor-preventie-die-zich-bij-lopende-opsporingsonderzoeken-aan dienen.aspx).

van der Schoot, C. (2006) *Organised Crime Prevention in the Netherlands*. PhD thesis, Erasmus University, Amsterdam.

van Duyne, P.C. (1995) 'The Phantom and Threat of Organised Crime', *Crime, Law and Social Change*, 24: 341–77.

Chapter 2

Situational crime prevention and cross-border crime

Edward R. Kleemans, Melvin R.J. Soudijn and Anton W. Weenink

Abstract

This chapter explores the consequences of cross-border crime for situational crime prevention. Many types of organised crime involve international smuggling activities – such as drug trafficking, money laundering, smuggling illegal immigrants, and other transnational illegal activities. Based on research in the Netherlands, this chapter explores cross-border crime from three different angles (export, import and transit) with regard to four different areas of organised crime: Ecstasy (production and export), cocaine (import and transit), money laundering (export), and human smuggling (transit). It highlights the opportunities for situational crime prevention, as well as its limitations and the attendant caveats when it comes to dealing with cross-border crime.

Introduction

Situational crime prevention and routine activity theory provide important new ways to understand and prevent crime problems. At the crossroads of theory and practice, studies by Clarke, Felson and others have demonstrated how situational crime analysis may help identify circumstances which facilitate crime and viable opportunity-reducing measures (Felson 1998; Felson and Clarke 1998). Many of these studies focus on 'local' problems such as public nuisance, street crime and burglaries. More recently, the scope of situational crime prevention has been extended to other types of crime, such as organised crime (e.g. Cornish and Clarke 2002) and terrorism (Clarke and Newman 2006).

The North American literature seems to equate organised crime with a distinct *local* profile, as 'Mafia-type' organisations which have gained control of certain economic sectors or regions, acting as an 'alternative government'. Organised crime is believed to make a profit by taking over two areas that are traditionally the exclusive province of the State: the use of force, and taxation. In the international literature, this kind of activity of organised crime groups is referred to as *racketeering* (e.g. Albanese 2008; Albini 1971; Fijnaut and Paoli 2004: 603–21; Finckenauer and Waring 1998; Gambetta 1993; Jacobs 1999; Jacobs and Peters 2003; Paoli 2002; Reuter 1983). However, in many European countries this concept of organised crime is at odds with the empirical facts. The nature of organised crime in the Netherlands, for example, can more fittingly be described as cross-border crime or *transit crime*: criminal groups are primarily involved in international illegal trade, using the same opportunity structure that facilitates legal economic activities. The major business of organised crime groups in the Netherlands boils down to international smuggling activities: drug trafficking, smuggling illegal immigrants, human trafficking for sexual exploitation, arms trafficking, trafficking in stolen vehicles, and other transnational illegal activities, such as money laundering and tax evasion (cigarette smuggling and European Community fraud). The Netherlands can be either a country of destination, a transit country, or, particularly in the case of synthetic drugs, a production country (Kleemans 2007).

This chapter explores the significance of cross-border crime for situational crime prevention. Based on research in the Netherlands, this chapter examines cross-border crime from three different angles (export, import, and transit) with regard to four different areas of organised crime: Ecstasy (production and export), cocaine (import and transit), money laundering (export), and human smuggling (transit). The first section starts with a brief discussion of the problems encountered in gathering data on organised crime. The next four sections highlight the transnational nature of organised crime, following the same basic structure: a general introduction to a specific type of crime, using data from research and police investigations, and a discussion of several actual or possible preventive measures and effects. The chapter concludes with a general discussion on the opportunities for situational crime prevention, as well as its limitations and the attendant caveats when it comes to dealing with cross-border crime.

Research into organised crime

Theoretically, situational crime prevention is applicable to all sorts of crime, including organised crime and terrorism. However, the problem with organised crime and terrorism is that these phenomena have to be scaled back to tangible events, offenders, and specific settings that can be studied. If we focus on organised crime, two problems are paramount. First, organised crime is in the eye of the beholder. Since researchers work from different definitions of organised crime, its characteristics range from loose networks to strict hierarchical groups, from shadow economies to immoral business practices, and from territorial control to monopolising the distribution of illicit goods and services. The second problem academic researchers face is the restricted access to primary source material. Whereas street crime, for example, can be studied in many ways drawing on diverse sources of data that are generally available to the researcher, the main data sources on organised crime are in many countries controlled by police or intelligence agencies which are reluctant to share them with the research and academic community.

In the Netherlands, the situation is rather different, as the Ministry of Justice acknowledges that it is important for academic researchers to study organised crime in an independent, systematic way. Many of the existing studies, such as the Dutch Organised Crime Monitor, have been carried out or facilitated by the Research and Documentation Centre of the Ministry of Justice (WODC) and police institutions. Compared with other countries, law enforcement institutions in the Netherlands are generally quite willing to cooperate in empirical research. The Netherlands Police Agency, for instance, employs researchers who have access to classified data on organised crime. Although many reports of law enforcement institutions are still confidential, there are more and more non-classified versions.

From 1996 to 2006, researchers at the Dutch Organised Crime Monitor systematically analysed 120 large-scale police investigations (40 case studies per sweep), involving 1,623 suspects. The main sources for this ongoing research project are the files of concluded Dutch police investigations into criminal groups, which often span a period of several years (for more information, see Kleemans 2007; Van de Bunt and Kleemans 2007; Kleemans and Van de Bunt 2008). Each case study always starts with structured interviews with police officers and public prosecutors. After these interviews, the police files are analysed and summarised, using an extensive checklist that elaborates on the following central questions. What is the composition of the group, and what form does cooperation between the offenders take? What kinds of illegal activities do they engage in and how do they operate? How do they interact with the opportunities and risks presented by their environment? What are the proceeds of the criminal activities, and how do the offenders spend these proceeds? Lastly, unobtrusive police methods, such as transcripts of wiretaps and data obtained from surveillance operations, as well as records of police interviews with victims and suspects, often additionally provide us with a detailed and interesting picture of the social world of organised crime. It is important to note that – compared with other countries – Dutch criminal investigations provide a lot of 'objective' evidence on offender behaviour, due to the extensive use of wiretapping, surveillance techniques and other special investigation methods, and the absence of plea bargaining. Since the researchers generally have access to the original police files, they can to a large extent check the evidence themselves.

An important analytical tool of the WODC researchers is the extensive checklist, which focuses on offenders, criminal activities, specific settings, and several aspects of the licit environment (Van de Bunt and Kleemans 2007: 205–17). Because the WODC checklist is easy to use and publicly available, other researchers have also made good use of this list (e.g. Soudijn 2006; Staring *et al.* 2005). For crime prevention purposes, the checklist has been translated and adapted for an international project on prevention of organised crime, involving the Netherlands, Italy, Hungary and Finland (Van de Bunt and Van der Schoot 2003).

As stated before, the major business of organised crime in the Netherlands amounts to international smuggling activities, such as drug trafficking, smuggling illegal immigrants, human trafficking for sexual exploitation, arms trafficking, trafficking in stolen vehicles, and other transnational illegal activities, such as money laundering and tax evasion (e.g. cigarette smuggling). Organised crime in the Netherlands can therefore be characterised as cross-border crime. In this chapter, we focus on four specific types of such crime. First of all, the Netherlands is one of the main producers and exporters of Ecstasy and other synthetic drugs. This provides a good example of the production and export of illegal goods. Second, the Netherlands (alongside Spain) plays a major role in the import of cocaine into Europe and its subsequent transit to other countries, such as the United Kingdom. Third, the cocaine import business also generates a reverse flow of money from the Netherlands to South America. Fourth, we analyse human smuggling, a criminal activity that is characterised by mutual interests and close cooperation between illegal migrants, their families, and smugglers. At least where the Netherlands is concerned, human smuggling is primarily focused on transit from Europe to other countries, such as the United Kingdom, Canada and the United States. We use cases from the Dutch Organised Crime Monitor and from the Netherlands Police Agency to illustrate the opportunities for and limitations of situational crime prevention (for more information on the cases from the Dutch Organised Crime Monitor, see van de Bunt and Kleemans 2007: 219–37).

Ecstasy

Since the 1990s, Ecstasy (MDMA) has been consumed worldwide. The major production of Ecstasy, however, is concentrated in a few countries, most notably the Netherlands and Belgium. The Netherlands is reportedly the origin of 42 per cent of the Ecstasy seized worldwide (United Nations Office on Drugs and Crime (UNODC) 2008: 135).[1] Since Dutch Ecstasy producers have a high level of expertise which results in good-quality products, their pills are in strong demand. The average production costs of an Ecstasy tablet amount to €0.15-€0.20, while each tablet sells in the Netherlands for an average price of €3.49. The street value is much higher in many major North American cities (€20–30), Australia and New Zealand (about €30), and Japan (€25–50) (Korps landelijke politiediensten, the Netherlands National Crime Squad (KLPD) 2005: 75–87). These price differences illustrate the logic of cross-border crime: export and transit produce major profits.

Ecstasy is created by chemical synthesis, which means that the production process requires certain essential chemicals (known as precursors), of which PMK (piperonylmethylketone) is the main ingredient. This presents an obvious opportunity for situational crime prevention. In order to prevent the production of Ecstasy, several of these precursors have been placed under strict international monitoring.

However, this has resulted in two new developments. First, it has created a lucrative sidebusiness in the smuggling of precursors. Second, as China is one of the few countries that can produce PMK in large quantities, it has also resulted in Chinese criminals entering the Dutch Ecstasy market. Moreover, because PMK is of such major importance, Dutch Ecstasy producers are now to a large extent reliant on Chinese precursor smugglers (Soudijn and Kleemans 2009).

> *Case* Chinese criminals are aware of the powerful position they hold. In an intercepted telephone communication, Chinese suspect A spoke with another Chinese criminal regarding precursor prices and suggested they should keep this 'water' back to boost prices. The ensuing investigation showed that after several seizures of precursors, the price of PMK in the Netherlands rose from €600 a litre to €1,500 a litre.

This example shows that it is important to block the flow of precursors with the aim of preventing the production of Ecstasy. It is interesting to note that we can also monitor the effectiveness of particular seizures by looking at price fluctuations. Nevertheless, we should not be under any illusion that a successful anti-drugs policy can be achieved by driving up the production costs. After a while the price per litre decreased significantly. Apparently, other PMK shipments had arrived unnoticed. Furthermore, even if prices remain high, extra costs are simply charged to the end-consumer. The production costs still remain merely a fraction of the price that end-consumers in other countries are willing to pay.

However, this precursor example, also shows us that Ecstasy producers face structural restrictions. Their dependence on precursors brings them into contact with other ethnic groups, with all the possible problems of miscommunication and social differences this entails. Precursors that are produced in a limited number of countries, in a limited number of factories, and that have limited legal use, make effective control of precursors more feasible than other chemical compounds that are widely produced and widely used.

Besides the supply of precursors, there are other bottlenecks that are faced by Ecstasy manufacturers. In the past, knowledge about producing Ecstasy was sparse and several criminal groups had to rely on the same laboratory experts. Now, it is access to precursors and equipment that is problematic. Offenders who can overcome these obstacles are attractive to others involved in this business, which leads to network formation:

> *Case* Suspect B has been operating in the synthetic drugs world for a long time and is well known for his knowledge of chemistry. He has been committing property crimes since he was 18 years old, and as a result he is well embedded in criminal circles and knows many people. Since the age of 22 he has specialised in manufacturing synthetic drugs. He did this for many years before moving on to selling everything required for the production of synthetic drugs, including portable labs and chemical knowledge. In this way, he successfully profits from the demand, because there are plenty of groups who want to produce synthetic drugs, yet only a few offenders possess the knowledge and requirements needed to do so independently. His legal company supplies precursors, other chemicals, and equipment to various criminal groups. He is also involved in manufacturing new designer drugs.

This example shows the importance of 'facilitators' in criminal networks. Although facilitators may not be in the top of criminal organisations, they do provide crucial services to various criminal groups (Kleemans 2007: 178–80). As many offenders face the same obstacles, facilitators that offer solutions for these problems are in high demand. The principal catalyst is the formation of networks around these facilitators: criminals tell one another about the specific expertise of these persons, and word gets around and contacts are formed. We find similar mechanisms at work with document forgers and currency exchangers (Kleemans and De Poot 2008).

A closer look at the production process reveals other peculiarities, not only involving people with a criminal background, but also the licit environment:

> *Case* A synthetic drugs producer ordered round-bottomed flasks and heating mantles from a glassblower. The glassblower called his legitimate supplier, from whom he ordered the equipment. After

delivery, the equipment was collected and transported to another city. A couple of days after this delivery a police raid was carried out at this location and a major production location was dismantled. It turned out that similar equipment had also been found in several other cases. The glassblower stated that he had modified the round-bottomed flasks several times, on the basis of instructions from the people who had ordered the equipment. Although the average selling price per heating mantle was €1,000, the drugs producer was prepared to pay between €1,500 and €1,725.

The production of synthetic drugs requires not only special chemicals, but also specialist apparatus (hardware), such as flasks and glass mantles. Of course, it is not illegal to buy or sell glasswork. Yet most glassblowers were unaware that their equipment was being used for the production of Ecstasy. The police therefore started an initiative to raise awareness among glassblowers. The objective was to provide information to make the companies in the sector aware of how they could recognise the purchasing methods of illegal buyers. They were also informed about possible liability issues with regard to Dutch penal law (preparatory actions) and about how they could report suspicious matters on a voluntary basis. The campaign proved fruitful: investigations have shown that synthetic drugs producers have been having difficulties in obtaining glassware and heating mantles (Huisman and Smits 2008). One major glass trader started to refuse risky customers and now sells about 10 per cent of his former annual turnover in special flasks. Criminals are therefore looking for novel solutions and displacement effects are taking place. Recently, a shipment of 750 flasks (of considerably lower quality) from China was intercepted.

The success of such awareness-raising initiatives means that foreign investigative partners are also planning on making these kinds of visits to relevant companies in order to provide them with information about possible abuses. Many foreign companies were unaware of liability issues in the Netherlands, particularly if their own country's legislation does not include similar provisions.

The focus on glassblowers can be seen as a local approach towards a transnational problem. This campaign was not focused on a particular criminal organisation or transnational network. Nevertheless, this local approach only became possible by analysing large-scale traffickers and their operations.

Cocaine

Between 2000 and 2003, a remarkable cross-border crime problem developed as thousands of couriers tried to smuggle cocaine on passenger flights from Hato International Airport on the island of Curaçao (part of the Netherlands Antilles) to Amsterdam Airport Schiphol. The number of intercepted couriers arriving at Schiphol from Hato rose steeply, from 618 in 1999 to 1,200 in 2000; the related amount of intercepted contraband rose from 2,067 to 3,500 kilograms (Ministerie van Justitie 2002a, 2002b, 2004).

Case In 2003, at the height of what had become a crisis situation, authorities on Curaçao counted up to 50 couriers per flight from Hato to Schiphol. Couriers either swallowed amounts of up to 800 grams of cocaine (in small pellets, bolitas), or carried larger amounts of up to 3 kilograms on their bodies, in suitcases, or in hand luggage. This meant that on a single flight couriers could traffic 40 to 150 kilograms. Since there were several flights a day, the problem was heightened.

The Dutch authorities suspected that criminal organisations orchestrated this trafficking (Ministerie van Justitie 2002a: 8). UNODC and World Bank described the modus operandi as traffickers using a 'shotgun technique' (UNODC and World Bank 2007: 97), suggesting they deliberately flooded flights with dozens of couriers in the expectation that enough would slip through. Since most couriers carried legitimate Dutch passports, it was impossible to stop them with visa requirements, as had been successfully done with the first waves of couriers in Hato, who came from Nigeria and Brazil.

In 2002, authorities took far-reaching measures both at Hato and Schiphol, where special teams of Customs officials and military and border police were formed. This team, known as the Hato Team, carried out pre-flight checks, working with a list of indicators of suspect behaviour that helped them identify likely couriers (e.g. a person travelling often for very short stays and without being able to give a satisfactory explanation; for obvious reasons, the list was not made public). Suspects had to face a body check or return home. Many couriers chose not to embark, and accepted the loss of the ticket fee. At Schiphol incoming flights from the Netherlands Antilles, Aruba, Venezuela and Suriname were subjected to '100 per cent controls'. This meant a check on *all* passengers, their luggage, and the aircraft. By the end of 2003, the measures at Schiphol were intensified, with *all* incoming flights from the Netherlands Antilles, Aruba, Venezuela and Suriname being subjected to '100 per cent controls'.

A second measure was the introduction of a body scan at Hato in February 2003. The scan detected cocaine in and on the body. At the same time, it also enabled suspected passengers to prove their innocence. In June 2004 a body scan was introduced at Schiphol as well.

Finally, in December 2003, to prevent a flooding of the judicial chain by thousands of couriers, authorities adopted a 'substance-oriented approach'. If a courier was found with less than 3 kg (in the Netherlands) or

2.5 kg (in the Netherlands Antilles) of cocaine, and if he was a first-time offender, the drugs were confiscated and, in the Netherlands, the courier would not be prosecuted. The Netherlands Antilles did continue to prosecute couriers, but a lack of detention capacity hindered execution of sentences (Openbaar Ministerie Nederlandse Antillen 2008: 23). Therefore, most couriers on Curaçao and in the Netherlands were sent home, and only faced travel restrictions. Their passports were confiscated, and their details were passed on to Schengen countries and airline companies, who blacklisted them. Due to the 100 per cent controls on all flights, couriers were likely to get caught, which meant losing the cocaine and being denied a second chance at smuggling.

The policy was as controversial as it was successful. Many travellers found the controls and body checks extremely intrusive and stigmatising. The results were undeniable, however. Between June 2002 and August 2005 at Hato 21,590 passengers were denied access on board, with the number of passengers refused falling rapidly from over 1,000 per month in 2003 to less than 40 per month in August 2005. The number of body scans, the number of people who refused to have their body scanned, and the number of positive scans declined to almost zero by the end of 2004 (Faber *et al.* 2009: 217; UNODC and World Bank 2007: 99). The numbers of arrested and prosecuted couriers at Hato fell sharply as well, from 1,231 in 2004 to less than 300 a year in 2008 (Openbaar Ministerie Nederlandse Antillen 2009: 14; data from Netherlands Antilles Customs). The 100 per cent controls have been maintained to the present day, so these trends were not the result of diminished controls. The number of suspicious transactions to the Netherlands Antilles also showed a clear correlation with the introduction of policy measures and the dwindling number of couriers. Once the situation became manageable again, authorities resumed prosecuting couriers in 2005. In recent years very few couriers from Curaçao have been intercepted at Schiphol airport.

The solution came at a price, though. Innocent travellers sometimes felt that they were being treated like criminals. It also placed a heavy burden on control capacity that implied a relaxation of checks on other flights. Moreover, there is evidence that traffickers still use the island as a transhipment point, be it perhaps less frequently than before. Coastguard and police forces continue to intercept wholesale amounts of cocaine in the waters around Curaçao, and on the island; in 2008 the amounts ranged from 77 to 800 kg. However the largest seizure of 800 kg was destined not for Curaçao but the Dominican Republic, which might indicate that traffickers look for new routes. Circumstantial evidence also suggests that smugglers are trying new routes on flights that are not subject to 100 per cent controls. Cocaine has also been found in mail parcels (96 intercepted parcels in 2005, 122 in 2007) (KLPD 2009: 118).

In the end though, it is noteworthy that authorities did not fall for the 'organized crime fallacy' (Felson 1998, 2006). They did not focus solely on identifying and prosecuting the 'criminal organizations behind the couriers', or on curing the social ills that explained why so many youngsters risked their lives as 'swallowers'. Instead, the authorities pragmatically tried to block a crucial step in a specific modus operandi, i.e. the use of couriers. Whether or not there were criminal organisations using 'shotgun techniques' was not relevant for the effectiveness of the measures taken. The policy may not have stopped the flow of cocaine to Western Europe, but it had a very important result. It reversed a process of criminalisation of thousands of youngsters in Curaçao and the Netherlands. It did so, without sending them to jail.

Money mules

The trade in narcotics is transnational in several respects. Besides the physical movement of the goods themselves (e.g. cocaine from South America to Europe, precursors from China to the Netherlands, Ecstasy and other drugs from the Netherlands to the United Kingdom), there are also reverse money flows, as shipments have to be paid for, and profits are distributed worldwide.

In order to prevent criminals from benefiting from their crimes, the international community has taken several measures. These amount to laws and regulations, transparency, compliance, the reporting of suspicious transactions, and customer due diligence.[2]

For research purposes, money laundering is often represented as a three-stage process: a placement phase (getting the dirty money into the legal system), a layering phase (obstructing the tracing of the money) and an integration phase (using the money in the legal economy). However, not every offender goes through this three-stage process. Most local drug dealers do not make enough profit to buy property or establish a company. More often than not, their income is consumed straight away (supporting their own habit, enjoying an expensive lifestyle). As was shown in the previous section, however, the smuggling of cocaine to the Netherlands also involves overseas suppliers. The problem for cross-border crime is that money and profits are often in the wrong place, in small denominations, and in the wrong currency. Money has to be changed into larger denominations, into different currencies, and it has to be wired or transported to different countries. Therefore, cross-border crime often involves simple solutions such as using money exchange offices, cash smuggling, and money transfers, as well as more complex money laundering methods (for an overview, see Levi and Reuter 2006).

> *Case* In 2005, a corrupt female bank employee, together with five other suspects working at that bank, exchanged large amounts of pounds sterling and euros in small denominations into €200 and €500 notes.

It turned out that they provided this service for one or more Colombian drugs organisation(s). It is estimated that over a three-year period, they exchanged at least €26 million. Because the bank employees did not follow the compliance rules, their activities remained undetected for a long time.

Money conversions of this kind constitute the first stage of concealing the criminal origins of drugs money. The next step involves actual transportation:

Case In August 2005, a passenger boarding a flight to South America was stopped and searched at Schiphol airport. She carried with her two specially prepared writing-cases, each concealing €260,000. The ensuing investigation uncovered a network of such money mules. It was estimated that in just over a year, about 80 money mules had transported about €36 million in a similar fashion.

From a situational prevention point of view, the money exchanges described should have been impossible. In accordance with international standards, Dutch banking regulations would have obliged the bank to report unusual or suspicious transactions. Yet in this particular case, the bank employees who fulfilled the so-called guardian role had become corrupt. In retrospect, the employees probably could not resist the opportunities. They worked at a small branch where they supervised themselves. Their customers offered them an illegal monetary reward of 2 per cent commission on every transaction. All employees had a South American background, which made them perfectly suited to cross the language barrier. South American clients (friends and acquaintances) did not have to identify themselves when they wanted to perform money transactions (which was in violation of standard procedures). The bank employees also assisted them in getting around other regulations, for instance by splitting up large amounts into smaller amounts (below reporting thresholds), coupling the transactions with the identity of innocent clients, or even changing money outside the building. As a result, the bank became very popular with the Colombian migrant community. In the end though, situational prevention prevailed, because it was finally noted by headquarters that the size of the branch did not justify the request for so many €500 notes.

Apart from the call for adequate supervision, these cases are also noteworthy because they tell us something about the criminal need for volume reduction. The euro is a 'global currency' that, similar to the American dollar, is used across the world. The large monetary value of €500 notes over 100 dollar notes has made the euro the perfect vehicle for clandestinely transporting huge amounts of money (Rogoff 1998). However, because compliance rules and banking regulations are already in place, the risks and efforts entailed in exchanging currency without attracting governmental attention constitute a serious barrier.

Although our analysis does not reveal whether the money mules were hired by the same persons as those who organised drugs transports to the Netherlands, we can safely assume there is a niche market for illegal financial service providers, i.e. people who can exchange and transport large amounts of euros. Tracking down such individuals or groups creates new opportunities for security services to hamper the drugs market.

Yet we might also pose the question: who, after all, uses €500 notes? The denomination is too large for everyday transactions and most shops in Europe refuse to accept these notes for fear of counterfeiting. If €500 notes were no longer issued, European citizens would hardly be troubled but it would reduce the amounts that money mules can physically transport. However, such measures cannot be decided locally or even nationally, as it is the European Central Bank that issues these notes.

Human smuggling

The media often relate human smuggling to organised crime and create images of cruel offenders and helpless victims. Nevertheless, unlike human trafficking (e.g. for sexual exploitation), human smuggling can be best described as the combined effort of immigrants, their social environment, and smugglers to circumvent immigration laws. Human smuggling basically involves mutual consent between illegal immigrants and 'smugglers', who are family members, friends, or more distant professional smugglers. There are many reasons why people want to migrate to affluent and safe Western countries: imminent danger, discomfort and poverty, combined with the prospect of a better life elsewhere. In addition to these push factors, major pull factors are wage differences, dual labour markets in Western countries (stable, high-paying jobs combined with labour shortages for unstable, low-paying jobs), and the welfare state, particularly in Europe (see for a review, e.g. Kleemans 2009; Soudijn 2006; Zhang *et al.* 2007).

Co-production is the basis of much human smuggling. Many of those involved – migrants, smugglers, family and friends, but also employers, organisations and some governments – may have a clear common interest in successful migration, through licit or illicit means. This also explains why much illegal migration occurs through entirely legal channels. With some creativity and manipulation, options that are open for legal immigration can also be used for illegal immigration. Zhang *et al.* (2007: 22–56) reviews the ways several legal channels are used: entering as a legal immigrant (by using forged documents), marriage fraud, the use of tourist, student or scholar visas, and business invitations. In Europe much attention has also been paid to the use of asylum procedures and counterfeit documents, providing access to the welfare state (e.g. Neske and Doomernik 2006).

Many police investigations highlight the centrality of forged documents in human smuggling:

> *Case* A and B, who lived in the Netherlands, smuggled illegal immigrants by aeroplane from Iran via Europe to Canada. Assisted by several compatriots in Iran and Canada, they smuggled on average 240 to 300 persons per year. A had a good reputation as a document forger, which stimulated his supply of clients as well as his supply of passports. So many suppliers and buyers of passports frequented his premises that a fellow smuggler called his house literally 'a passport market'. At a certain moment, A had a stock of as many as 400 passports at his disposal, enabling him to find a 'plausible' passport for any client, travel route and destination, which was subsequently adapted by a relatively simple 'photo change'. The investigation not only highlighted the many opportunities this document forger seized upon, but also the weak links in the visa provision procedures, the weaknesses of the decentralised production of passports, the circulation of blank passports, the habit of 'losing' passports (and applying for a new one), and the habit of 'lending' passports to human smugglers. This case also illustrates the direct link between global crimes such as human smuggling and the very 'local' world of burglars, robbers and receivers. Local thefts of cash, passports and credit cards, involving addicts and frequent offenders, are related to global crimes such as human smuggling.

In many cases, human smuggling is interrelated with local ethnic communities. People speak relatively openly about human smuggling, and family members, friends and acquaintances often assist in buying tickets, transporting people or providing shelter (Kleemans 2009). In the past, Dutch centres for asylum seekers emerged as convenient places for temporary accommodation and as full-service facilities for smugglers. In one case, a human smuggler even refused the offer of a place of his own, because the asylum centre provided him with so many opportunities for his smuggling business.

Although a traditional view on combating human smuggling focuses on border controls, research shows that prevention should also target 'regular' migration channels and forged documents: entering as a legal immigrant (using forged documents), marriage fraud, business invitations, and the use of tourist, student or scholar visas. Forged documents are a central theme in human smuggling investigations, and this is a perfect focus for situational crime prevention (see also Van de Bunt and Van der Schoot 2003).

Besides general living conditions and dual labour markets, an additional attractive feature of EU countries involves the welfare state and access through asylum systems. During the 1990s the rate of migrants applying for asylum in Europe rose to unprecedented numbers, partly because the asylum system provided one of the few opportunities to enter Europe legally (Neske and Doomernik 2006). The sheer number of applicants, and the difficulty of distinguishing between true political refugees and economic migrants, seriously undermined the efficiency and legitimacy of asylum adjudication processes. Careful, protracted and individualised procedures were an easy prey for smugglers and immigrants, who forged or destroyed documents and used fabricated stories about countries of origin and travel routes. As a result, many procedures, for true political refugees and economic immigrants alike, have become shorter, stricter and less individualised (e.g. general 'safe' areas and regions) and are accompanied by less generous facilities. Furthermore, visa regulations have been changed, pre-boarding checks have been strengthened, and carrier sanctions have been imposed (for instance making airline companies responsible for checks on irregular migration). All these initiatives may be regarded as opportunity-reducing measures, targeting mechanisms that are actually used by human smugglers and illegal immigrants (Kleemans 2009).

Another policy strategy involves demand-reducing initiatives such as curbing access to the welfare state and making employers or companies responsible for contracting illegal labourers (e.g. sanctions, inspections). These initiatives may indeed reduce demand, yet at the same time they make life much harder for illegal immigrants and their families. Engbersen, van der Leun and van der Boom (2007) point to the unintended side effects of the very effective way Northern European welfare states are able to exclude illegal immigrants from the formal economy and public services: illegal immigrants have to participate in various informal economies or, when lacking access through social networks, engage in criminal activities. In the United States, access to labour markets seems to be less restricted, and the welfare state plays a less dominant role than in many Northern European countries.

Conclusion

Cross-border crime poses new challenges for situational crime prevention and routine activity theory. As offenders face different bottlenecks from street crime, situational crime prevention measures are highly dependent on knowledge of the logistics of cross-border crime. In Ecstasy production and export, crucial logistical bottlenecks relate to importing scarce basic chemical compounds (precursors such as PMK), acquiring specialised equipment (hardware), and arranging export (as export generates the major profits). Each bottleneck may be the focus of situational crime prevention measures: regulation of and checks on precursors, raising awareness in the legal business community (e.g. among glassblowers, and other producers and distributors of equipment), and regulation of export. Export is often a 'blind spot', as the Customs services focus mainly on import and import duties. Cocaine import by couriers travelling from Curaçao to Amsterdam is another clear example of the potential of a situational approach towards cross-border crime. Tightening controls at airports, particularly at Curaçao, virtually wiped out this specific route that was used by many couriers. Interestingly, for several crime prevention measures the answer to the question of whether or not criminal groups were 'organising' these huge flows of couriers turned out to be irrelevant. Similarly, targeting money mules in the money laundering cases did not necessarily require elaborate insights into the networks behind the crime. Sufficient insight into the specific modus operandi often suffices: the use of large denominations (€500 notes), money exchange offices, physical transfers (money mules), and money transfers by relatives. Finally, the example of human smuggling shows how this phenomenon is characterised by co-production and mutual interests, and is related to 'regular' migration mechanisms: entering as a legal immigrant (by using forged documents), marriage fraud, the use of tourist, student or scholar visas, business invitations, asylum policies, and access to labour markets and the welfare state. These insights produce many options for situational crime prevention that go beyond building higher fences and tightening border controls.

Nevertheless, cases of cross-border crime also illuminate several limitations of situational crime prevention, and highlight various caveats. First, many cross-border crime problems are 'hidden' problems. If airline traffic is not checked systematically, flows of couriers go unnoticed or may be disregarded as a minor problem. If intrusive police investigations do not produce insight into crucial bottlenecks of Ecstasy producers, many options for situational measures may never enter the policy arena. Similarly, opportunities for crime prevention may be overlooked if police investigations focus solely on prosecuting offenders, impeding options to change opportunity structures in more structural ways.

Second, cross-border crime problems are often global or transnational problems with foreign 'problem owners' and 'local' solutions. Ecstasy production in the Netherlands creates spillover effects, affecting receiving countries such as the United States. Conversely, flows of couriers from Curaçao flooded Amsterdam Airport Schiphol and the Dutch criminal justice system. Many cross-border crime problems are discovered by foreign 'problem owners' and may be targeted by 'local solutions' in other countries. This makes the policy environment of situational crime prevention much more complex than where local street crime is concerned. One example is precursor flows from China. Fundamentally, it is clear that such a problem calls for international cooperation between the Netherlands and China in criminal justice operations or prevention. However, views on human rights and the death penalty may impose high barriers for effective cooperation.

Third, cross-border crime is often related to licit economic transit and passenger transit, and creates trade-off problems between economic interests and criminal justice interests. Balancing economic interests with adequate border controls is a very real problem for open Western economies. For example, 100 per cent controls on the legitimate flow of containers in a port the size of Rotterdam would have a devastating impact on the (European) economy. Furthermore, freedom of movement in the European Union is at odds with collective action. Entrepreneurs in cross-border crime know that checks in most places do not come even near to 100 per cent, and they act accordingly.

Fourth, criminal justice resources are limited, and cross-border crime may compete with more 'local' crime problems. For example, 100 per cent controls at Schiphol on flights from the Netherlands Antilles, Suriname and Venezuela stretched manpower to the point where controls on flights from other destinations had to be relaxed.

Finally, there is always a catch. We would be falling to a 'Soviet fallacy' if we assumed administrative measures and controls could completely annihilate crime. As the banking sector case illustrates, where rules are in place, opportunities for corruption may arise. Tightening rules and controls raises the rewards for those crime entrepreneurs who succeed in circumventing them. Corrupting 'guardians' becomes more attractive, and they become better positioned to demand higher bribes. So, strengthening guardianship can create new opportunities for crime, in this case corruption, and raises the classic but awkward question of who will guard the guardians.

All in all, identifying and solving problems of cross-border crime seems to require more effort, creativity and international cooperation than standard 'local' situational crime prevention. Cross-border crime poses many new theoretical and practical challenges that are yet to be met.

Notes

1 See Blickman (2005) for a discussion on worldwide figures.
2 For an in-depth overview, see also the recommendations by the Financial Action Task Force (FATF): http://www.fatf-gafi.org.

References

Albanese, J.S. (2008) 'Risk assessment in organized crime: Developing a market and product-based model to determine threat levels', *Journal of Contemporary Criminal Justice*, 24: 274–95.

Albini, J.L. (1971) *The American Mafia: Genesis of a Legend*. New York: Appleton.

Blickman, T. (2005) 'The ecstacy industry in the Netherlands in a global perspective', in P.C. van Duyne, K. von Lampe, M. van Dijck and J.L. Newell (eds), *The Organised Crime Economy: Managing Crime Markets in Europe*, pp. 231–59. Nijmegen: Wolf Legal Publishers.

Clarke, R.V. and Newman, G.R. (2006) *Outsmarting the Terrorists*. Westport: Praeger Security International.

Cornish, D.B. and Clarke, R.V. (2002) 'Analyzing organized crimes', in A. Piquero and S.G. Tibbetts (eds), *Rational Choice and Criminal Behavior: Recent Research and Future Challenges*, pp. 41–62. New York: Garland.

Engbersen, G., van der Leun, J.P. and van der Boom, J. (2007) 'The Fragmentation of Migration and Crime in the Netherlands', *Crime and Justice*, 35: 389–452.

Faber, W., Mostert, S., Nelen, J.M., Van Nunen, A.A.A. and La Roi, C. (2009) *Baselinestudy 'Criminaliteit en rechtshandhaving Curaçao en Bonaire'*. Oss/Amsterdam: Faber Organisatievernieuwing BV/Vrije Universiteit Amsterdam.

Fijnaut, C. and Paoli, L. (eds) (2004) *Organised Crime in Europe: Concepts, Patterns and Control Policies in the European Union and Beyond*. Dordrecht: Springer.

Felson, M. (1998) *Crime and Everyday Life* (2nd edn). London: Pine Forge Press.

Felson, M. (2006) The Ecosystem for Organized Crime, HEUNI paper No. 26. Helsinki: HEUNI.

Felson, M. and Clarke, R.V. (1998) *Opportunity Makes the Thief: Practical Theory for Crime Prevention*. London: Police Research Series.

Finckenauer, J.O. and Waring, E.J. (1998) *Russian Mafia in America: Immigration, Culture, and Crime*. Boston: Northeastern University Press.

Gambetta, D. (1993) *The Sicilian Mafia: The Business of Private Protection*. Cambridge: Harvard University Press.

Huisman, S. and Smits, E.M. (2008) *Synthetic Drugs and Precursors Subreport Crime Pattern Analysis 2007*. Driebergen: KLPD.

Jacobs, J.B. (1999) *Gotham Unbound: How New York City was Liberated from the Grip of Organized Crime*. New York and London: New York University Press.

Jacobs, J.B. and Peters, E. (2003) 'Labor Racketeering: The Mafia and the Unions', in M. Tonry (ed.), *Crime and Justice. A Review of Research*, 30: 229–82. Chicago: University of Chicago Press.

Kleemans, E. (2007) 'Organized crime, transit crime, and racketeering', in M. Tonry and C. Bijleveld (eds), *Crime and Justice in the Netherlands. Crime and Justice. A Review of Research*, 35: 163–215. Chicago: University of Chicago Press.

Kleemans, E.R. (2009) 'Human smuggling and human trafficking', in M. Tonry (ed.), *Oxford Handbook on Crime and Public Policy*, pp. 409–27. Oxford: Oxford University Press.

Kleemans, E.R. and de Poot, C.J. (2008) 'Criminal Careers in Organized Crime and Social Opportunity Structure', *European Journal of Criminology*, 5(1): 69–98.

Kleemans, E.R. and Van de Bunt, H.G. (1999) 'The social embeddedness of organized crime', *Transnational Organized Crime*, 5(2): 19–36.

Kleemans, E.R. and Van de Bunt, H.G. (2008) 'Organised crime, occupations and opportunity', *Global Crime*, 9(3): 185–97.

KLPD (Korps Landelijke Politiediensten)(2005) *Criminaliteitsbeeldanalyse Synthetische drugs 2002–2004 (Crime Analysis Synthetic Drugs 2002–2004)*. Driebergen: KLPD.

KLPD (Korps Landelijke Politiediensten) (2009) *Criminaliteitsbeeldanalyse Curaçao 2008 (Crime Analysis Curaçao 2008)*. Driebergen: KLPD.

Levi, M. and Reuter, P. (2006) 'Money laundering: a review of current controls and their consequences', in M. Tonry (ed.), *Crime and Justice: A Review of Research*, 34. Chicago: University of Chicago Press.

Ministerie van Justitie (2002a) 'Plan van aanpak drugssmokkel Schiphol', Tweede Kamer, vergaderjaar 2001–2002, 28 192, nr. 1.

Ministerie van Justitie (2002b), 'Vierde voortgangsrapportage drugssmokkel Schiphol', Tweede Kamer, vergaderjaar 2002–2003, 28 192, nr. 16.

Ministerie van Justitie (2004) 'Aanpak drugskoeriers Schiphol succes', 3 maart 2004.

Ministerie van Justitie (2006) 'Zevende voortgangsrapportage drugssmokkel Schiphol', Tweede Kamer, 5441455/06.

Neske, M. and Doomernik, J.M.J. (2006) 'Comparing notes: Perspectives on human smuggling in Austria, Germany, Italy and the Netherlands', *International Migration*, 4(4): 39–58.

Openbaar Ministerie Nederlandse Antillen (2008) *Jaarverslag 2007*. Willemstad.

Openbaar Ministerie Nederlandse Antillen (2009) *Jaarverslag 2008*. Willemstad.

Paoli, L. (2002) 'The paradoxes of organized crime', *Crime, Law and Social Change*, 37: 51–97.

Reuter, P. (1983) *Disorganized Crime: Illegal Markets and the Mafia*. Cambridge, MA: MIT Press.

Rogoff, K. (1998) 'Blessing or curse? Foreign and underground demand for euro notes', *Economic Policy*, 13(26): 263–303.

Soudijn, M.R.J. (2006) *Chinese Human Smuggling in Transit*. The Hague: Boom.

Soudijn, M.R.J. and Kleemans, E.R. (2009) 'Chinese Organized Crime and Situational Context: a Comparison of Human Smuggling and Synthetic Drugs Trafficking', in *Crime, Law and Social Change*, 52(5): 457–474.

Staring, R.H.J.M., Engbersen, G.B.M., Moerland, H., De Lange, N.E., Vermeulen, E.H. and Weltevrede, A. (2005) *De Sociale Organisatie van Mensensmokkel*. Amsterdam: Kerckebosch.

UNODC (2008) *World Drug Report 2008*. Vienna: United Nations Office on Drugs and Crime.

UNODC and World Bank (2007) *Crime, Violence, and Development: Trends, Costs, and Policy Options in the Caribbean*, Report No. 37820.

Van de Bunt, H.G. and Kleemans, E.R. (2007) *Georganiseerde Criminaliteit in Nederland. Derde Rapportage op basis van de Monitor Georganiseerde Criminaliteit* (Organised Crime in the Netherlands. Third report of the Dutch Organised Crime Monitor). The Hague: WODC/Boom.

Van de Bunt, H.G. and Van der Schoot (eds) (2003) *Prevention of Organised Crime: A Situational Approach*. Cullompton, UK: Willan Publishing.

Zhang, S.X., Chin, K.L. and Miller, J. (2007) 'Women's participation in Chinese transnational human smuggling: a gendered market perspective', *Criminology*, 45(3): 699–733.

Chapter 3

Preventing organised crime: the case of contraband cigarettes

Klaus von Lampe

Abstract

This essay examines the potential of situational crime prevention for curbing the smuggling and illicit distribution of cigarettes, specifically focusing on the situation in Germany during the 1990s. Data were mainly obtained from closed investigative files, media reports and official reports. For the purpose of analysis the cigarette black market is broken down into scripts of illicit activities taking place in particular situational settings. On this concrete level the usefulness of the 'Twenty-Five Techniques of Situational Crime Prevention' is discussed.

The lesson to be learned is that overall situational crime prevention appears to be an effective approach to tackling the trafficking in contraband cigarettes. The implementation of situational crime prevention techniques can take on fairly traditional forms in some instances while being unique and specific to the peculiarities of the illegal market in other instances. Some preventive measures have already been applied with some success, although adaptation and displacement have also occurred.

Introduction

In the first ever treatise on crime prevention, Cesare Beccaria (1986 [1764]: 63-4) noted that the crime of smuggling, citing tobacco as the only concrete example, 'arises from the law itself, since its advantages always grow with the tariff, and hence the temptation to smuggle'. Beccaria also noted the ease with which borders can be crossed as an important factor. Finally, he observed 'that offenses that men do not believe could be done to them', because they are not the sovereign collecting duties, 'do not interest them enough to arouse public indignation against perpetrators'. Men, therefore, 'do not see as much reason to disapprove of a smuggler'. Without too much effort it is possible to translate these observations from the eighteenth century into the language of routine activity theory and situational crime prevention by saying that cigarette smuggling is the result of motivated offenders in the presence of lucrative targets ('boundaries') in the absence of capable guardians (bystanders who 'do not see as much reason to disapprove of a smuggler'). The purpose of this chapter is to explore the usefulness of situational crime prevention in tackling the smuggling and illicit distribution of cigarettes, with a special focus on Western Europe and, more specifically, Germany.

The illegal cigarette business, in a nutshell, is a form of tax evasion. Through a number of different schemes, suppliers and customers circumvent the taxation of cigarettes. In many countries cigarettes are highly taxed commodities. In the member states of the European Union, for example, the level of taxation has been ranging between about 60 and 80 per cent of the retail selling price (European Commission 2005). Given the intricate link between the illicit cigarette trade and excise duties, as already recognised by Beccaria some 250 years ago, and the addictive nature of cigarettes, one might be tempted to reduce the problem to one of political will and to argue that all it would take to reduce or to entirely eliminate the illicit cigarette trade is to reduce or eliminate the taxes on cigarettes. For various reasons, however, the problem is more complex and more difficult to address. Political support for high tobacco taxes seems to be unfaltering, if not gaining momentum, so that any short- and medium-range preventive approach needs to accept high tax levels as a given. Moreover, the relationship between high tax levels and black market developments is less than clear. Illegal markets for cigarettes are not necessarily most prevalent in high-tax countries, and least prevalent in low-tax countries (Joossens and Raw 2002: 5–6). Likewise, there are substantial regional variations in illegal market prevalence within particular countries despite uniform tax rates nationwide (von Lampe 2006). It makes sense, therefore, to examine the illegal cigarette trade in a more comprehensive way, beyond the 'root cause' of taxation, when one wants to approach the problem from a crime prevention perspective.

The conceptual framework

Situational crime prevention aims to reduce opportunities for crime. It focuses on highly specific forms of crime, and considers the immediate environment in which the crime takes place with a view to increasing the effort and risks and reducing the rewards from crime (Clarke 1993: 3;

Cornish and Clarke 1986: 2). In principle, any type of crime lends itself to this kind of close scrutiny. To capture the complexity of some criminal activities 'crime-commission scripts' have been developed (Cornish 1994). These highlight the procedural nature of crime and help identify points of intervention in the process of crime.

It is assumed that the cigarette black market, analytically, consists of a variety of interlocking and parallel scripts which market participants follow. For the purpose of the present analysis, the illegal cigarette business is conceptualised in terms of sequential patterns of activity, or scripts, that violate the integrity of particular 'systems', including, but not confined to, the system of collecting excise duties. Particular phases in the sequential patterns of black market activity will be examined with a view to the applicability of the 'Twenty-Five Techniques of Situational Crime Prevention' (Cornish and Clarke 2003; Clarke and Eck 2005; see also Bouloukos *et al.* 2003). The 'Twenty-Five Techniques' are a classification scheme which brings the diverse opportunity-reducing measures that have been developed so far into a systematic order. It is essential to understand the mechanisms through which a technique will achieve its preventive effect. The 'Twenty-Five Techniques' are grouped in five broad categories: increase the effort (or difficulties) of crime, increase the risks of being apprehended, reduce the rewards, reduce provocations, and remove excuses (Clarke and Eck 2005: 75). The classification is used here as a heuristic device, not as a rigid framework. Therefore, the exact classification of the measures that appear to be relevant in the context of the cigarette black market is not a primary concern for the analysis.

Data

The data on which the following discussion is based pertain primarily to developments during the 1990s in Germany, more specifically the Berlin area which is by far the country's most significant regional illegal cigarette market in terms of both volume and visibility (von Lampe 2005). Three main kinds of data have been collected and analysed as part of a larger research project: criminal files (n = 104), hundreds of media reports retrieved, *inter alia*, from various press archives, and interviews with black market participants, Customs officers and representatives of the tobacco and transport industries. In addition to Germany, some references are made to the United Kingdom for illustrative purposes or to highlight certain aspects which are less prominent in Germany. With regard to the UK only open-source material has been collected (see also von Lampe 2006).

Overview: the main characteristics of the illegal cigarette market in Western Europe

Since the 1990s, Germany and the United Kingdom appear to have emerged as the major retail markets for contraband cigarettes within the European Union, with France, Belgium and the Netherlands also being identified as main destination countries (Council of the European Union 2003: 2; Lakhdar 2008; Regional Intelligence Liaison Office for Western Europe (RILO) 2001: 10, 12–13), although the role of the latter two may in fact be predominantly that of transshipment centres (van Dijck 2007; Vander Beken *et al.* 2008).

In the 1990s and well into the 2000s, cigarettes were supplied to the illegal market in three main ways: bootlegging, large-scale smuggling and counterfeiting.

1. Bootlegging which 'involves the purchase of cigarettes [...] in low-tax jurisdictions in amounts that exceed the limits set by customs regulations for resale in high-tax jurisdictions' (Joossens *et al.* 2000: 397). In these cases taxes on tobacco are paid, though not in the country of consumption.

2. Large-scale smuggling involves cigarettes procured in bulk directly or indirectly from manufacturers at a stage in the legitimate distribution process where Customs duties, excise taxes and VATs have not yet been paid. This applies to cigarettes 'in transit' to non-EU countries (Joossens *et al.* 2000: 398).

3. Counterfeiting involves the production of fake brand cigarettes by unauthorised manufacturers (HM Treasury 2004). For the most part, counterfeit cigarettes are said to be produced in 'outlaw factories' (Levin 2003) and tend to differ in every respect from their legal counterparts, including tobacco, paper, filter tips and packaging. Illegal cigarette factories producing such fakes have been located in many countries, primarily in China, but also in consumer countries including Germany and the United Kingdom.

Since 2004, a new phenomenon has begun to shape the cigarette black markets across Europe: cigarettes legally manufactured in Kaliningrad, Russia, and other locations in Eastern Europe under the brand name 'Jin Ling'. These cigarettes appear to be readily available to smugglers and, indeed, appear to be primarily distributed through illegal market channels (Candea *et al.* 2008a, 2008b).

The cigarettes which are procured for illegal distribution through these various schemes may go through similar and at times identical channels on the lower levels of the illegal market. This is especially true for the illegal cross-border transport of cigarettes, the modes of which vary not so much according to the source of the cigarettes but rather with the size of the consignments that are being moved. Large loads of about 1,000,000 sticks and more are typically transported concealed in or behind legal goods under the guise of legal cross-border commerce, whereas smaller consignments are typically embedded in the flow of non-commercial cross-border traffic, or are brought across the 'green border' on foot or by boat. Small consignments of cigarettes have also been smuggled through parcel post. This is especially prevalent in connection with the illicit sale of cigarettes over the internet (House of Commons 2005: Ev. 81).

Cigarettes may be directly passed on to consumers without any further activity other than the transportation to the place where suppliers and customers meet. In most cases, however, there is a separate pattern of activities linking procurement and retail distribution. On this intermediate level, which, in fact, may consist of several broadly similar sub-levels, the consignments of cigarettes are reconfigured and typically broken up into a number of smaller consignments which are then passed on to buyers positioned further down the distribution chain.

A variety of patterns have emerged by which contraband cigarettes are sold to consumers. These patterns can be grouped into three broad categories: open distribution at public places, 'under-the-counter' distribution in semi-public places such as bars and kiosks, and clandestine distribution through social network relations. Interestingly, the dominant distribution scheme varies geographically. Street vending has been prevalent only in parts of Germany, namely the greater Berlin area, while clandestine distribution networks appear to be most common in West Germany. In contrast, there seems to have been very little overlap between legal and illegal distribution channels for cigarettes (von Lampe 2002).

Crime commission scripts and targeted systems

As a consequence of the complexity of the illegal smuggling and distribution of cigarettes there are numerous possible points of intervention from a situational crime prevention perspective. At the same time, the diversity of partly overlapping, partly interlocking and partly parallel schemes makes it difficult to devise a simple single measure. Conceptualising the illegal cigarette market in terms of crime commission scripts (Cornish 1994) and targeted 'systems' (Ekblom 2006; Tilley 2005) is an attempt to facilitate the analysis by better fitting this phenomenon into the framework of situational crime prevention.

Scripts are 'hypothesized knowledge structures' by which individuals are guided in routinised, yet inherently flexible goal-oriented behaviour through a sequence of steps or sub-goals (Cornish 1994: 157, 176). As already indicated, there are certain patterns of activity typically occurring in sequence as cigarettes are being moved down the distribution chain from the procurement level through various intermediate distribution levels to the level of retail selling. On each of these levels, in turn, offender conduct may follow particular sub-scripts.

The links between any two steps in the process can be understood as critical decision points where a given situation determines the choices offenders have on whether or not and how to proceed towards accomplishing the ultimate goal of a criminal endeavour. These decision points are also potential points of intervention to disrupt the crime script (Cornish 1994: 187). This implies that in principle for every step in the sequence of a crime event the full range of the techniques falling within the scope of situational crime prevention (see Cornish and Clarke 2003; Clarke and Eck 2005) have to be considered with regard to their potential for influencing the concrete offender decisions in that specific situation. It also implies that the situational crime prevention measures that are potentially relevant may vary from one phase to the next in the crime commission process (Cornish 1994: 164–5).

In order to understand the situational variations across the different levels of the illegal cigarette market it is important to clarify what the 'target' comprises. The concept of 'target' is of significance here for three reasons. First, as already indicated, direct victims or tangible objects as targets such as they appear in violent and property crimes, are absent or difficult to discern in the illegal cigarette market, given that the procurement of the cigarettes appearing on the black market normally does not involve theft but rather a chain of voluntary transactions (see e.g. Joossens and Raw 2002, 2008). Therefore it appears necessary to define 'targets' in more abstract terms; that is in terms of 'systems' which are negatively affected by particular types of illegal market activity (Ekblom 2006). Second, the sequential nature of the smuggling and illegal distribution of cigarettes means that while each endeavour is geared towards attaining a particular goal, which in turn is defined by a particular 'target', the proximity to this 'target' may vary across the whole crime sequence. This has obvious consequences for the degree of illegality of the offender conduct in light of the limited criminalisation of preparatory acts. But it also seems that the remoteness or closeness of a 'target' influences the possibilities for interventions on the micro level. For example, the presence of individuals who could function as discouragers of crime is likely to decrease with the distance to a 'target'. Third, it is assumed that the 'targets' broadly defined as vulnerable 'systems' vary across the different levels of the black market, and that with the 'targets' also the potential 'guardians' differ. This means that as one follows the sequence of black market activities step by step, offenders may well face fundamentally different constellations, defined by different sets of targets and potential guardians.

In the situational crime prevention literature the conceptualisation of 'targets' in terms of 'systems' has not gone beyond the broad formulation presented by Ekblom, who referred to a 'system' as one possible object of crime that is 'vulnerable, provocative or attractive' (Ekblom 2006: 248). Tilley has written about 'systems', but in a much broader sense. He defines systems as 'any set of organized or consciously-developed habitual human behaviours' as opposed to 'unorganized, though not necessarily unstructured, human action' (Tilley 2005: 267). While this broad conceptualisation is useful, the perspective adopted here is much narrower. Tilley's concern is with the various ways in which the design of systems influences opportunities for crime and, conversely, how changes in the design of systems can reduce opportunities. The following analysis will look at systems only insofar as they are designed to promote or safeguard certain interests which are compromised by some aspect of the cigarette black market, or by the illegal cigarette market as a whole.

The system most directly and most profoundly affected by the illegal cigarette market is the one for collecting excise duties on cigarettes. At the same time, it is also the least tangible system because, as will be explained in more detail below, black market participants do not have to deal with the procedural and institutional structures of this system in any way in the course of their activities. Less elusive systems that black market participants may be interfering with include the Community Transit System as the prescribed mode of transport of untaxed cigarettes within the EU, the tobacco companies' distribution systems in destined non-EU markets, the external EU border (including Customs borders as they exist around Customs warehouses within the territory of the EU), and the system of legal wholesale and retail distribution of cigarettes within the EU member states in question.

It is not possible in this chapter to analyse exhaustively all aspects of the illegal cigarette market with the same detail. Rather, in the following sections an in-depth look will be provided only with regard to small-scale smuggling and the open retail sale of contraband cigarettes. This brings into focus the two areas which were central to the initial development of the cigarette black market in Germany (see von Lampe 2002). Other aspects of the cigarette black market which reflect later stages in the historical development, namely large-scale smuggling and counterfeiting, will be mentioned but briefly and only with regard to the successful application of crime prevention measures.

A close-up look at small-scale smuggling

Script

The patterns of small-scale cigarette smuggling have varied considerably over the years. The following script analysis of small-scale smuggling will take an ideal typical smuggler as an example who brought cigarettes from Poland to the Berlin area in the 1990s.

The first step in the script, following the initial decision to engage in cigarette smuggling, was to obtain a specific quantity of cigarettes. At least in the early phase of the black market this did not pose a practical or legal problem in light of the significant price differentials between the licit cigarette markets in Poland and Germany. Cigarettes for profitable resale in Germany could be easily obtained from legal outlets within Poland, including valuta stores ('Pewex') which sold Western brand cigarettes for hard currency.

In the second step the smuggler needed to prepare the cigarettes for transport across the border into Germany. A number of alternative sub-scripts were available, largely linked to the means of transport. Smuggling by bus required the hiding of contraband in pieces of luggage. The same applied to travel by train unless the cigarettes were hidden inside the train, for example behind the wall covering of rail cars, a technique that had long been popular among Polish smugglers in Soviet times with respect to other contraband, notably salami (Irek 1998: 58).

Motor vehicles offered a wider range of possibilities to conceal contraband. Various hollow spaces inside a car, for example behind the dashboard and underneath the rear bench, could be used as hiding places. Additional hidden compartments could be created with some technical expertise, for example by modifying the petrol tank so that it was internally divided into a smaller container holding the petrol while the rest of the original petrol tank was filled with contraband. In many cases, however, smugglers did not go to great efforts to conceal contraband.

After the cigarettes were stowed in whatever means of transport had been chosen, the actual criminal operation was set in motion by bringing the contraband across the border. There seems to have been little the smuggler could do to purposefully influence whether or not (and with what intensity) Customs controls occurred, in addition to the way the contraband was concealed.

Once the cigarettes had successfully been brought into Germany, the smuggler needed to link up with a buyer. While business relations between Polish smugglers and Vietnamese distributors of cigarettes seem to have developed over time, in many of the cases included in the sample of investigative files studied here, finding potential buyers posed a key challenge to smugglers. One pattern entailed taking the contraband cigarettes to 'dormitories' occupied by former Vietnamese contract workers and to randomly approach Vietnamese-looking individuals. In another common pattern, Polish smugglers sought out Vietnamese street vendors at their public selling places.

In the subsequent step of the script a price was negotiated and the smuggled cigarettes were sold and handed over to a Vietnamese buyer, either on the spot, or at some other, agreed upon location.

The script concluded with the smuggler departing from the scene of the transaction. Originally, the script had taken a different direction after the border crossing, containing a step for finding a suitable location for retail selling, a step for publicly displaying the contraband cigarettes, and a step for selling the cigarettes to passers-by.

Points and modes of intervention

The ideal typical script of small-scale smuggling from Poland to Germany took the offender essentially through three phases and three different situations: the preparatory phase in Poland, the border crossing, and the disposal of the contraband in Germany. In the process, the integrity of two systems was targeted: the Customs border between Poland and Germany, and the system for the collection of excise duties within Germany.

Procurement of cigarettes and concealment in means of transport

The first two steps in the script, procurement of cigarettes and concealment in the means of transport, were characterised by the remoteness of any affected targets, which translated into a largely non-hostile environment. From a crime prevention perspective this meant in effect that interventions would have had to be implemented at a meso or macro level rather than in the concrete situation in which the preparations for the smuggling operation took place.

One potentially effective macro-level intervention at the initial phase of the smuggling script would have been to decrease the cross-border price differentials by increasing tobacco taxes in Poland. This would have reduced the expected rewards from smuggling as a result of increased procurement costs and correspondingly it would have led to decreased profit margins. The European Union has long made efforts towards a harmonisation of excise duties, however, only with limited success (van der Hoek 2003).

The possibilities for intervention were similarly limited at the second step in the smuggling script, the concealment of contraband in the means of transport, namely cars and trains. An obvious measure which would have increased the efforts of smugglers would be to reduce the number and size of hollow spaces in the types of vehicle used. In the case of cars this would have had to be implemented by car manufacturers and could have borne fruit only in the long run. Modifications on trains would have appeared to be feasible, theoretically speaking, even when already in service, given the smaller overall number. In practice, however, new train cars were introduced which no longer permitted the concealment of contraband behind the wall covering (Irek 1998: 62).[1] It is not clear if that had been done with the intention of curbing smuggling, and what actual effect this has had on the nature and extent of cigarette smuggling.

The use of motor vehicles for transporting contraband opened up another entry point for manipulating the opportunity structure of small-scale cigarette smugglers. From the criminal file analysis it seems that a number of smugglers tried to avoid the confiscation and forfeiture of motor vehicles by using cars registered in the name of third persons. Extending liabilities so that third persons would have been at greater risk of having their cars impounded or at least withheld for an extended period of time could have discouraged smugglers directly, or it could at least have made it more difficult for potential smugglers to obtain necessary tools by inducing the owners of cars to turn down requests to use their vehicles. In this context it should be noted that the rigorous application of confiscation laws by British Customs against the so-called 'white van trade' is believed to have significantly contributed to a reduction in cross-Channel smuggling of cigarettes in the year 2000. The term 'white van trade' referred to the smuggling of duty-paid goods in light vehicles through the Channel ferry ports and the Channel Tunnel by small-scale operators who exploited cross-Channel tax differentials, especially with regard to Belgium and Luxembourg. The goods were bought ostensibly for personal use and were illegally sold on in the UK. The zero tolerance policy adopted by Customs meant that vehicles used for smuggling could be seized and even destroyed (HM Customs and Excise 2001: 9; House of Commons 2003: Q 173, 2005: Ev. 62, 83; Seely 2002: 13).

Cross-border transport

The actual smuggling of the cigarettes across the border constituted the third step in the smuggling script. Unlike the previous steps, the situation was defined by a clear target. The activity aimed at compromising the integrity of the border as a system to control and monitor the movement of goods and persons and to collect duties on certain types of goods, including cigarettes, except when they were moved under the strict regulations of the 'in-transit' system.

An obvious crime prevention strategy would have been to increase the efforts necessary for smugglers to bring contraband across the border. As with modifications of doors and windows to prevent trespassing and burglary, target hardening techniques could have been applied against cigarette smuggling, namely the erection of physical barriers such as fences to reduce the opportunities for irregular border crossings. While border fortifications were politically undesirable, there was at least one instance where target hardening reduced the permeability of the German–Polish border for contraband cigarettes. An important border crossing connecting Germany and Poland is a bridge spanning the Oder River on high grounds between the towns of Frankfurt (Oder) and Slubice. For some time during the 1990s, smugglers took advantage of the fact that one could walk over to the German side and drop packages containing cigarettes from the bridge down to the riverside walkway below before having to go through Customs at the end of the bridge. The packages, reportedly containing 10,000 cigarettes each, were picked up by accomplices and carried away. After a member of one smuggling group was accidentally hit and killed by a package (weighing about 15 kilograms), high wire fences were installed on the bridge. The measure did not entirely eliminate this form of smuggling because cigarettes could still be slipped through the fence. But for a while the measure significantly reduced the size of the packages that were dropped from the bridge to only 1,000 cigarettes each (Runkel 1995: 25). Interestingly, smugglers eventually adapted to the fence with a brazen new modus operandi involving a new pattern of offender cooperation. A group of about 50 men would gather near the fence so as to block from view one accomplice who cut a large hole in the fence using a bolt cutter. Others would then run up and drop large packages, reportedly containing 5,000 cigarettes and more, through the hole in the fence down to yet other waiting accomplices who stood ready to load the cigarettes into cars and quickly drive away. This new scheme prompted the authorities to install a net underneath the bridge out of the reach of any smugglers and positioned in such a way that any cigarettes dropped from the bridge would be caught in it (Prutean 1996). In response, smugglers reportedly switched to the use of boats and rafts to bring cigarettes across the Oder River (Steyer 1996).

In addition to physical barriers, the strengthening of formal surveillance to increase the risks of apprehension seems to be an obvious choice. More intense formal surveillance should increase the likelihood that a given smuggling operation is uncovered. This, in turn, should enter into the cost–benefit calculation of those who engage in smuggling on a continuous basis (see Irek 1998: 59). Increased formal surveillance at the border can occur in two basic forms, the monitoring of cross-border traffic at designated border crossings, and the control of the 'green border' in order to detect irregular movements. Prior to the accession of Poland and the Czech Republic to the European Union, Germany had increased its control efforts along the Eastern border, though primarily, it appears, in an effort to curb illegal migration. Increased surveillance was achieved through increasing manpower and by technological means including night vision devices and motion sensors (Lüdi and Busch 1998; Witt 2003: 125–6). From the available data it is not clear what effect this had on the extent and modus operandi of cigarette smuggling. What can be said is that in the initial phase of the illegal market, in 1989 and early 1990, smugglers profited from lenient or absent controls at designated border crossings. The East German authorities only monitored Polish smugglers to ensure that no merchandise remained in East Germany. In West Berlin, no border checkpoints existed so that smugglers did not have to pass through any formal control. The removal of formal border controls along the German–Polish border in 2007 as a consequence of the eastward expansion of the

Schengen Region may have had a similar effect, at least for small-scale smuggling (Steyer 2008).

Apart from formal surveillance 'natural surveillance' by persons who serve as 'guardians' can potentially help to increase the (perceived) risk of apprehension of smugglers. One case in point involves anonymous travellers on crowded trains who inevitably observe how cigarettes are retrieved from hiding places in rail cars, if they have not already been privy to the cigarettes being stowed away in the first place (Irek 1998: 58). However, the available evidence indicates that the discouraging effect of the presence of anonymous others is limited. It seems that these individuals are usually not willing to interfere with smuggling activities and that this is taken into account by smugglers.

Given that apprehended small-scale smugglers often claim ignorance of the legal framework governing the importation of cigarettes, the posting of highly visible instructions at border crossings, or distributing information brochures could be effective in removing excuses and in alerting the conscience of potential smugglers. This pertains not only to the allowed limits for cross-border shopping. Another interesting detail gleaned from the analysed sample of criminal files is that smugglers often pretended they did not bring the cigarettes over the border but that they had received them from someone within Germany. Presumably these individuals believed that the *receiving* of contraband cigarettes did not constitute a criminal offence similar to the *smuggling* of cigarettes. However, the German law, since 1994, is only more lenient towards receivers of contraband cigarettes in cases of small amounts (up to 1,000 sticks) obtained for personal consumption (30a German Tobacco Tax Act). Prior to 1994 no distinction had been made at all.

In the UK, Customs has distributed flyers to cross-Channel travellers containing detailed information on the legal limits for bringing cigarettes into the country, and they have also aimed at the conscience of potential smugglers by pointing out the negative consequences of smuggling for tax revenues and legal cigarette vendors in Britain (HM Customs and Excise 2002). It is not clear what effect, if any, this awareness campaign has had.

Disposal of the contraband

The phases in the small-scale smuggling script following the crossing of the border were characterised by the absence of a tangible 'target'. The aim of the smuggler was to dispose of the contraband for a profit and to avoid apprehension.

From a situational crime prevention perspective, one aspect in this part of the script is of particular interest: the linking-up of Polish smugglers and Vietnamese dealers, because it commonly occurred at one of two distinct types of location, the immediate vicinity of 'dormitories' inhabited by Vietnamese and the vending places of Vietnamese street sellers. This meant that suppliers did not approach buyers based on pre-existing direct ties or through reference by a third person, but simply based on the expectation that at these places individuals could be found who would be willing and able to purchase contraband cigarettes. This expectation was fostered by the fact that Vietnamese people had indeed come to dominate the retail sale of contraband cigarettes as the result of a unique combination of factors (von Lampe 2002). The phenomenon of the street sale of contraband cigarettes will be discussed below. At this point it will have to suffice to point briefly out the significance of the Vietnamese dormitories as 'convergence settings'.

Offender convergence settings, as defined by Felson (2006: 9), are places that set the stage for crime by assembling accomplices and getting an illicit process started. Illicit transactions might occur in these settings, or might occur later. The concentration of the Vietnamese community in ethnically homogeneous dormitories had been a product of the segregation policies adopted by the East German Government towards foreign labourers. An attempt was made to keep contract labourers under tight surveillance and to separate them from the rest of the population outside their respective place of work. Even after German unification, former contract labourers continued to live in their previously assigned dormitories. As numerous similar cases confirm, it became a common pattern for smugglers to take their contraband directly to one of these dormitories and randomly to approach Vietnamese-looking persons. Even after business contacts had developed out of initial encounters, smugglers apparently found it easy to locate a buyer wherever the intended customer could not be located; not an unusual turn of events given the difficult communication between smugglers from Poland and Vietnamese dealers who usually did not share a common language (see also Irek 1998: 59). The dormitories became notorious as logistical centres of illegal market activity and some of them were closed down in the early 1990s (Schulz 1995). This, in effect, reduced the opportunities for smugglers to link up easily with potential suppliers, although there is no indication of a profound impact on the functioning of the overall supply chain connecting Polish smugglers and Vietnamese dealers.

'Natural surveillance' is another potentially risk-increasing factor in this context and, in fact, a number of investigations in the sample of criminal files were triggered by reports from onlookers, including members of the Vietnamese community, who observed the delivery of cigarettes by small-scale smugglers to Vietnamese dealers. Similar effects could have been expected from a strengthening of place management, especially in the case of the Vietnamese dormitories, which had on-site administrative staff. Finally, the strengthening of formal surveillance around the Vietnamese dormitories would most likely have increased the risk for smugglers, given that the surveillance that had been put in place proved highly efficient. In a number of analysed cases smugglers were apprehended by plain-clothes Customs agents who patrolled the streets around dormitories.

A close-up look at open retail selling

The selling of cigarettes to consumers marks the end of the illegal market distribution chain. As already indicated this can take on different forms with varying degrees of public exposure. At this point the focus will be only on open selling in public places, specifically that involving Vietnamese street vendors in the Berlin area.

Open retail selling had developed from simple, straightforward activities involving only one street vendor, to complex structures of a number of participants with different positions in a division of labour, including lookout, storage manager, money manager and street vendor (von Lampe, 2003). Notable changes had also occurred with regard to the volume of cigarettes in the possession of a street vendor. Originally, street vendors brought to the vending place all the cigarettes they hoped to sell on a given day, sometimes putting the entire inventory on display on blankets or on makeshift stalls made from cardboard boxes. Later, street vendors shifted to hiding the cigarettes near the vending location while only using an empty carton or a pack of legally purchased cigarettes to attract customers (von Lampe 2002, 2003).

Leaving aside a number of details, the open retail selling followed a fairly straightforward script. The first step was to select a suitable vending location. The primary criterion appears to have been the presence of a large number of people passing by, which was typically the case near supermarkets and subway stations. Another factor presumably was the availability of facilities to store and hide the cigarettes near the vending location. Storage facilities included bushes or holes dug in the ground, but also kiosks and other businesses which allowed vendors to stash their cigarettes there.

The second step was to bring the cigarettes to the vending location or to the hiding place. The actual selling activity began at the vending location with the public display of merchandise, or objects representing the merchandise, such as a legally purchased pack of cigarettes. Once the attention of a potential customer had been attracted, the vendor entered into negotiations about the kind of cigarettes, the amount and the price. When an agreement was reached, the cigarettes were either directly handed over, retrieved from the secret storage facility, or the customer was directed to another place where the transaction took place. After the transaction, the money was usually put in a place separate from the vending location and the stored cigarettes in order to camouflage its illicit origin.

Points and mode of intervention

A number of situational factors come into play in the script of street vending. However, it is questionable whether measures could realistically be implemented, given the politically problematic nature of some of them. The possibilities of hiding cigarettes near vending locations could, for example, have been reduced by removing public green spaces near supermarkets and subway stations. Opportunities to stash cigarettes could have been removed by closing nearby businesses which provided (or could have provided) support for illicit vendors. Legal and political issues aside, this could have been achieved at least with the more easily removable businesses operating from trailers, vans or stalls. A more indirect measure would have been to redesign the street layout so that there was less space for the illegal vendors to occupy, which might have increased the effort of street vending.

The strengthening of 'natural' and formal surveillance appears to be another, and perhaps more feasible approach, one which could have been directed both at the preparatory stages, including the hiding of cigarettes, and selling them. However, one of the problems of tackling the open illegal cigarette market had been not a lack of awareness of the time and place of illegal activity but a lack of resources on the part of the Customs service and the police to intervene at the numerous vending locations which in Berlin have ranged between about 350 and 1,200. Reports of illegal vending by 'guardians', then, did not necessarily increase risks. Rather, calls, for example, from legal cigarette retail outlets who reported illicit selling activity nearby, merely exerted pressure on the authorities to reallocate scarce resources and to intervene at a specific location.

The sheer number of vending places would also have rendered futile strategies to deflect offenders. Had there been only a few hot spots for selling the cigarettes, it might have been possible to seal off the area, so forcing street vendors into areas less suitable for street vending because, for example, of additional efforts that would have had to be made to attract customers. Such a strategy appeared feasible only during the early stages of the black market when open retail selling was concentrated at a few places in West Berlin.

As already mentioned, makeshift open-air markets had sprung up shortly after the Polish Government lifted travel restrictions for its citizens in January 1989. One location in particular emerged as the central marketplace, quickly dubbed 'Polenmarkt' (market of the Poles) by the media, in the desolate area adjacent to a flea market near the buildings of the Berlin Philharmonic Orchestra and the National Library. Up to several tens of thousands of Polish tourists congregated here to sell a wide range of merchandise of which smuggled cigarettes and alcohol constituted only a rather small share. Accordingly, illegal activities were only one of the concerns raised by the 'Polenmarkt'. Despicable sanitary conditions, the sale of meat in violation of public health regulations, and competition with the traders of the adjacent flea market fuelled demands to close down the 'Polenmarkt'. After some debate the West Berlin city government did indeed crack down on the 'Polenmarkt' and effectively interdicted all illegal market activity. The result was, according to observers, a dispersal of the illegal market over numerous other locations (Gast 1989). Eventually, Polish tourists were permitted to return to the original site. It was only a year later that the 'Polenmarkt' was irrevocably shut down when the area was fenced in. This measure was not aimed primarily at any illegal market activity, which had subsided as a result of price increases and stricter export controls in Poland. The fence was mainly set up in preparation for construction work on what, since the fall of the Berlin Wall, had become prime real estate property. In the meantime, vending places for contraband cigarettes had been established elsewhere in the city so that the closing down of the 'Polenmarkt' had little if any impact on the illegal cigarette market as far as can be judged in hindsight.

So far, the focus of this chapter has been on measures which have a potential to influence the opportunity structure for suppliers of contraband cigarettes. In illegal markets, however, actors on the demand side, the consumers of illicit goods and services, are also offenders who can potentially be influenced by increases in the costs and decreases in the benefits of illicit activities. On the retail level of the illegal cigarette market, therefore, there are two types of offenders which have to be taken into account, sellers and buyers. In part, the situation for buyers is defined by the same factors which are relevant for sellers as well, given that the 'target', the system for collecting excise takes, is the same. Such factors include, for example, 'natural' and formal surveillance.

Alerting conscience, through awareness campaigns, is also a possible technique. The German ministry of finance launched campaigns in the mid 1990s which reminded smokers of the lost tax revenues, the threat to legal retail dealers, and the alleged link to 'organized crime'.[2] Similar campaigns have been initiated by the tobacco industry in more recent years, including one sponsored by Philip Morris and the association of tobacco retailers in 2008.[3] As far as can be seen, there is no evidence that these campaigns had the intended impact of discouraging smokers from buying contraband cigarettes.

Crime prevention measures on other levels

In the previous section, the typical scripts of small-scale smuggling and open retail selling in Germany, specifically the Berlin area, have been examined step by step with a view to identifying possible points of intervention using the broad range of techniques of situational crime prevention. It should be obvious that these measures tackled only some of the elements of the overall phenomenon of smuggling and illicit distribution. A number of preventive measures have been adopted on other levels of the illegal cigarette market which should be briefly mentioned without being able, within the limits of this chapter, to go into them in any more detail.

A series of steps was taken during the 1990s to curb the diversion of cigarettes 'in transit' to the black market. These steps included the banning of cigarettes from the TIR system (Transport International Routier) which allows the transport of goods across various Customs borders without the payment of duties and taxes and using only a single document (European Parliament 1997: 30; Kampf 1996). In consequence, from then on untaxed cigarettes had to be transported under the Community Transit System, a concession system aimed at facilitating trade by allowing the temporary suspension of Customs duties, excise and VAT payable on goods originating from and/or destined for a third country while under transport within the EU (European Parliament 1997: 26). The System requires, in cases of road transport, that the principal, usually the freight forwarder, provide Customs with a legally enforceable guarantee. In February 1996, the so-called 100 per cent guarantee was introduced for sensitive goods, including cigarettes. The principal had to provide a specific guarantee covering 100 per cent of potential liability for each transit operation. Previously, the required guarantee only covered an amount corresponding to 30 per cent of the potential liability on an estimated one week's turnover of the respective principal (European Parliament 1997: 27). The introduction of the 100 per cent guarantee, according to an inquiry by the European Parliament, has been followed by a marked decline in transit fraud and a shift towards the legal export of cigarettes and subsequent illegal reimport, using traditional smuggling techniques and the false declaration of goods (European Parliament 1997: 56).

The shift from the diversion of cigarettes within the EU to their legal export and illegal reimport meant that the target of offenders operating on the procurement level of the black market shifted from the TIR system and the Community Transit System to the distribution systems that tobacco companies had established abroad. Somewhere along the distribution chain connecting tobacco manufacturers with wholesale distributors and retail dealers in a non-EU country, the cigarettes were redirected towards the black market within the EU. It has been alleged for many years that tobacco manufacturers knowingly supplied cigarettes to distributors who in turn supplied these cigarettes to smugglers. However, under increasing public and political pressure the tobacco industry has adopted a number of measures in recent years to prevent the diversion of its products into illegal channels. The most effective, and also most drastic, measure apparently was to discontinue export and to entirely withdraw from a particular market where cigarettes had previously returned to the domestic black market (House of Commons 2003: Q 310, appendix 3).

Other measures include markings on cigarette packages to determine leaks in the distribution chain, and the monitoring of business partners down to the retail level (Joossens and Raw 2008).

Closely related to the shift to illegal reimports of cigarettes is an increased need for the control of the cross-border movement of goods. Illegal reimport, as well as the smuggling of counterfeit cigarettes and, most recently, 'Jin Ling' cigarettes, is typically embedded in the flow of legal goods. A number of measures have been introduced in the past 10 years to make it more difficult to bring contraband cigarettes into the European Union. These measures include the introduction of stationary or mobile scanners and the use of tobacco sniffing dogs which substantially reduce the time needed for the control of a truck or container (Bundesministerium der Finanzen 1998: 62; van de Voort and O'Brien 2003: 10–11). Intensified controls of freight traffic have been linked to decreases in the number of cigarettes confiscated by Customs as they have been observed since 2000 in Germany, the Netherlands and most other Member States (Bundesministerium der Finanzen 2003: 57; Council of the European Union 2003: 2; van Duyne 2003: 287). Scanners and detector dogs, it has been argued by some, have led to an overall reduction in smuggling, or at least have forced smugglers to divide shipments into smaller consignments, thereby increasing transport costs, or to seek out new routes for their contraband shipments (van Duyne 2003: 287; House of Commons 2005: Ev. 77).

By necessity, large-scale smuggling is connected with facilities where a shipment can be stored until further distribution, or at least broken down into smaller consignments for immediate redistribution. These facilities, typically warehouses or barns, have to meet certain requirements, namely accessibility for trucks so that the unloading of the cargo can take place outside of the view of third persons. They may also have to be suitable for operating forklifts unless sufficient manpower is available to quickly remove the cargo from a truck. The Berlin-Brandenburg branch office of the German Customs service, as was related in an interview conducted in 2006, has tried to reduce the supply of such facilities. Officers systematically went to town council meetings with sets of photos to disseminate information about typical patterns of cigarette smugglers to raise awareness among property owners. This campaign was credited with an increase in reports of smuggling activity. It was also seen potentially to have contributed to the observed withdrawal of smugglers from the Berlin area as the preferred place for storing and reloading large-scale shipments of contraband cigarettes in the early 2000s.

Conclusion

In the preceding analysis the illegal cigarette market has been presented as a complex crime phenomenon which can be broken down into

Preventing organised crime: the case of contraband cigarettes

numerous scripts of illicit activity. An attempt was made to frame the steps in these scripts as crime settings which can be manipulated by situational crime prevention techniques. This has proven to be rather difficult. It has been argued that central to the definition of each crime setting is the presence of a target and that in the case of the illegal cigarette market a tangible target in the classic sense does not always exist. The conceptual framework of situational crime prevention seems to fit well the concrete situation of smuggling where contraband is physically brought across the border. The border lends itself to various methods of target hardening and increased surveillance, including the use of tobacco sniffing dogs and scanners. While there is no research into the effectiveness of these measures it seems that they have increased the risk of detection for cigarette smugglers. However, the border is only one of many potential points of intervention in the illegal market overall. Other situations where preventive measures might be applied can be found further up and down the chain of events between the original procurement of cigarettes for illicit distribution all the way to the retail selling of contraband cigarettes. Here the targets of illicit activity are more elusive and more remote, like the 'system' for collecting excise duties, the integrity of which is compromised not by any form of intrusion or manipulation, but simply by way of being circumvented by participants in the illegal market.

The absence of a tangible target not only makes it more complicated to apply the conceptual framework of situational crime prevention. It can also be hypothesised that the absence, or remoteness, of a tangible target translates into the absence of capable guardians in the broad sense. It is one of the striking features of the illegal market that offenders tend to operate in a complex 'social microcosm' characterised by interaction with and exposure to a large number of individuals, and that these individuals, even if they are outsiders, do not seem to discourage illegal activity by their mere presence (von Lampe 2007), as is the original assumption of Routine Activity Theory (Felson 1995: 53). An important strategy to tackle the smuggling and illegal distribution of cigarettes would therefore be to extend guardianship by increasing the awareness and the level of responsibility of those who come into contact with the participants in the market. Some approaches which have been taken in that direction have been mentioned. This includes increasing the stakes car owners have in preventing their vehicles being used for smuggling, or increasing the awareness of property owners and local communities in general about the attractiveness of certain facilities for storing and reloading bulk loads of contraband cigarettes. Awareness campaigns could presumably also be launched with regard to other target audiences, including the transport business which provides crucial logistical support for large-scale smuggling operations (von Lampe 2007; Vander Beken *et al.* 2005). In the latter case, awareness campaigns may well simultaneously be a means to remove excuses for those actors in the transport business who seemingly turn a blind eye to obvious indicators of illicit activity.

Another aspect which could only be touched upon briefly in this chapter is the situational contingency of offender structures. As indicated, the establishing of links at a crucial point in the distribution chain in the German illegal cigarette market, the point where smugglers and distributors meet, has been facilitated by the existence of two particular types of convergence settings. It seems worth exploring further more generally how the expansion of networks between illegal market participants is facilitated by situational factors.

Notes

1 Anecdotal evidence suggests that hidden compartments in trains on the railway lines between Germany and Poland continued to be used for smuggling. However, the cigarettes apparently were stowed in places only accessible from the outside, from where they could only be retrieved once the train had been brought to the depot (Bundesministerium des Innern, 2003: 33).
2 BMF-Finanznachrichten, 'Bundesfinanzministerium startet Antischmuggelkampagne', 53/1994, 3–4; Gast (1995); Seher (1995).
3 http://www.tabakwelt.de/cms/branchenthemen/schwarzrauchen.php (last viewed 25 February 2009)

References

Beccaria, C. (1986) *On Crimes and Punishment*. Indianapolis: Hackett.
Bouloukos, A., Farrell, G. and Laycock, G. (2003) 'Transnational Organised Crime in Europe and North America: Towards a Framework for Prevention', in Kauko Aromaa *et al.* (eds), *Crime and Criminal Justice in Europe and North America 1995–1997: Report on the Sixth United Nations Survey on Crime Trends and Criminal Justice Systems*. Helsinki: HEUNI, pp. 176192.
Bundesministerium der Finanzen (1998) *Die Arbeit des Zolls*. Bonn: Bundesministerium der Finanzen.
Bundesministerium des Innern (2003) *Bundesgrenzschutz-Jahresbericht 2002*. Berlin: Bundesministerium des Innern.
van de Bunt, H. and van der Schoot, C. (2003) *Prevention of Organised Crime: A situational approach*. The Hague: WODC.
Candea, S., Campbell, D., Lavrov, V. and Shleynov, R. (2008a) *Going Undercover: Inside Baltic Tobacco's Smuggling Empire*. The Centre for Public Integrity, http://www.publicintegrity.org/investigations/tobacco/articles/entry/843/ (last viewed 25 February 2009).
Candea, S., Campbell, D., Lavrov, V. and Shleynov, R. (2008b) *Made To Be Smuggled: Russian Contraband Cigarettes 'Flooding' EU*. The Centre for Public Integrity, http://www.publicintegrity.org/investigations/tobacco/articles/entry/763/ (last viewed 25 February 2009).

Clarke, R.V. (1993) 'Editor's Introduction', in R.V. Clarke (ed.), *Crime Prevention Studies*, Vol. 1. Monsey, NY: Criminal Justice Press, pp. 1–6.
Clarke, R.V. (1997) 'Introduction', in Ronald V. Clarke (ed.), *Situational Crime Prevention: Successful Case Studies* (2nd edn). Guilderland, NY: Harrow and Heston, pp. 1–43.
Clarke, R.V. and Eck, J.E. (2005) *Crime Analysis for Problem Solvers: In 60 Small Steps*. Washington DC: US Department of Justice.
Cohen, L.E. and Felson, M. (1979) 'Social Change and Crime Rate Trends: A Routine Activity Approach', *American Sociological Review*, 44(4): 588–608.
Cornish, D.B. (1994) 'The Procedural Analysis of Offending and Its Relevance for Situational Prevention', in R.V. Clarke (ed.), *Crime Prevention Studies*, Vol. 3. Monsey, NY: Criminal Justice Press, pp. 151–96.
Cornish, D.B. and Clarke, R.V. (1986) 'Introduction', in D.B. Cornish and R.V. Clarke (eds), *The Reasoning Criminal*. New York: Springer, pp. 2–16.
Cornish, D.B. and Clarke, R.V. (2003) 'Opportunities, Precipitators and Criminal Decisions: A Reply to Wortley's Critique of Situational Crime Prevention', in M.J. Smith and D.B. Cornish (eds), *Crime Prevention Studies*, Vol. 16. Monsey, NY: Criminal Justice Press, pp. 41–96.
Council of the European Union (2003) *The Smuggling of Manufactured Tobacco Products in the European Union and its Links with Organised Crime*, CRIMORG 90, 4 December, 15618/03.
van Dijck, M. (2007) 'Cigarette Shuffle: Organizing Tobacco Tax Evasion in the Netherlands', in P.C. van Duyne *et al.* (eds), *Crime Business and Crime Money in Europe: The Dirty Linen of Illicit Enterprise*. Nijmegen: Wolf Legal Publishers, pp. 157–93.
van Duyne, P.C. (2003) 'Organising Cigarette Smuggling and Policy Making, Ending up in Smoke', *Crime, Law and Social Change*, 39(3): 285–317.
Ekblom, P. (2006) 'Organised crime and the Conjunction of Criminal Opportunity framework', in A. Edwards and P. Gill (eds), *Transnational Organised Crime*. London: Routledge, pp. 241–63.
European Commission (2005) *Excise Duty Tables, Part III – Manufactured Tobacco*. Brussels: European Commission.
European Parliament Committee of Inquiry into the Community Transit System (1997) *Report on the Community Transit System*. Strasbourg: European Parliament.
Felson, M. (1995) 'Those Who Discourage Crime', in J.E. Eck and D. Weisburd (eds), *Crime Prevention Studies*, Vol. 4. Monsey, NY: Criminal Justice Press, pp. 53–66.
Felson, M. (2003) 'The Process of Co-Offending', in M.J. Smith and D.B. Cornish (eds), *Crime Prevention Studies*, Vol. 16. Monsey, NY: Criminal Justice Press, pp. 149–67.
Felson, M. (2006) *The Ecosystem for Organized Crime*, HEUNI Paper No. 26. Helsinki: HEUNI.
Gast, W. (1989) 'Handeln ist gefährlich geworden', *die tageszeitung*, 27 June.
Gast, W. (1995) 'Ähnlich wie das Rotlichtmilieu strukturiert', *die tageszeitung*, 31 March.
HM Customs and Excise (2001) *Tackling Indirect Tax Fraud*. London: HMCE.
HM Customs and Excise (2002) *Shopping Across the Channel? Bringing Back Cigarettes or Alcohol? Don't be taken for a smuggler*. London: HM Customs and Excise.

van der Hoek, M.P. (2003) 'Tax Harmonization and Competition in the European Union', *eJournal of Tax Research*, http://www.austlii.edu.au/au/journals/eJTR/2003/2.htm

HM Treasury (2004) *Counterfeit Cigarettes 2004*. www.hm-treasury.gov.uk

Hornsby, R. and Hobbs, D. (2007) 'A Zone of Ambiguity: The Political Economy of Cigarette Bootlegging', *British Journal of Criminology*, 47(4): 551–71.

House of Commons, Committee of Public Accounts (2003) *Third Report: Tobacco Smuggling*. London: The Stationery Office.

House of Commons, Treasury Committee (2005) *Excise Duty Fraud: Fourth Report of Session 2004–05*. London: The Stationery Office.

Irek, M. (1998) *Der Schmugglerzug: Warschau – Berlin – Warschau*. Berlin: Das Arabische Buch.

Joossens, L., Chaloupka, F.J., Merriman, D. and Yurekli, A. (2000) 'Issues in the smuggling of tobacco products', in P. Iha and F. Chaloupka (eds), *Tobacco control in developing countries*. Oxford: Oxford University Press, pp. 393–406.

Joossens, L. and Raw, M. (2002) *Turning Off The Tap: An update on cigarette smuggling in the UK and Sweden, with recommendations to control smuggling*. London: Cancer Research UK.

Joossens, L. and Raw, M. (2008) 'Progress in Combating Cigarette Smuggling: Controlling the Supply Chain', *Tobacco Control*, 17(6): 399–404.

Kampf, H.-J. (1996) 'Zollrechtliche Versandverfahren: Probleme der Gegenwart und Prognosen für die Zukunft', *AW-Prax*, January: 11–14.

Lakhdar, C.B. (2008) 'Quantitative and qualitative estimates of cross-border tobacco shopping and tobacco smuggling in France', *Tobacco Control*, 17(1): 12–16.

von Lampe, K. (2002) 'The Trafficking in Untaxed Cigarettes in Germany: A Case Study of the Social Embeddedness of Illegal Markets', in P.C. van Duyne, K. von Lampe and N. Passas (eds), *Upperworld and Underworld in Cross-Border Crime*. Nijmegen: Wolf Legal Publishers, pp. 141–61.

von Lampe, K. (2003) 'Organising the Nicotine Racket: Patterns of Criminal Cooperation in the Cigarette Black Market in Germany', in P.C. van Duyne, K. von Lampe, J.L. Newell (eds), *Criminal Finances and Organising Crime in Europe*. Nijmegen: Wolf Legal Publishers, pp. 41–65.

von Lampe, K. (2005) 'Explaining the Emergence of the Cigarette Black Market in Germany', in P.C. van Duyne *et al.* (eds), *The Organised Crime Economy: Managing Crime Markets in Europe*. Nijmegen: Wolf Legal Publishers, pp. 209–29.

von Lampe, K. (2006) 'The Cigarette Black Market in Germany and in the United Kingdom', *Journal of Financial Crime*, 13(2): 235–54.

von Lampe, K. (2007) 'Criminals are Not Alone: Some Observations on the Social Microcosm of Illegal Entrepreneurs', in P.C. van Duyne *et al.* (eds), *Crime Business and Crime Money in Europe: The Dirty Linen of Illicit Enterprise*. Nijmegen: Wolf Legal Publishers, pp. 131–55.

von Lampe, K. (2008) 'Organized Crime in Europe: Conceptions and Realities', *Policing* 2(1): 2–17.

Levin, M. (2003) 'Counterfeit Cigarettes Force Tobacco Firms to Fight Back', *Los Angeles Times*, 24 November.

Lüdi, J. and Busch, H. (1998) 'Nicht "undurchdringlich": Kontrolle und Überwachung der Schengener Außengrenze', *Bürgerrechte and Polizei/CILIP*, 59(1): 23–27.

Machowski, H. (1990) 'Polens schwieriger Weg in die Marktwirtschaft', *Aus Politik und Zeitgeschichte*, B12–13: 29–38.

Prutean, S. (1996) 'Ständig werden Löcher in die Gitter geschnitten', *Der Tagesspiegel*, 25 May.

RILO (Regional Intelligence Liaison Office for Western Europe) (2001) LASSO 2000: *Review on Cigarette Smuggling in Europe*. Cologne: RILO.

Runkel, W. (1995) 'Operation Blauer Dunst', *Die Zeit magazin*, 4 August: 16–25.

van der Schoot, C.R.A. (2006) *Organised Crime Prevention in the Netherlands: Exposing the Effectiveness of Preventive Measures*, doctoral dissertation, Erasmus Universiteit Rotterdam.

Schulz, G. (1995) 'Kriminalitätsbekämpfung durch Wohnheimschließung', *die tageszeitung*, 31 March.

Seely, A. (2002) *Cross Border Shopping and Smuggling*, House of Commons Library Research Paper 02/40.

Seher, D. (1995) 'Den Dealern auf der Spur', *Berliner Zeitung*, 17 February.

Steyer, C.-D. (1996) 'Mit vollbeladenem Autoreifen über die Oder', *Der Tagesspiegel*, 25 July.

Steyer, C.-D. (2008) 'Schwarzer Rauch im Grenzgebiet', *Der Tagesspiegel*, 26 June.

Tilley, N. (2005) 'Crime Prevention and System Design', in Nick Tilley (ed.), *Handbook of Crime Prevention and Community Safety*. Cullompton, Devon: Willan Publishing, pp. 266–93.

Vander Beken, T., Verpoest, K., Bucquoye, A. and Defruytier, M. (2005) 'The Vulnerability of Economic Sectors to (Organised) Crime: the Case of the European Road Freight Transport Sector', in P. C. van Duyne *et al.* (eds), *The Organised Crime Economy: Managing Crime Markets in Europe*. Nijmegen: Wolf Legal Publishers, pp. 19–41.

Vander Beken, T., Janssens, J., Verpoest, K., Balcaen, A. and Vander Laenen, F. (2008) 'Crossing Geographical, Legal and Moral Boundaries: the Belgian Cigarette Black Market', *Tobacco Control* 17(1): 60–5.

van de Voort, M. and O'Brien, K.A. (2003) *'Seacurity': Improving the Security of the Global Sea-Container Shipping System*. Santa Monica, CA: Rand.

Witt, A. (2003) *Die deutsch-polnische und die US-mexikanische Grenze: Grenzüberschreitende Zusammenarbeit zwischen regionaler Identität, nationaler Priorität und transkontinentaler Integration*. PhD dissertation, Humboldt-Universität Berlin, Germany.

Chapter 4

Sex trafficking: a target for situational crime prevention?

James O. Finckenauer and Ko-lin Chin

Abstract

One of the controversial issues surrounding sex trafficking is its links to prostitution. Among the points of disagreement are the degree to which sex trafficking feeds prostitution, and whether all prostitution is sex trafficking. Such disagreements aside, there is no question that the profit from sex trafficking derives from the exploitation of victims as prostituted persons. Thus, any preventive efforts focused on containing and reducing sex trafficking must, we believe, take account of its connections with prostitution.

Drawing largely on information from three empirical studies, our chapter examines this linkage. Subsumed within the general question of just how sex trafficking is connected to commercial sex and what the implications are for prevention, we examine how women are recruited, and what role their consent may play in possibly putting them on the road to victimisation. We look at who the traffickers are and how they are related to intermediaries at different stages in the process. Then we consider the character of the commercial sex industry itself to discern possible points for intervention and interference. From all this we formulate potential situational crime prevention approaches for reducing sex trafficking.

Introduction

> Sexual slavery is like any other business: raise the operating costs, create a risk of jail, and the human traffickers will quite sensibly shift to some other trade. (Kristof 2009)

Sex trafficking: a target for situational crime prevention?

This chapter will explore the applicability and possibilities for using various situational crime prevention approaches to combat sex trafficking; a crime that has been widely linked with organised crime. To do so, we will first develop the context for that exploration – a context that includes several themes or threads. First, just what is *organised crime* and how is it different from other crime that requires some organisational capability (but not necessarily 'real' organised crime as defined below) for its commission? Then, why is sex trafficking particularly apropos for consideration in this context? What do we see when we look closely at sex trafficking – especially with respect to who is trafficked, by whom, how, and to what end? What situational crime prevention methods have been used or suggested with respect to crimes that are organised in this fashion? What 'rational choices' are the various players in sex trafficking exercising? What are the costs and benefits related to those choices? And finally, might it be possible, as Kristof suggests in the quote above, to alter the costs/benefits equation so as to actually change those choices and thereby reduce sex trafficking?

To address these questions, we draw upon three original studies. These were conducted using different research methods in different parts of the world. All, however, are based upon in-depth interviews with women who had left their countries and were or had been participating in some form of prostitution at the time of interview. We examine these research findings to discern the situational factors that seem to be associated with commercial sex and the providers of sexual services, under the assumption that the demand generated by the various commercial sex venues is a major pull factor in transnational sex trafficking. Lastly, we consider how some of these situational factors linked to prostitution and sex trafficking might be defused through increasing the effort and risks, reducing the rewards and provocations, and removing the excuses.

Background and context

Because we are talking here about the ostensible role of organised crime in sex trafficking, we should first be clear about the terms which will define our discussion. 'Organized crime' is not *a* crime. Instead, it is a collection of crimes, carried out by some number of individuals who have a modicum of organisation. As others have noted, the problem with defining organised crime is not with the crime part, but with the organised part. Ironically for this purpose, however, the focus of situational crime prevention efforts is specifically on the target of the crime and not on the particular organisation or level of organisation of the criminals. As Natarajan and Clarke put it:

In applying situational prevention, we must focus not on criminal organizations, but on specific kinds of crime that rely for their accomplishment on cooperation and organisation among criminals. Organized crime syndicates might undertake some of these crimes, but many others, especially the newer forms of transnational crimes, might be undertaken by much more loosely structured enterprises consisting of temporary alliances of criminal entrepreneurs. (Natarajan and Clarke 2004: 7)

How then might this be addressed? Relevant here, we think, is the distinction between 'organised crime' and 'crimes that are organised'. The former is crime carried out by sophisticated criminal organisations that have continuity over crimes and over time. These organisations have both the ability and the reputation for the use of extreme instrumental violence, the capacity to gain monopoly control over criminal markets, and the resources and connections to corrupt law enforcement and political authority at the highest levels. It is these particular criminal organisations that are deservedly labelled organised crime. They are not, however, by any stretch of the imagination the only organisational form for committing crime.

There are a host of crimes that cannot be successfully carried out by individual criminals acting alone. For example, the trafficking of stolen goods such as cars requires procurement, transportation, storage and distribution. It is hard to envisage a lone person accomplishing all of this. Because crimes like these have a number of tasks that must be completed, more than one person is required. Thus, there must be some structural form, planning, direction, etc. That does not necessarily mean, however, that a criminal organisation of the kind previously described is required.

For purposes of this discussion, we will assume that whoever is doing it, and however they are organised (except with particular respect to the unique organisational structure necessary to facilitate the particular crime), the commission of the crime can be made more difficult and riskier, and the cost/benefit ratio of that crime can be altered. In other words, the 'organisation' of the crime can be attacked. With respect to sex trafficking, there is a potential negative side effect in doing this. Assuming a continuing demand from the various parties that drive the sex industry, making trafficking more difficult and riskier may mean driving up the cost and creating a more lucrative criminal enterprise for the 'real' organised crime groups, while at the same time driving out those who are simply criminal opportunists. Given who the real traffickers are, as you will see, we believe this is a risk worth taking.

One of the associations of sex trafficking with organised crime derives from its link to the sort of vice crimes that have long been connected with organised criminality. Because sex trafficking is related to vice, and in particular prostitution, special difficulties for prevention are posed. Unlike predatory crimes where there are clear victims, in vice crimes – such as those involving commercial sex – what is 'victimisation' and who exactly are the 'victims' is much less clear. Then there is also the special clandestine character of these crimes. Because there is a substantial demand from otherwise 'respectable' and 'legitimate' sectors of society for commercial sex, there is an ambiguous and ambivalent law enforcement stance and often significant official corruption. All this complicates the prevention picture.

Even within the realm of criminal activities that typically require some level of organisation for their completion, sex trafficking has a certain unique character. For instance, among the crimes that include providing goods and services that are illegal, regulated or in short supply, humans are a commodity that is reusable. They can be bought and sold, or even sell themselves, numerous times. As a result, victimisation can occur over and over. But at the same time, the criminals' exposure to the risk of being caught is also occurring over and over.

The matter of who are the victims in sex trafficking is important in part because it relates to the rational choice underpinnings of situational crime prevention. Rational choice theory (see Cornish and Clarke 1986) assumes that offenders make reasoned decisions about committing crimes after deciding that the chances of getting caught are relatively low, and the possibilities for a relatively good pay-off are high. It is, in other words, a kind of cost–benefits decision in economic terms. It seems not too much of a stretch to extend this notion to crime facilitators, i.e. persons not generally viewed by themselves or others as being criminals, but whose actions enable the commission of crimes. An example in this instance would be the consumers of commercial sex. We can extend it even further to persons who because of a 'rational choice' end up becoming victims themselves. Examples of the latter might be persons who choose to frequent drug hot spots in order to buy drugs, and gamblers who borrow money from mob-connected loan sharks.

The issue of so-called victimless crimes – crimes in which the victim's own choices and actions facilitate their victimisation – is a controversial one in part because it can lead to accusations of blaming the victim. This is not our intention. Nevertheless, it seems obvious that if one is considering who it is that is making decisions that result in commission of a crime, then choices made by victims that lead to crimes that would not have otherwise occurred are relevant to crime prevention.

We will present a case here for taking account of the rational choices not only of those who might be most directly labelled as criminals, but also of the various intermediaries and facilitators, and especially of the 'victims' themselves. All play roles in the sex trafficking process, and indeed it could not take place without the active participation of all these players. Let us begin with the female subjects who may or may not ultimately end up being victims.

Representatives of the US Immigration and Customs Enforcement (ICE) indicated at a 2006 conference on human trafficking that many (most) trafficking cases begin as human smuggling cases. Human smuggling is defined by the UN as 'the procurement, in order to obtain, directly or indirectly, a financial or other material benefit, of the illegal entry of a person into a State Party of which the person is not a national or permanent resident' (United Nations 2000). The participants in smuggling are willing illegal immigrants. This is not true of human trafficking, which is characterised by force, abduction, fraud, deception, coercion, or debt bondage. The participants are unwilling victims.

As witness the ICE conclusion cited above, however, the distinction between smuggling and trafficking may often become blurred. At least in the initial stages, there may be voluntary participation in the process by most of those who then subsequently may end up being victimised. With reference to transnational sex trafficking, some desire to migrate is an important characteristic of potential trafficking victims. It stands to reason that individuals who are not willing to migrate are much less likely to become victims of trafficking. Based upon her research, Galma Jahic concluded: 'While they [sex trafficking victims] are not willing participants in their abuse, the beginning of their journey tends to start with them seeking a way to migrate to a country where they see more opportunities for themselves' (Jahic 2009: 25). The fact that eventual victims have played an active role in a process that put them in a vulnerable position is an important consideration for prevention. Is that circumstance true in each and every case? No, as we will see; but it is true in the vast majority of cases.

If among the first persons making choices are the female subjects, we must ask what motivates their choices, and whether those factors are susceptible to remedy through the application of situational crime prevention measures. How might we deter/prevent possible victims from consenting to steps that ultimately lead them to becoming actual trafficking victims? As we know from a considerable body of research, the major driving factors in human trafficking are macro conditions, e.g. poor economies (no jobs), gender discrimination, civil strife, war and so on – all factors that particularly affect women because of their greater vulnerability. These obviously do not readily lend themselves to remedy through any means, and certainly not via typical situational crime prevention measures. It is still the case, however, that decisions are taken and choices are made based upon available information and understanding. This might be the avenue for intervention in attempting to shape victims' choices. We will come back to this.

The group that includes sex trafficking victims is also not homogeneous. At one end of a spectrum in this group we see women who have been labelled 'migrant sex workers'. These are commercial sex workers who migrate from one place to another to make more money through continuing their sex work. This should not be taken to mean that they cannot end up as trafficking victims. As researchers have pointed out, sex workers who decide to move and work abroad in hopes of making more money sometimes end up being victimised in a variety of ways, such as by having their earnings withheld, or being confined, or being physically abused. They thus become trafficking victims (see Banwell *et al.* 2000; Skeldon 2000).

Then there are women who, driven largely by the socio-economic conditions mentioned above, choose to migrate and knowingly become sex workers as the quickest way to make the most money. Just as in the first case, they too can end up being victimised through threats, beatings, deception or other forms of coercion.

Next are women for whom sex work is not originally part of their consideration, but who instead are promised any of a variety of jobs – entertainers, models, au pairs, domestic workers, etc. These jobs do not materialise, and they too end up in sex work. Although the end result may be the same, the choices at the outset, and at least some of the factors that shape those choices, are clearly quite different.

The exceptions to this rule of being willing and choosing to migrate (whether or not for sex work) are victims who are kidnapped and trafficked against their will, or child victims who are sold to sex traffickers by their parents or relatives. Such victims, whose circumstances are horrendous, and whose plight has received a great deal of attention in the media, nevertheless – as the available evidence indicates – constitute a small part of the sex trafficking victim population. For example, in data from the International Organisation for Migration to be discussed shortly, only a small minority (under 4 per cent) of the sex trafficking victims assisted by IOM between 1999 and 2003 reported being kidnapped (see Jahic 2009). The IOM further reported that of 7,711 cases of trafficking victims in 26 countries whom they assisted between 1999 and 2005, only 13 per cent were minors – and those cases involved all forms of trafficking, not just sex trafficking (IOM 2005). Such cases certainly need to be dealt with and stopped to the greatest extent possible. It should be recognised, however, that doing so will not necessarily make much of a dent in the overall sex trafficking problem.

The second group of choosers comprises the various functionaries in the sex trafficking process: the multiple actors with various responsibilities and a division of labour, including recruiters, middlemen, and the traffickers themselves. These actors are usually arranged in a kind of loose network, with shifting responsibilities and degrees of involvement. There are often blurred distinctions among the different roles. For example, the operator of a commercial sex business may do his or her own recruiting of women and act as their pimp, or contract through a trafficker for women, or he may work with one or more pimps. Zhang (2008) describes 'dyadic cartwheel networks' comprising multiple one-on-one relationships, that he says characterise Chinese human smuggling organisations, and possibly human traffickers as well. This means that the two parties to a transaction, e.g. the recruiter and a transporter, or a transporter and the operator of a safe house, know each other but not necessarily anyone else in the network. Our study of the sex trafficking of Chinese women, to be described shortly, suggests that this seems to be true in this case as well. Thinking of this network of individuals as making up a coherent, hierarchical, well-defined criminal organisation with the kind of harm capacity that we associate with true organised crime is a mistake.

Also in the network are the various trafficking facilitators such as drivers, corrupt officials (corruption is, indeed, a central element in human smuggling and trafficking because it makes it easier to get the migrants across the borders), the owners of hotels, motels, bars and discos, and others. These individuals also have shifting roles and degrees of involvement. For example, a driver, who may or may not be a regular taxi driver, simply delivers women to hotels or other establishments as ordered by clients, and then awaits their call to retrieve them. On the other hand, the manager of a bar or disco might directly engage in recruiting dancers/prostitutes and make the arrangements for bringing them to his establishment, or he might hire someone else to do this, or he might have an ongoing arrangement with traffickers to supply him with women as ordered and needed. The point is there is no single network model. Each model has a variety of actors, and these actors play different parts and have different levels of criminal culpability. This too creates a considerable challenge for prevention.

Next are the first line 'consumers' of sex trafficking victims, the so-called sex industry. These are the owners/operators of the various commercial sex establishments, for example, brothels, massage parlours, karaoke lounges, etc. Linked to these businesses are the pimps and so-called mommies, who have the most direct responsibility for managing the women as sex workers. They are usually the ones who deal with the women on a daily basis. The pimps may be intermediaries between the traffickers and the sex industry, or they may be traffickers themselves, or they may operate sex establishments. Whatever their specific role and modus operandi, they are all economic entrepreneurs – their interest in sex trafficking is making money from it. As such, despite being a multifaceted group, they are the closest to being similar to the typical offender targets for whom situational crime prevention is used to shift their rational choices. Again, however, the complexity and versatility adds to the challenge.

The final group of choosers is the actual customers, the consumers of commercial sex. They might pick up prostitutes on the street, sign in to a karaoke lounge for an evening of eating, drinking and entertainment (including sex), or order an 'escort' delivered to their hotel room while on a business trip. Among the most egregious examples of sex customers are those who sign on to sex tours where child sex is the 'entertainment', and those who are consumers of child porn.

According to a recent comparative examination of sex tourism and trafficking in Jamaica, Japan, the Netherlands and the United States by a non-governmental organisation called Shared Hope International, and presented in a report entitled simply *DEMAND* (2008: 3), 'the buyers of sexual services can be placed in three categories: situational, preferential and opportunistic'. Situational buyers are said to seek out and engage in commercial sex simply because it is available and tolerated. For example, when we (the authors) were in Singapore in 2007, we observed that at the end of their workday, migrant construction workers from Indonesia, Malaysia, etc., who were housed in a local hotel near the construction site, were loaded on a flat-bed truck and driven into the red light district of Singapore. After the evening's entertainment, they returned to the truck and were driven back to their hotel. It appeared that this entertainment was one of the perks of their employment.

The *DEMAND* report indicates that preferential buyers have a 'sexual preference and ... shop specifically in the markets providing the preferred victim or service' (p. 3). These consumers are obviously not new to the commercial sex scene. Because they are a category of buyers that would include paedophiles, consumers of child pornography, and other such specialists, they are likely to be the most difficult to effectively reach with any sort of prevention or deterrence programme.

The third group of buyers is described as 'opportunistic buyers'. Opportunistic buyers are those who 'purchase sex indiscriminately because they do not care, are wilfully blind to the age or willingness of the female, or are unable to differentiate between adults and minors' (*DEMAND* 2008: 3). According to the report, they are especially susceptible to the intensive marketing of sex via the internet, movies, cable television, video games, etc., and the increased normalisation of commercial sex in society. What the *DEMAND* report calls a culture of tolerance that enables commercial sex, but also facilitates exploitation and victimisation, surrounds each of these categories.

The cost–benefits equations that would influence the rational choices of all these various players are clearly going to be different. As a result, any effort to increase costs and reduce benefits is likewise going to have to be different. For instance, with the last combination of buyers, increasing costs might include public exposure, shaming, arrest, etc., and decreasing benefits could include increasing awareness of the exploitation/victimisation involved in commercial sex and of the risk of sexually transmitted diseases (STDs) and AIDS.

Mining some data

In order to discern more specifically exactly how sex trafficking operates, we have tapped into three different and original sets of empirical data.

The first data were compiled from our (Finckenauer and Chin) National Institute of Justice (NIJ)-sponsored study entitled 'A Case Study of Human Trafficking: The Transnational Movement of Chinese Women for Sex Work'. As part of this study, 350 subjects were interviewed in 10 different sites. The subjects consisted of sex workers (N = 164), sex ring operators (N = 76), law enforcement authorities (N = 76), and representatives of non-governmental organisations and other key informants (N = 34). The sites included major cities in Asia as well as the United States. For purposes of this chapter, we have analysed the specific responses of a subset of the Chinese sex workers (those for whom English translations of the interview transcripts were then available; N = 51). They were interviewed by Ko-lin Chin in Macau, Taipei, Bangkok, Kuala Lumpur, Singapore and Jakarta.

These female subjects were located in a variety of sex establishments, including some who were street walkers. The basic approach to finding and approaching the women was through the use of local informants and contacts. The women are purposely referred to as sex workers and not sex trafficking victims. Briefly, our assumption is that if there is abuse, coercion and exploitation, we should be able to discern it from this sex worker pool, since deliverers of commercial sex have to be sufficiently accessible and available to potential clients to make the sex business profitable. Does this mean that there are not sex trafficking victims being controlled and held in clandestine out-of-the-way settings? No, but in general if such settings are so hidden as to be inaccessible, they are unlikely to be profitable enterprises. An exception, which would have been beyond the scope of our study, would be special sex venues dealing in, say, child prostitution, wherein the clientele are like the preferential buyers described earlier.

The local contacts in our research, who were persons (men and women) knowledgeable about the street scene in each city, made introductions, and assisted Professor Chin in gaining the trust and cooperation of the female subjects. The selection criteria included requirements that they be at least 18, from mainland China, and currently employed as a sex worker.

The second study was conducted by Galma Jahic, as part of her doctoral dissertation research at Rutgers University. Ms Jahic used data from two sources compiled by the International Organization for Migration (IOM). One contained data on 717 sex trafficking victims assisted by IOM between 1999 and 2003. A second source of data, also from IOM and also covering the period 1999–2003, included more extensive information on the victims' background and the nature of exploitation. Data for 551 victims were available in this second source. Since some of the same victims are included in both sources, the precise total number of victims from whom data are available from IOM cannot be discerned. The major limitations of these sorts of data are that they may not represent the universe of trafficking victims, and that victims may lie to agency representatives, either out of fear of retribution or to secure benefits for which they may otherwise be ineligible.

In addition, Jahic conducted 25 interviews in Bosnia-Herzegovina in 2004. Interviewees included representatives of law enforcement agencies and investigators from the immigration unit who were responsible for interviewing potential trafficking victims (N=15). Also interviewed were representatives of non-governmental organisations and service providers who worked directly with trafficking victims (N=6), as well as representatives of governmental and international organisations that deal with trafficking issues, either through policy or through services (N=4).

The third study was conducted by Oguzhan Demir, a captain with the Turkish National Police. This research too was the basis for a doctoral dissertation at Rutgers University completed in 2008. Demir's study was based in part on information compiled from victim interviews conducted by the Turkish police, as well as approximately 20 interviews of key law enforcement and non-governmental personnel by Demir himself.

Interviews of 430 alleged sex trafficking victims in Turkey were conducted between January 2004 and June 2007. The interviewers were especially trained personnel of the provincial city police departments of the Turkish National Police, assisted where necessary by a translator and/or a psychologist. The interviews collected background information on the victims, the details of the time, conditions, and process of their trafficking, and information about their traffickers.

This study too risks having an unrepresentative sample. It may well again be that some victims have special reasons to lie to the police or to withhold information. In response to such points, Demir emphasises that the interviewers were all experienced officers who had received special training in human trafficking and victim identification. In addition, the victims' accounts were compared for reliability with some combination of the particular traffickers' confessions, witness statements (such as those from customers), statements of sex workers who had been detected in the same place or incident, and other evidence collected during investigations. Thus, no information with respect to particular victims came solely from them. Again, is this foolproof? No, but then again neither are any other data on this topic.

Results

Following Clarke's (1997) prescriptions for devising situational crime prevention measures, we have collected data on the nature and dimensions of the specific crime phenomena of prostitution and sex trafficking. We can now use these data to analyse the situational conditions that both permit and facilitate their commission.

Push factors

It is clear from the three studies, as well as from a host of other work on human trafficking, that the principal motivating factors – factors that put people, in this case young women, in a position of vulnerability and susceptibility to recruitment – are economic. In case after case, the women interviewed mentioned economic hardship and unemployment or underemployment as the main factors that motivated them to want to migrate. Also mentioned are other circumstances such as domestic and marriage problems.

To illustrate, when Chin asked his Chinese subjects what prompted them to come to the country in which they were working as a sex worker, the vast majority (two-thirds) said they came to get involved in sex work and to make money. Demir found that a third of the women in his sample reported having no job in their home country. When the women were asked about their main reason for travelling to Turkey, half of them reported that their main motivation was to find jobs as domestic workers. But interestingly, almost a third reported an intention to work as sex workers. The others came as tourists or seeking marriage. A Ukrainian woman explained her rationale as follows:

> I used to work as a barmaid in a club and was making good money. I was living with my family; however, I had lots of problems with them because they did not like me. I had heard from my friends that they could make good money in Turkey in exchange of sex work. I asked one of them to take me to Turkey with her. She paid my passport and ticket expenses and we left for Turkey together.

Almost half of the Chinese women reported having already been sex workers in China before migrating. The great majority, whether or not they were already prostitutes, knew they would be sex workers once they arrived at their destinations. Typical stories of these women are the following:

> The main reason [prompting her to come to Singapore] is for money. I make 400–500 RMB [US$54–67] per day in China, but I make 400–500 Singapore dollar [US$266–333] per day here, it is incomparable. I have planned to work as a prostitute before I came here. (Singapore sex worker)

> The main reason is to make money. I have heard before I came here that sex workers in Singapore can make lots of money. I came to Singapore as a tourist for several days three years ago. I have a relative here and I went to Geylang when I was here as a tourist. I

Sex trafficking: a target for situational crime prevention?

made a decision to come here and 'stand street' (street prostitute) one month ago because I cannot stand that kind of life with only 1,200 RMB [US$162] income each month. (Singapore sex worker)

When I did business in Shenzhen [China], the business is not good. I have a friend whose boyfriend is Taiwanese. He exclusively introduces women to foreign countries to work as prostitutes. He introduces women to go to Taiwan, Singapore, Japan, and Indonesia. He always told me how nice Indonesia is; it is easier to make money; and there is a good chance for me to marry an Indonesian if I go to Indonesia. He talked this in front of me for one year and tried to change my mind. He also made it clear that I would be a sex worker. (Jakarta sex worker)

Victimisation

The Chinese women interviewed fall by and large into the category of being migrant sex workers. They were asked explicitly whether anyone had used physical force, had deceived them, or had coerced them into sex work, and in literally every case the women indicated that they were not deceived, forced or otherwise coerced to become sex workers. The only hint of deception in just a handful of cases was when a subject said she had been led to believe that she would not have to service as many clients as she did, and that she would be making even more money than she was. Nearly all of the Chinese sex workers thus denied being victims of force, fraud or coercion. Where there was any indication of deception, and again this was in a very small minority of cases, it was of the kind illustrated in the answers below:

No. The person who took me here told me clearly what I would do in Malaysia. The only difference is that she over-evaluated how much we could earn. It is not that easy as she said to make money. (Chinese sex worker in Malaysia)

No. If there is deception, they just said that you need to accompany patrons to talk, drink, sing; this is what *zuotai* [sitting table] requires you to do. But how can you make money by *zuotai* only? Everyone knows that you need to sleep with patrons [provide sex service]. Only those who did not earn money in Malaysia will go back and say that they did not anticipate that they need to sleep with patrons; they refused [to sleep with patrons], so they did not make money and went back to China. Let them go to hell! They went back to China because no patrons like them. And because of them, my hometown villagers know what we are doing in Malaysia. How can those who have earned money and go back to China tell villagers what they actually did in Malaysia! (Chinese sex worker in Malaysia)

These elements of force, fraud and coercion – which are the defining elements of human trafficking in contrast to human smuggling – seem much more evident in the data compiled by Demir and Jahic. We should reiterate, however, that migrant sex workers can indeed become trafficking victims if and when these elements enter into the process.

Demir cites cases that likewise fall into the migrant or knowing sex worker category, but also some that are more obvious cases of sex trafficking. A young woman from Moldova explained:

> I decided to come to Turkey to make money by having sex with men. I have a couple of friends who previously came and made lots of money here. I came to Turkey by plane and went to a hotel which I heard about from my friends. I was going to discos and bars to find customers and have sex with them.

Similarly, a Ukrainian woman said:

> I used to work as a masseuse in my country. I heard from my friends several times that one could make much money in sex work in Turkey. I heard about a woman pimp who was famous among women that she was a good person, had a wide network, and paid good money to the women working with her. Women working with her had never problems in money and living conditions. Then, I decided to go to Turkey to find that woman.

But there was also this from a Moldovan girl, who came to Turkey expecting to work in a factory, but who was forced to have sex, finally escaped, but then began working on her own:

> When I came to Turkey, someone met me at the sea port and we went to a hotel. He told me there was no need for a worker at the factory, so I had to have sex with men, and I desperately agreed. I was going to different hotels to have sex with customers. My pimp did not pay me well. He was paying me a little and taking the big portion of the money that I made. I worked with him for about two and a half months. Then, I left him and went to another hotel in around Aksaray, Istanbul where a friend of mine from Moldova was working as prostitute. I started to work for my own.

In the Jahic study, only a small minority of the victims reported being kidnapped (3.6 per cent or 26 of 717 cases). She found that most of the women were recruited through personal contacts and newspaper advertisements. Demir found that the majority of the women in Turkey were offered a job (73 per cent), whereas 13 per cent reported being kidnapped or smuggled. In all three studies, the great majority of the potential migrants made a decision about whether to migrate or not, based on the information they had. While they had a clear understanding of why they wanted to leave their village and their country, they were much less clear about where they were going and what they would be doing when they got there. This was comparatively less true of the Chinese women.

The process

The potential victims' choice was usually based on an image, rather than on reality. And that image was shaped by the recruiters. Therefore, knowing just who the recruiters are, and what their message is, are critical to this initial stage of the sex trafficking process. As Jahic points out, the fact that most women were not kidnapped means that recruiters had to offer or promise something to them that would be attractive enough for these women to take the risk and to venture into international migration. The recruiters manipulate the information that they give to potential migrants about the amount of money they will earn. They generally misrepresent the costs and the benefits of moving to a new country in order to get the women to agree to migrate, using their assistance and services. Such agreement is important because cooperative migrants are much easier to get across national borders than are kidnap victims who may try to get attention and to escape. The manipulations and misrepresentations used by traffickers represent the kinds of deception that help define human trafficking.

In the case of the Chinese sex workers, girlfriends or at least female acquaintances who were often former prostitutes were usually instrumental in their recruitment. Boyfriends and in one case, the migrant's husband, were also recruiters. In only a few cases was recruitment by a third party such as the so-called 'chickenheads' or 'fake husbands'.

Jahic found that 43 per cent of the IOM subjects reported that they were recruited by a woman. In the Turkish study an even higher portion of recruiters were females (70 per cent). One police official said: 'Female recruiters can easily fool women and girls. They are more reliable and trusted than men.' Also, slightly more than half of all the Turkish study recruiters (56 per cent) were acquaintances of the women, i.e. friends, relatives and neighbours. One IOM official in Turkey said: 'Neighbours, friends and boyfriends are extremely trusted people engaging in recruitment, and that is why it is difficult to get information from victims about their recruiters.' Both Demir and Jahic suggest that females are more likely to recruit their clients through their social networks (families, relatives or friends) than are males.

This picture of the reality of how recruitment actually works is quite different from the one usually portrayed by the media – one in which innocent victims are abducted by organised crime figures. Does this happen? Yes, kidnapping does occur, and perhaps sometimes involves traffickers connected to organised crime. But based upon these data, this is the exception rather than the rule. Any efforts at prevention will have to take account of this reality.

Another finding relevant to potential preventative interventions is the fact that most of the women in these studies legally entered the countries where they were sex workers. Demir found many young women who were recruited (or at least believed they had been recruited) for work in the entertainment industry, and they arrived at the border with valid paperwork. Likewise among the Chinese women, they travelled with legal passports and visas. When asked whether they came to the country on their own or were helped by someone, three Chinese sex workers in Thailand described the process as follows:

> Yes. Somebody helped me when I went to the UAE and I spent 30,000 RMB [about US$4,000]. But I had passport already when I planned to go to Thailand. I applied a tourist visa and bought an air ticket by myself.

> It is my cousin who took me here. But I applied a passport and a visa on my own. They cost me only several hundred RMB [about US$50]. You can ask travel agency to apply a visa, it is very simple.

> No. I applied a passport by myself. My friend applied a visa and bought the air ticket for me.

Demir found that many of the Turkish women had little money and limited means for obtaining a passport and buying a travel ticket abroad. Therefore, recruitment offers were accompanied by offers of free travel tickets and assistance in obtaining a passport. These offers were particularly important in persuading the women to decide to leave their countries. The interviews showed that more than 60 per cent of them had accepted recruiter assistance in obtaining travel tickets or a passport.

One can get a sense of how these businesses operate and certain choices are made from the following account of a sex worker in Taiwan:

> I moved to Taiwan six years ago and did not work in the beginning. But, three years ago, I realised that I must have money. What will I do if my husband passed away? Who would give me money when I become old? So I decided to look for a job. I applied for a job at a massage parlour advertised in a newspaper.

> The owner's wife asked me to serve two customers when I came to the store for the interview. This is a fairly big store. There are more than 10 prostitutes and sometimes even up to 20, especially at night. The store is called a hair salon and massage parlour. But it is actually a 'black' store. We prostitutes sit in the lounge. Customers select one

of us and then go to a room. They have to take a shower themselves [we do not help them to shower in case there is a police raid].

Customers can also take prostitutes to nearby hotels. But most of them just have sex in the store in order to save money. People know the nature of the services we provide and it is impossible for customers to come here for other purposes [like just having a massage].

Some customers bring guns with them when they come; others have tattoos. Even so, they [the gangsters] are not bad customers. They do not have excessive demands and they are generous. For example, they usually buy 'overnight' and pay us a lot of tips if we are taken out.

There are also some police officers. The owner does not charge them but the owner will pay us after the officers leave. There are some *sanqi* [pimps] guys in front of our store. They solicit patrons outside. Taxi drivers bring customers to our store too. The owner pays them tips and this does not have any effect on our income.

With respect to the role of organised crime, the following information was provided by an individual who assisted Professor Chin in arranging contacts with sex workers in Taipei, Taiwan:

Why do [organised] gangs not do this business involving mainland sisters? It is because this is not a business with a lot of profit. The gangs look down on this business. In addition, you must be patient to do this business. You need to coax the women. Gang members tend to either beat them or spoil them. These are not solutions. It is impossible for them to run the business with patience and hard work. At best, they open a store and hire a manager. This business is between black and white (illegitimate and legitimate). People who run this business are those who are afraid of getting into trouble. They will not offend anybody, and bear whatever they have to. But they are also very suspicious, do not trust anyone.

Implications for situational crime prevention

The situational crime prevention framework divides into five broad categories of preventive effort: increasing the effort, increasing the risks, reducing the rewards, removing the excuses, and reducing the provocation. Returning to the notion that the first 'choosers' (from a rational choice perspective) in the string connecting sex trafficking and prostitution are the women/victims themselves, we can envisage two overlapping sets of factors that influence their choices and create a pool of potential victims: 'push/pull' factors, and 'supply/demand' factors. As long as there is a ready supply of young women being pushed by their circumstances to migrate, it will be difficult (impossible) to shut off the sex trafficking pipeline. So how might we reduce this supply and increase the effort necessary on the part of recruiters to recruit?

Building on the findings by Demir and Jahic that the women are presented with rosy pictures of well-paying jobs, and most importantly that these pictures are usually painted by women and/or other 'trusted' acquaintances, there is a need to counter this misinformation by demonstrating the stark reality of sex trafficking in order to increase their awareness of the risks and dangers. That reality often includes more and different working demands and less pay than promised, harsh living and working conditions, limited freedom, and physical and psychological abuse. Critically important to the credibility of the prevention effort would be that the facts be likewise presented by women and trusted messengers. One possibility is a cadre of former victims and female law enforcement agents who might visit schools and other groupings of young women to deliver the message. Respected women in the community, such as teachers and community leaders, might be similarly enlisted in this effort. Films or TV spots might be used in conjunction with these efforts, but not as substitutes for them.

Prior research has demonstrated that traditional public information campaigns are relatively ineffective in getting across the necessary message. Government-sponsored ads, posters, public service announcements, fact sheets, and so on are especially distrusted as propaganda. Poorly targeted awareness campaigns, propaganda and overblown scare tactics are unlikely to be effective (Lange 2008). The key seems to be a personal message from a trusted messenger. Since the studies also indicate that newspapers are being used to advertise overseas jobs for young women, and that these are a cover for recruiting sex workers, a system for monitoring such ads might be implemented.

Both Demir and Jahic found that many young women are recruited for the entertainment industry – in the Jahic study 44 per cent of sex trafficking victims had been offered jobs as dancers or other entertainers. Given this reality, increased border control attention and surveillance could be focused upon young women who have worked in the entertainment sector and/or who claim to be migrating because they have or they are seeking jobs as entertainers.

Corruption in the source countries, like their socio-economic and political conditions, is a macro problem. One way in which official corruption can touch directly on the crime of sex trafficking is through the counterfeiting or theft of visas, passports, and other immigration documents. Although the data reported here indicate that most of the women were travelling with legal documents, e.g. nearly all of the Chinese women and over 90 per cent of the victims interviewed in Turkey reported that they entered the country through legal border crossings with legal travel documents, this is not true in every case. In any event, better protecting these documents would increase the difficulty and the risk for traffickers using false documents. In their report on preventing organised crime, van de Bunt and van der Schoot (2003) recommend the following situational crime prevention steps in this regard:

> To reduce the opportunity of forging documents or the availability of forged documents . . . .[f]irstly, governments should pay more attention to the security of places where official documents are stored, e.g. town halls, to counteract the theft of blank passports. Greater security measures should also apply to the materials which are used to fabricate official documents, such as copper stamps and watermarks. Secondly, official documents should be made foolproof, making forgery almost impossible or at the very least, more difficult. To this end, modern techniques such as biometrics could be used. Finally, greater investments should be made in the verification of documents. Customs should have well-educated employees and hi-tech equipment at their disposal.

Once the women have been located in their particular commercial sex venue, there are a variety of facilitators who enable the businesses to actually operate. Cases in point are drivers or jockeys, who are often cab drivers. For example, the Chinese women reported that cellphone-equipped cab drivers delivered them to hotels or their other places of assignation, and then remained on call to pick them up again. Assuming there is some kind of licensing requirement for taxicabs and drivers, a rigorous licensing and enforcement regime could be instituted whereby participation in a commercial sex business would result in licence revocation, thus increasing the risk from enabling sex trafficking.

Major beneficiaries of sex trafficking are the numerous public or publicly available venues in which commercial sex services are offered. Most, if not all, of these venues have legitimate covers. They are hotels, motels, discos, nightclubs, bars, cafes, massage parlours, karaoke lounges, etc. The pimps and the street walkers, for example, have arrangements with nearby hotels for the use of their rooms. If law enforcement focuses on these venues, via frequent unannounced raids, they can target sex workers who are illegal aliens, i.e. those who do not have their paperwork or their paperwork is counterfeit. We observed such a practice in Taipei, Taiwan where we accompanied a police raid of a karaoke lounge. Although the lounge and its various sexual entertainments were not outlawed, the employment of illegal aliens was. Consequently, the raids disrupt business and alienate customers, but especially put the owners/operators on notice and deter the employment of foreign women (some of whom may be trafficking victims).

Where any form of licensing or registration is required to remain in business, the potential loss of that licence or registration is also a deterrent threat. One can get a sense of how hotel operators benefit from sex trafficking in Demir's quote from an Uzbek trafficking victim:

> There is a disco on the first floor of the hotel. Girls go to the customers, join them at their tables, and drink until the late hours. Then they agree on a price and take customers to their rooms. They have sex with them. If girls find customers that night, they pay $40 for the room and keep the remaining money which goes directly to the pimps. If they can't find customers, they stay in the hotel as usual, but don't pay for the room. It is an unwritten agreement with the girls and the hotel manager.

When we asked about the complicity of hotel owners/managers in the prostitution being conducted in their establishments, the Singapore police denied such complicity and claimed to be closely and regularly monitoring these places. It was apparent to us, however, that this was not so. For hotel/motel owners and others, rigorous licensing, monitoring and enforcement would deter the acquiescence of these establishments (for a price) to the needs of pimps and their sex workers. Likewise, unfavourable and unwanted publicity through the media could be bad for business and have a deterrent effect. Thus, the media should be enlisted in this effort.

Sex workers, who may include trafficking victims and who are working in public settings such as hotels and motels, bars and discos, are relatively exposed. It is the private settings, mainly apartments, that are more clandestine and therefore difficult to find. But these venues cannot be so hidden that potential customers are unaware of them. Private settings include apartments, houses/villas, etc. These have to be advertised in some fashion to potential customers. One of the findings of Demir's study was that more than half of the women were confined in private settings such as apartments and houses – places usually not visible to the public. Often, however, there are other people living in the same premises. In a step to increase the awareness of these other people, a Turkish municipality sent utility bills to customers with a refrigerator magnet attached. It included hotline numbers and encouraged customers and potential victims to contact officials and inform them if they thought someone was in danger. The Turkish National Police reported that roughly 80 per cent of the callers to their hotline were clients (who took pity on the victims), or were relatives or friends. They further indicated that 116 trafficking victims were rescued in 2006 as a result of a hotline contact.

In a similar instance, Dutch authorities found that clients were willing to report on the hard-to-detect involuntary prostitution. A campaign called 'Appearances Are Deceptive' stimulated clients to call an anonymous hotline, and was found to be a useful approach in combating sex trafficking (Kleemans 2009).

Service agencies and other companies, such as mail carriers, utility companies, rental managers and cleaning crews, can be enlisted in this effort via awareness campaigns. In these cases of victims being confined in private settings, such as apartments, the strategy should be to increase the awareness of utility workers, postal workers and others who have contact with such places, to alert them to the signs of sex trafficking. Here, too, exposure by means of unwanted publicity for these facilitators could act as a deterrent. Media attention can be focused on apartment buildings being used to confine sex trafficking victims. This would have the added value of enlisting the occupants of other apartments in the prevention effort.

In general, much more needs to be done to identify this 'hidden' crime. Extensive consciousness raising among the public, including educating citizens about suspicious activities that they should be aware of in their own neighbourhoods, may help to lessen the trafficking of people. Van der Schoot (2006) indicates that there is a greater need for 'guardianship', and for the government to introduce new 'watchdogs'. Those watchdogs could include citizen groups comparable to neighbourhood watch groups, or persons working with local community policing initiatives, as well as auditing authorities for bars, hotels and other venues that may become hot spots for commercial sex.

Last in the line of 'choosers' whose choices help fuel the crime of sex trafficking are the buyers of sexual services. Any logic model that delineates the roles and linkages among the actors who sustain a criminal enterprise or market would tell us that these buyers are critically important to sex trafficking. Unfortunately, none of the three studies referenced here collected information directly from buyers. We will, therefore, have to look briefly to other sources to see if we can learn anything that might help in formulating situational crime prevention strategies.

In the *DEMAND* report, reference is made to a 'culture of tolerance' that surrounds the commercial sex business. This culture of tolerance provides an environment in which behaviour that in other places or at other times would be regarded as deviant becomes normalised. In other words, commercial sex is normal and acceptable. In each of the cities where the Chinese sex workers were interviewed, for example, there was evidence of this culture of tolerance. In some cases prostitution was legal, although public solicitation might not be. The prostitution was sometimes linked to gambling casinos such as in Macau. Usually there was drinking and often drug use associated with the buying of sex services. Seeking sexual pleasure is just part of an entertainment package – an entertainment package that is an important source of revenue in many jurisdictions.

The culture of tolerance, which is both official and unofficial, presents an enormous challenge for crime prevention. Because the venues for commercial sex are critical elements of the profitability of the entertainment sector, officials are very reluctant to shut down those venues. The various venues in turn have to have a constant supply of new providers of sexual services, and thus the connection to sex trafficking. Within the culture of tolerance, it is still ultimately the individual buyers who drive the demand. And there have been a number of initiatives that have focused on increasing the risks and removing the excuses for these buyers. These initiatives include the following:

- Across the United States and Canada, a number of cities have implemented programmes for men arrested for soliciting sex acts. Known as 'john schools', their purpose is to eliminate recidivism for men who purchase sex acts. One such programme, the SAGE First Offender Prostitute Program in San Francisco, California, has won numerous awards for its innovative approach, and was recently found to be highly effective in substantially reducing recidivism among men arrested for soliciting prostitutes (see Shively et al. 2008). There is a caveat to these findings, however. Most of the men in these programmes were caught by the use of female decoys on the street. They may thus learn to recognise and avoid such decoys or to purchase sex acts in venues, such as from escort services and massage parlours, where decoy police officers cannot or do not work.

- Some cities in the US have implemented car confiscation programmes for men arrested for soliciting prostitutes.

- Some countries have passed laws to curb sex tourism. These extraterritorial laws permit prosecution of nationals for crimes committed abroad, regardless of whether the offence is punishable under the law of the country where it occurred.

- New laws also make the promotion of travel for the purpose of prostitution a felony crime and the grounds for denial or revocation of a travel agent's licence. This is obviously intended to increase the risk for agents who facilitate sex trafficking.

What, to sum up, should we conclude from these and the other examples? One conclusion is that adopting any or all of these measures is unlikely to have much impact upon *organised crime*. This is because true *organised crime* plays such a small role in sex trafficking. Just how small we do not know, but the evidence from the three studies cited here showed practically no role for organised crime. As we said earlier, the distinction between *organised crime* and crimes that are organised becomes less relevant when the target of the prevention effort is the crime and not the particular organisation and level of organisation of those committing the crime. Therefore, whoever is doing it, and however they are organised, committing the crime of sex trafficking can be made more difficult and more risky, and thus the cost–benefit ratio can be altered. Sex trafficking can be made less attractive and less lucrative, but doing so will require recognising that the links among a culture of tolerance, prostitution and sex trafficking are critical to prevention.

References

Banwell, S., Phillips, R. and Schmiechen, M. (2000) *Trafficking in women: Moldova and Ukraine*. Minneapolis, MN: Minnesota Advocates for Human Rights.

Clarke, R.V. (ed.) (1997) *Situational Crime Prevention: Successful Case Studies* (2nd edn). New York: Harrow and Heston.

Cornish, D.B. and Clarke, R.V. (eds) (1986) *The Reasoning Criminal – Rational Choice Perspectives on Offending*. Secaucus, NJ: Springer-Verlag.

Demir, O. (2008) *Characteristics of the Victims, the Traffickers and the Methods of Trafficking of Women for Sexual Exploitation in Turkey*. Newark, NJ: Rutgers University Graduate School.

Finckenauer, J. and Chin, K. (2006) *A Case Study of Human Trafficking: The Transnational Movement of Chinese Women for Sex Work*. Washington, DC: National Institute of Justice, NIJ 2006 IJ CX 0008.

International Organization for Migration. (2005) *IOM Data and Research on Human Trafficking: A Global Survey*. Geneva, Switzerland.

Jahic, G. (2009) *Analysis of Economic and Social Factors associated with Trafficking in Women: Thinking Globally, Researching Locally*. Newark, NJ: Rutgers University Graduate School.

Kleemans, E. (2009) 'Human smuggling and human trafficking', in M. Tonry (ed.), *The Oxford Handbook of Crime and Public Policy*. Oxford: Oxford University Press.

Kristof, Nicholas D. (2009) 'Striking the Brothel's Bottom Line', *New York Times*, 11 January.

Lange, A.G. (2008) 'Successes and failures in identifying human trafficking victims: why the domestic violence model has not worked.' Paper presented at the American Society of Criminology Annual Meeting, St Louis, MO, 13 November.

Natarajan, M. and Clarke, R.V. (2004) 'Understanding and controlling organised crime: The feasibility of a situational approach.' Paper presented at the annual Environmental Criminology and Crime Analysis Seminar, Wellington, New Zealand, July.

Shared Hope International (2008) *DEMAND. A Comparative Examination of Sex Tourism and Trafficking in Jamaica, Japan, the Netherlands, and the United States*, www.sharedhope.org.

Shively, M., Jalbert, S.K., Kling, R., Rhodes, W., Finn, P., Flygare, C., Tierney, L., Hunt, D., Squires, D., Dyous, C. And Wheeler, K. (2008) *Final Report on the Evaluation of the First Offender Prostitution Program*. Washington, DC: National Institute of Justice, 2005-DD-BX-0037, March.

Skeldon, R. (2000) 'Trafficking: A perspective from Asia', *International Migration*, 38(3): 7–30.

United Nations (2000) *Protocol against the smuggling of migrants by land, sea and air, supplementing the United Nations convention against transnational organized crime*. www.undoc.org/pdf/crime/final_instruments/383e.pdf

van de Bunt, H. and van der Schoot, C. (2003) *Prevention of Organised Crime: A Situational Approach*, Research and Documentation Centre of the Ministry of Justice in the Netherlands (WODC).

van der Schoot, C. (2006) *Organised Crime Prevention in the Netherlands*. PhD thesis, Erasmus University, Amsterdam.

Zhang, S.X. (2008) *Chinese Human Smuggling Organizations*. Palo Alto, CA: Stanford University Press.

Chapter 5

Situational prevention of organised timber theft and related corruption

Adam Graycar and Marcus Felson

Abstract

Organised theft of timber is a large and significant worldwide enterprise. Corruption in every step of the timber harvesting and selling process involves substantial criminal cooperation, with bribes paid at every stage of the way. The authors review several situational crime prevention measures that could be brought into play. The timber theft example has general significance, offering ideas for preventing criminal enterprise from expanding and for containing public corruption of other processes.

Introduction

At any time there is more timber being transported on the seas than there is oil. Illegal timber could not move on this scale without considerable organisation and corruption.

In 2007 the Indonesian Environment Minister estimated that over 70 per cent of the total timber harvest in that country was illegal (Environmental Investigation Agency 2007: 11). In recent years this has cost the government over $20 billion in revenue forgone and enforcement. Illegal cuts impair tree conservation, have implications for climate change, threaten endangered species and neglect scientific forestry (the science and art of cultivating, maintaining and developing forests, including harvesting that balances sustainability, regeneration and consumption).

The World Bank (2006) estimated the global forestry trade to be worth around $150 billion, and as much as 10 per cent of that was illegally sourced or traded. Thus the losses to illegal logging were likely to be between $10 and $15 billion per year, totalling around 2 billion cubic metres of illicit roundwood (logs, bolts or other round sections cut from trees for industrial or consumer uses), lumber (partly prepared timber, usually sawn into rough planks or otherwise roughly prepared for further processing) and plywood (boards consisting of two or more layers of timber glued, pressed or otherwise bonded together with the grain of adjacent layers crosswise to give it increased strength). The illegal trade in one wood species, ramin – which ends up as baby cribs, paintbrushes, pool cues and dowels – was alleged to be more profitable than drug smuggling (Khatchadourian 2008: 66)

Burma's rare old-growth teak is highly prized, and teams of Chinese loggers cross the border to cut what they can to take back across the border. Bribes are paid at every step of the way to either government or rebel forces (Environmental Investigation Agency 2007: 9). In many countries illegal timbering becomes a threat to government stability and the proceeds are used to kill people. 'Conflict timber', like conflict diamonds, engenders a special criminality, an example of crimes that are sometimes under the radar screen, yet have important human consequences.

Criminologists have paid little attention to illegalities in the timber trade, though there have been some papers (Green *et al.* 2007; White 2003; White 2008, for example). However, these works have not focused on organised crime or situational crime prevention. A situational approach is worthy of further analysis because traditional criminological approaches, telling people not to behave illegally and working on improving social conditions on the one hand, or using the might of law enforcement on the other, have had little effect on illegal timber markets. Exploring how to make the crime harder, how to increase the risks, reduce the rewards and remove excuses is worth a shot. Situational approaches to minimising corruption have received scant attention in the literature though Angela Gorta addressed the issue over a decade ago (Gorta 1998).

In addition, timber theft can become highly elaborate in its organisation, and can involve substantial corruption of public officials. That corruption has a market basis. A truckload of timber is worth over $US10,000 if legally harvested, but if illegally harvested this timber is likely to cost half the legal price. Asian furniture manufacturers, especially in China, Vietnam and Taiwan, are aware that illegal sources are considerably cheaper. After being manufactured into furniture, the product usually finds its way to the shelves of a major retailer in the US or Western Europe. Merbau timber stolen in Indonesia is worth $120 per cubic metre in the port, $250 upon arrival in China and $2,200 when sold for high-quality flooring in an American store (Environmental Investigation Agency 2007: 3).

Andreas Schloenhardt (2008) examines the illegal trade in timber products in the Asia/Pacific region, and this paragraph and the next report his findings. The largest forest area in the Asia/Pacific region is in Indonesia (second globally to Brazil), and it is variously estimated that over 70 per cent of the logging is illegal, and as much as three times the sustainable yield. While much of the logging in Indonesia involves logging without government permits 'corruption and bribery are perhaps the greatest facilitators of illegal logging in Indonesia' (Schloenhardt 2008: 53). This comes in a variety of forms, the military extorting fees from illegal loggers, and local and provincial officials accepting bribes to ignore illegality or corruptly to issue permits. There have also been allegations of judges taking bribes not to prosecute illegal loggers (*ibid.*: 53).

In Cambodia and Papua New Guinea there is commercial logging on a wide scale and it is generally undertaken in accordance with the issuing of commercial logging concessions. The introduction of these concessions increased the amount of illegality as activities that were formerly legal had become illegal, and widespread allegations have been made of corruption against government officials, politicians, police and military, all of whom supposedly have ignored illegal logging, and have manipulated the concession system. In Papua New Guinea, the second largest Asia/Pacific exporter of tropical logs (after Malaysia) it is suggested that 70–90 per cent of all logging is illegal and involves a high level of organisation.

China, the largest importer of timber and the largest consumer of illicit timber (Environmental Investigation Agency 2007), has relatively little logging because central controls have been implemented to counter severe environmental damage. China is a global intermediary for high-risk wood, transforming illegal timber from many countries into manufactured products for major consumer markets in the US and Europe (Environmental Investigation Agency 2007: 5). Much of the illegal wood in China comes from Russia, and in that country illegal logging has expanded enormously since the collapse of the Soviet Union, and Schloenhardt (2008: 67) lists several types of illegality in Russia – logging of protected species, logging outside authorised areas, excessive logging, logging using unauthorised methods of cutting trees, and logging without a permit or with a fake permit.

Schloenhardt surveys the situation across the Asia/Pacific region and describes the situation in about a dozen countries (2008: 51–133). All these countries are signatories to CITES, the Convention on International Trade in Endangered Species of Wild Flora and Fauna. This is the major international instrument in this field which deals with the illicit trade in timber. CITES, which has 169 signatories, is widely praised in international law as it is the only convention that requires state parties to criminalise the illicit trade in protected species and that enables importing countries to seize illegally sourced timber (Schloenhardt 2008: 11). Implementation unfortunately lags far behind the aspirations of the Convention.

Significance for organised crime

Some of the illicit timber trade requires complex criminal organisation with international activities. Consider that on a normal day a railyard in Suifenke, China, receives hundreds of rail cars carrying contraband timber from Primorski Krai, the neighboring province in the Russian Far East (Pye-Smith 2006). This amounts to more than 2.3 billion kilograms of hardwood per year, over half of which is harvested in violation of Russian law. To quote the Russian Minister for Natural Resources,

> There has emerged an entire criminal branch connected with the preparation, storage, transport and selling of stolen timber. (Quoted in Khatchadourian 2008: 64)

As noted above, wood items made in China and sold in the US are often made from timber imported from Russia and transported through Suifenke. Investigative journalists tell of protection money, payments to organised crime groups, and of business people and environmental activists murdered for interfering in the business practices of organised crime. Writing about the Russian Far East, Vandergert and Newell (2003: 304) have claimed that criminal organisations increasingly control much of the industry and that corrupt officials are linked with organised crime operations. These examples illustrate a complex network taking illicit products from the forest to the ultimate consumer.

A recent report (2007) by the Environmental Investigation Agency, an independent NGO with offices in Washington and London, noted that in numerous countries illegal logging is financed and conducted by criminal syndicates with high-level connections who maintain immunity with police and courts. Timber barons in countries as diverse as Indonesia, Malaysia, Honduras, Peru, Liberia and Papua New Guinea are well connected, often linked to other organised crime groups, and participate in international business on a huge scale, thus blending illegal activities with legal activity.

This chapter examines how situational crime prevention ideas have been applied to the illicit timber issue. We draw upon existing work by others and relate that work to the field of situational crime prevention. We are particularly interested in techniques which reduce the corruptive influence of organised criminal transport of timber products.

Fundamentals

Not all illicit timber trade is highly organised. We do not deny that some people steal limited amounts of wood for their own purposes or for direct sale to a few others. We acknowledge that unorganised timber thefts by lone individuals can add up. In many parts of the world, human populations are very large, tree populations are dwindling, and alternative fuel sources are non-existent or very expensive. Poor women scavenging for firewood perpetrate small-time thefts and this can have environmental significance, and can deplete the store of fuel for the future. Yet we maintain a focus in this chapter on more organised criminal efforts, especially when timber is imported and exported. With sufficient scale, timber theft is nearly always an organised crime because to fell, transport and sell trees of substantial volume and weight, several persons are required and they need to coordinate their efforts to a significant degree.

Sorting out the organisation process for timber theft is not always easy. The process is complicated by a fundamental fact of the illegal timber trade: that illegal and legal timber are often mixed together, with legal timber providing camouflage for contraband. Once processed the end consumer is not able to distinguish legal wood from illegal wood. As the span of the illicit timber trade widens and its complexity multiplies, so do the social, environmental, financial and economic consequences of the crimes. We can expect illegal cutting, illegal transport, and bribery at so many levels to involve organisation. As the illicit enterprise grows in size and complexity, more persons are involved and more corruption also emerges.

Many of these issues come into play when licit and illicit come together and legal provides camouflage for illegal. Markets in diamonds, wildlife, pharmaceuticals, art and antiquities, intellectual property to mention a few, have components where organised crime has a significant, but not necessarily a comprehensive role. The complexity of the processes of illegal trade in timber does raise some important questions of whether any one group can control the whole process from beginning to end. While this is not a likely scenario, there are multiple points at which illegal activities can occur, and empirical work should be undertaken to identify how and where the organised illegality and corruption occur.

The corruption issue

The impacts of corruption disproportionally affect the poorest and most vulnerable in any society, and when widespread, corruption deters investment and weakens economic growth. If system integrity is dubious then the rule of law cannot be maintained, and business cannot be well regulated. Corruption and bribery at all levels of government are common at every stage of this illicit and highly organised trade. Corruption, for simple purposes, can be defined as the abuse of entrusted power for personal gain (Transparency International 2008). For the illicit timber to have value added it must be cleared and then transported, often across a border. Documentation can be forged, or those approving the documentation can be bribed, as can the permits for clearing the timber in the first place. Corruption plays a major role in the component parts of timber theft. Timber trade involves many processes, from sourcing the timber to selling it in a distant country. Thus illicit timber trade readily becomes transnational organised crime, fostering substantial corruption in more than one nation.

Weak governance enhances the corruptive process for illegal logging, offering little counterweight to the illicit timber trade. That corruption process includes bribery, graft, kickbacks, extortion, misappropriation, abuse of discretion, self-dealing, patronage, nepotism, favouritism, conflict of interest and political corruption. The enormous profits also make it worthwhile for loggers to corrupt, and for government officials and politicians to accept illicit benefits from loggers. Moreover, nations with stronger governance are not immune to these corruptive influences.

Varieties of corruption

A long list of corrupt practices is found in the illicit logging process. Many of these practices can be sorted into three categories: *simple corruption* – officials provide normal services for an extra illicit charge; *corrupt complication* – officials insist upon providing new services, for an illicit charge; *corrupt enactment* – in response to a bribe, officials add new regulations or procedures to the legal regime, benefiting those who pay, and/or costing their rivals.

First, examples of simple corruption include taking bribes to

- grant a permit to cut trees in the public forest;
- allow harvesting beyond permit limits;
- speed up issuing a timber transit permit (so labour and capital can be optimised);
- speed up weighing the timber (also so labour and capital can be optimised);
- write down a lower or higher weight (depending on who is being defrauded);
- allow a heavy or illicit load to pass unimpeded;
- ignore forest laws, including laws forbidding harvest in parks and laws protecting endangered species.

Simple corruption also includes these actions during the transit process:

- officials stop legal log shipments on the road, demanding extra money to pass;
- customs agents taking bribes to ignore duties or endangered species protections;
- officials taking bribes to allow export of illegally harvested timber.

Second, more complex corruption includes the following:

- infrastructure development (new roads, new facilities, etc.) is dependent upon officials or politicians receiving kickbacks;
- ministers siphon timber money for personal enrichment – they take a cut on all transactions, or divert money that would normally go to the Treasury;
- politicians use timber receipts to fund political campaigns. The commodity of timber is embedded in the political process (and vice versa), and the wealth generated is used not only for personal gain, but also for the achievement of political office and political pay-offs. Sometimes politicians are beholden to senior officials without whom the money cannot be misapplied or stolen.

Third is an illegal enactment of new legal procedures. This means bribing politicians to write legislation, shape forest policy, develop favourable taxation policies, or grant large-scale concessions. Once enacted, the procedures become authoritative and legal.

Corruption and illegal organisation are quite complex processes. For the duration of this chapter we narrow down our concerns to consider the harvest, transit and sale of illegal timber.

Specific analysis of the timbering process

Perhaps the most important feature of situational crime prevention (Clarke 1997, 2008) is its emphasis on very specific analysis of each crime process. Magrath and associates (2007) offer such specificity in their study of timber thefts and frauds. Among the specific questions they raise about illicit forestry are these: Exactly which forest species are to be sold? From what specific locations are they taken? How is the volume of timber determined? When and where is ownership transferred? What is the sale design? Who are the parties involved at each step? What are the prices, rates and specific terms of the harvest, transfer, approval and taxing process?

They also specify periods during which timber transactions can be corrupted or defrauded, and put these periods in rough temporal order. Paraphrasing Magrath *et al.* (2007), these are as follows:

1. *During pre-harvest.* Collusion and deception occur in the pre-harvest contracting process, including bidding and negotiations. These frauds can occur in the earliest stages of logging, can involve substantial corruption, and set the stage for subsequent illegality. For example, at this stage there are opportunities to designate illegal wood as legal.
2. *During harvesting and transport.* During these stages, timber can be diverted. Loggers and truck drivers, sometimes with connivance of others, can deliver to unauthorised locations or falsify invoices.
3. *At the time of delivery, scaling or inventory.* At these stages those responsible for accepting deliveries or for measuring or recording quantities and weights can manipulate the records. They can commit many types of fraud or conceal frauds by others.
4. *At point of sale.* Those involved in logging or their agents can misrepresent the process to buyers who may or may not be aware that the source is illicit.

The timing of fraud depends on such factors as convenience, which private officials are directly involved in the fraud, and which government officials are corrupted. Although we have not offered a complete list of corrupt practices, we have explained that such practices have a certain logic and order that assists the design of situational measures against them. These measures are possible because theft of timber and its transport are crimes of opportunity, depending at several stages upon the complicity of others. As these crimes become more complex and corrupt, the offenders become more vulnerable to interventions at critical points in their illegal efforts.

Working with a commodity that is so thoroughly transformed and goes through so many processes, most of which add value along the way, and which occur in so many settings, often in many countries, creates an oversight nightmare. Fraud would be considerably limited if there were one body or office which had oversight of the whole process. There are still many tension points at which fraud could occur, or corrupt officials can make demands or take what is offered.

At some point most of the illegal timber finds its way into the legitimate economy, and regular commercial and regulatory processes come into play. There are two general sets of processes (and many shades within each). First, there is legally harvested timber which has, along the long road of transportation and value adding, been allowed to move to the next process only on payment of a corrupt consideration. Second, there is timber that is illegal when harvested, and corrupt considerations are required to keep it moving and integrated into the legitimate economy.

Situational prevention of timber theft

Magrath et al. (2007) detailed numerous situational prevention measures for forestry purposes. We have used Magrath et al.'s examples and have adapted Clarke's situational prevention measures to illustrate the specifics of the activities in timber theft, organised crime activity and corruption. We have repackaged these measures into seven categories:

1. Improve how timber is traced (increase risks [of being caught]);
2. Improve the technology of labelling timber (increase effort);
3. Make vehicles more traceable (increase risks);
4. Enhance inventory control and chain of custody (reduce rewards);
5. Reduce official discretion (increase effort);
6. Reduce procedural complexity (remove excuses);
7. Create simpler and more visible accounting formats and systems (increase risks).

The first three categories deal with tracing timber. A simple way to improve how timber is traced is to use labels. A commercial log labelling system tracks logs from stump to mill. Such a system makes it more difficult to hide the origins of timber, hence to conceal illicit origins. For example, a plastic tag indicating tree and log number can be attached to each log when harvested. A matching tag is placed on the stump, thus linking the two and producing a chain of custody. Chain of custody 'is the custodial sequence that occurs as ownership or control of the wood supply is transferred from one custodian to another along the supply chain. It is the method by which logs are tracked from the stump to the processing facility' (Magrath et al. 2007: 58). Simple technologies like fluorescent paint to identify logs through to more technological means such as transponders embedded in trees or logs, or microdot technology to identify assets, can assist the labelling and tracking process. They can be detected by authorities, but not as easily modified for criminal purposes.

In the third category vehicles can be tracked with mandatory truck or trailer identification. This can be either large numbers on both sides of the truck or Automatic Licence Plate Recognition (ALPR) which can be installed at main entrances to logging operations and designated checkpoints. Combined with CCTV, licence plates and vehicle ID can be checked against various databases of inventory on the move, of vehicles, and on people authorised to be in particular vehicles at particular times. With this in place, real travel time and real location can be plotted and confirmed with satellite-based navigation systems. Multiple methods can trace a truckload of timber, and it is this multiplicity that authorities can use, but criminals cannot easily circumvent, as there are too many linkages and connections.

The fourth category assists authorities to understand their product and its value, and identify fraud, corruption or collusion. Measuring and weighing the logs can produce enormous variations. If corruptly scaled (undermeasured) the loss can be large, and something as simple as a coloured crayon or marker notation on the end of the log can send a signal that the log has already been measured. This reduces the opportunity for a corrupt worker to falsify the record. It obliges a potentially corrupt scaler to measure correctly to avoid a possible discrepancy. Measuring and weighing the logs at the scale house can create opportunities for corruption and the process of issuing tickets can create a significant fraud situation, so means can be implemented to prevent fraudulent ticket processes. Cameras at the scale house can record every transaction and the record will maintain the chronological order. Cameras can also pick up the vehicle ID as well as the driver and the load. The chain of custody is a sequence of documentation from harvest to final sale.

The next three categories (5–7) have to do with the role of officials in potentially manipulating the process. Officials can make processes very complex, and for a consideration can cut through the complexity. They can exercise discretion, and not be accountable, and for a consideration exercise it in a particular way. Reducing official discretion serves to enhance accountability and makes it harder for officials to be corrupted. This includes making clear, consistent and coherent criteria for decisions about counting and grading timber, thus reducing the opportunity for officials to be corrupted. Reducing procedural complexity is part of this process. Very complex rules and bureaucracies are very easily corrupted, and hide the corruption that is there. Conversely, streamlining forestry rules and organisations serves to increase transparency and reduce the illicit opportunities. Finally, simpler accounting formats and systems make it more difficult to carry out and conceal corruption, especially if accounts are publicly available.

Conclusion

Underlying this chapter is a challenge – to apply situational thinking to a transnational crime that involves substantial organisation and corruption at many levels. Clearly, situational analysis and situational crime prevention may help reduce large-scale timber fraud, and the resulting corruption. More generally, we believe that corruption and organised crime are amenable to situational measures that are carefully applied at the right pressure points.

To find these pressure points, it is essential first to break each legal activity and routine into its smallest and specific components and sequences. Doing so gives us the ability to devise countermeasures. In timber theft, as we discover the process in strategic terms we begin to understand how to counter illicit acts. Two basic efforts are needed. First, one must ensure that there is a tracing process – a process that identifies the timber at all stages, from pre-cut to cut to transit, and to identify every step in the process, and break down every part of the custody chain into the smallest units. The second is to harness organisational auditing techniques to follow the transit process. This involves identifying and documenting each step that is taken and each process along the way, as a tree, perhaps illegally and corruptly, is transformed into a highly desirable value added commodity.

We suggest, too, that some of the principles offered here can in the future apply to other transnational organised offences and other issues in corruption. With more specific analyses of how goods and services move, it becomes possible to improve their auditing and to make them more difficult to corrupt. The pioneering work by Magrath and his colleagues at the World Bank demonstrates the applicability of situational crime prevention to natural resource management. It also points to the importance of blending criminological skills with environmental skills. Using situational analysis of forestry, experts in the future will be able to sort out the components and sequences of crime systems, find critical junctures at which corruption occurs, and figure out measures to interfere with the illicit process.

References

(All URLs correct at 27 June 2009)

Asher, W. (1999) *Why Governments Waste Natural Resources: Policy Failures in Developing Countries.* Baltimore: Johns Hopkins University Press.

Clarke, R.V. (2008) 'Situational crime prevention', in R. Wortley and L. Mazerolle (eds), *Environmental Criminology and Crime Analysis.* Cullompton, UK: Willan Publishing.

Clarke, R.V. (ed.) (1997) *Situational Crime Prevention: Successful Case Studies.* Albany New York: Harrow and Heston.

Environmental Investigation Agency (2007) *No questions asked: the impacts of US market demand for illegal timber.* Available from http://www.eia-global.org/forests_for_the_world/forests_for_the_world_reports.html

Gorta, A. (1998) 'Minimising corruption: Applying lessons from the crime prevention literature', *Crime, Law and Social Change*, 30, 67–87.

Green, P., Ward, T. and McConnachie, K. (2007) 'Logging and Legality: Environmental Crime, Civil Society, and the State', *Social Justice*, 34(2): 94–110.

Khatchadourian, R. (2008) 'Stealing the forests', *The New Yorker*, 84: 64–73 (6 October).

Magrath, W.B., Grandalski, R.L., Stuckey, G.L., Vikanes, G.B. and Wilkinson, G.R. (2007) *Timber Theft Prevention: Introduction to security for forest managers*. Washington: World Bank.

Naim, M. (2005) *Illicit: How Smugglers, Traffickers and Copycats are Hijacking the Global Economy*. New York: Doubleday.

Pye-Smith, C. (2006) *Logging in the Wild East: China and the forest crisis in the Russian Far East*. Royal Institute of International Affairs, http://www.illegal-logging.info/textonly/papers/Forest_Trends_China_Russia.pdf

Schloenhardt, A. (2008) *The illegal trade in timber and timber products in the Asia-Pacific Region*. Research and Public Policy Series no. 89. Canberra: Australian Institute of Criminology.

Seneca Creek (2004) *'Illegal' logging and global wood markets: the competitive impacts on the US wood products industry*. Seneca Creek Associates, LLC Poolesville, Maryland USA and Wood Resources International, LLC University Place, WA USA.

Soreide, T. (2007) *Forest concessions and corruption*, U4 Issue 3: 2007. http://www.cmi.no/publications/file/?2818=forest-concessions-and-corruption

Transparency International (2008) *Frequently Asked Questions about Corruption* http://www.transparency.org/news_room/faq/corruption_faq#faqcorr1 (accessed 16 May 2009).

Vandergert, P. and Newell, J. (2003) 'Illegal logging in the Russian Far East and Siberia', *International Forestry Review*, 5(3): 303–6.

White, R. (2003) 'Environmental issues and the criminological imagination', *Theoretical Criminology*, 7(4): 483–506.

White, R. (2008) 'Environmental harm and crime prevention', *Trends and Issues*, No. 360. Canberra: Australian Institute of Criminology.

World Bank (2006) *Strengthening Forest Law Enforcement and Governance: Addressing a Systematic Constraint to Sustainable Development*. Report No. 36638-GLB. Washington: World Bank.

Chapter 6

Situational organised crime prevention in Amsterdam: the administrative approach

Hans Nelen

Abstract

In this chapter, the programme theory and practical application of the three projects that are part of the administrative approach in the City of Amsterdam, are scrutinised from a situational crime prevention perspective. The analysis shows that the emphasis in Amsterdam has been put on 'increasing the efforts', 'increasing the risks' and 'reducing the rewards'. Less attention has been paid to situational crime prevention techniques in the categories 'removing excuses' and 'reduce provocations'. Despite the fact that the Van Traa project, the Integrity Bureau and the SBA Bureau are officially considered to be inter-related, the three projects developed independently and are not geared to complementing one another. Additionally, all projects have drifted away from their original raison d'être: preventing organised crime. Although the administrative approach in Amsterdam in many respects is innovative and promising, it cannot be denied that some assumptions that lie at the root of the approach are debatable, contradictory or have proven hard to implement in practice. As a result, it is far from clear that the approach is effective.

Introduction

In September 2007, one of the key players in the sex industry in the Amsterdam Red Light District, a man with the nickname Fat Charles, sold 18 of his premises to a housing corporation. The City of Amsterdam is a large shareholder in this corporation. The transaction, valued at 25 million euros, was the final step in a long-lasting procedure of the local authorities to get rid of Fat Charles in this notorious part of the city centre. The brothel-keeper allegedly had been involved in organised crime and money laundering activities for decades but, except for a minor fiscal offence, was never convicted.

Fat Charles was targeted not only by the police and public prosecution department for a large number of years, but was one of the subjects of the administrative approach the city administration had launched in the mid 1990s. As a result of one of the main findings of a criminological study on organised crime in Amsterdam, that indecisiveness of the local authorities had created a fertile breeding ground for illegal and criminal activities in the city, in particular in the Red Light District (Fijnaut et al. 1996), the city administration decided to introduce three interrelated projects:

- First is the Van Traa Project, named after the former chairman of a parliamentary inquiry into police misconduct. The trailblazer of this project was the Red Light District manager, who was appointed in 1997 at the request of the city council, with the objective of improving the prevention of organised crime in the area. The Red Light District manager and his team were asked to develop a methodology for the administrative approach to organised crime. In 2000, the Van Traa Project was launched. Since then, the methodology developed by the Red Light District manager has also been applied in other city districts and in specific economic branches. Some examples of the selected areas are rundown streets in deprived areas with a high number of immigrants; the most expensive shopping street in the city; and the industrial harbour district. Some examples of the selected branches are the so-called *smart shops* that may participate in drug trafficking; phone centres that may be used for informal value transfer systems; and the prostitution sector that may be used for trafficking women.

- The second pillar of the administrative approach covers the activities of the Bureau for Screening and Auditing (in Dutch abbreviated to SBA), that operates under the direct authority of the mayor. This bureau is responsible for the screening and monitoring of all parties involved in tender procedures of large infrastructural projects in relation to construction activities, communication, data transfer, and so on.

- The third component of the administrative approach is linked with the Integrity Bureau, which was established in 2001. This bureau is mainly responsible for the regulation of the internal municipal departments. The main objective of the Integrity Bureau is to develop and promote a municipal integrity policy and to monitor the developments in this area.

The introduction of this new threefold strategy was accompanied by new legislation as well. One of the new tools city administrations can use in supporting this administrative approach is the Public Administration Probity Screening Act, hereinafter (in Dutch abbreviation) the BIBOB Act. This Act, which came into effect in mid 2003, allows the refusal or withdrawal of approval decisions and the refusal of participation in public tenders or contracts. This is applicable if there is a serious risk that the approval will also lead to criminal acts or to financial benefits which have been or are to be gained through criminal activities. Before the Amsterdam city administration and Fat Charles agreed on the sale of his 18 premises, the local authorities had withdrawn his permits to exploit his sex houses under this Act. Fat Charles contested this administrative decision. To avoid a long-lasting administrative legal procedure both parties decided to settle the case.

The case of Fat Charles has led to a controversy in the media and in the academic arena. The huge amount the local authorities have paid to an alleged money launderer has been challenged and has triggered cynical responses. Some critics even claim that the Amsterdam city administration has assisted in laundering illegal funds that allegedly had been invested in the sex industry.[1] However, most commentators tend to judge the deal with Fat Charles positively. According to them, it shows that the local government is anything but powerless in its efforts to contain organised crime. The case is being presented as a classic example of a watchful local government that puts a check on the provision of facilitators of organised crime.[2]

The judicial and administrative measures are not isolated responses but are accompanied by a large-scale renovation of the old Amsterdam city centre, including the Red Light District. The renovation is a form of public-private partnership in which the local authorities cooperate with hotels, housing corporations, project developers and major financial institutions. The goal of this project is to give the area a different complexion and to upgrade the prestige of the neighbourhood. Parts of the Red Light District in which the sex industry, coffee shops and other 'vices' are concentrated will be transformed into an area destined for 'legitimate' and 'bona fide' entrepreneurs. Already some brothels have been replaced by studios and fashion centres. Instead of prostitutes, the passer-by is being confronted with fashion mannequins.

The administrative approach thus encompasses a wide variety of tools and interventions with both repressive and preventative dimensions. However, most scholars (van der Schoot 2006; Huisman *et al.* 2005; Nelen and Huisman 2008) tend to link it with situational crime prevention on the grounds that most of the intervention strategies aim to eliminate opportunities for crime and money laundering, rather than to focus on specific perpetrators. In this respect, the case of Fat Charles is atypical.

The application of the principles of situational crime prevention in criminological studies in relation to organised crime is rather new, yet increasingly popular. In the Netherlands, during the past seven years the theoretical framework has been used in a number of empirical studies.[3] Due to the fact that I was involved in three empirical studies that were conducted in relation to the three pillars of the Amsterdam administrative approach – the Integrity Bureau, SBA and the Van Traa Project – I have a fairly good overview of the way the local authorities have tried to implement the theoretical notions of situational crime prevention in daily practice. In this chapter I will take the 25 techniques of situational crime prevention, as developed by Cornish and Clarke (2003), as a starting point. These opportunity-reducing techniques are grouped under five main headings: (1) increase the effort, (2) increase the risks, (3) reduce the rewards, (4) remove excuses, and (5) reduce provocations. The goal of the chapter is to describe which of these five techniques have featured in the administrative approach in Amsterdam and which techniques have been (almost) unused. The programme theory of all three subprojects will be scrutinised from a situational crime prevention perspective. Special attention will be paid in this respect to the social and behavioural mechanisms that underlie the three interventions and to the assumptions of policy-makers and programme managers as to why and how these interventions should have an impact in their specific local context (Leeuw 2003).

The Van Traa Project

The reports of both Van der Schoot (2006) and Huisman *et al.* (2005) reveal that the Van Traa Project – and its successor project, *Emergo* – involve a multi-agency approach in which several agencies cooperate by sharing information and integral enforcement. A small team – the Van Traa team – coordinates all activities. Besides using its own methodology, the Van Traa team also coordinates the implementation of the BIBOB Act on behalf of the City of Amsterdam. The Van Traa team works closely together with the local BIBOB bureau, that was established to enforce the BIBOB Act.

The methodology used in the Van Traa Project comprises two components: first, the collection and analysis of information on the selected areas or economic sectors; and, second, the formulation of measures on the basis of this information. The team is given access to all the relevant information on the housing situation and the use of the real estate in the selected areas and branches, from the local authorities, and, if appropriate, from the police, the judiciary and the tax authorities. The second step is to select measures on the basis of analysis of these data. Because different partners work together in the Van Traa Project, a wide range of measures can be applied, including the refusal or withdrawal of licences and permits, the levying of taxes, the closure of certain establishments, the start of a criminal investigation, and, under certain circumstances – as is shown in the case of Fat Charles – the acquisition of real estate by the city itself, in order to prevent criminals from investing their money in specific projects.

Nelen and Huisman (2008) conclude that the impact of the Van Traa Project is hard to assess, because no clear target was set for the project and no solid, reliable threat analysis of the problem of organised crime in Amsterdam had been conducted. Furthermore, simultaneously with the implementation of the administrative approach, other developments have taken place that may have influenced the local operation of organised crime and its containment.

Despite these limitations some conclusions can be drawn in relation to the programme theory of the Van Traa Project. These reflect the normative assumptions underpinning the moral foundations of the project. The case of Fat Charles contains a clear message in this respect: the City of Amsterdam no longer wants to do business in the sex industry with (alleged) criminal entrepreneurs. This message seems to be straightforward at first sight, but implicitly starts from the assumption that it is rather easy to separate the wheat from the chaff within the sex industry. This starting point neglects the historical and cultural roots of the sex industry in Amsterdam, as from way back this line of business has attracted 'adventurers', 'pioneers', and 'free-riders', who have never cared much about legal restrictions or moral condemnation in the first place. Thus, the expectation that due to the Van Traa Project and Project Emergo the Red Light District may be transformed into a decent and transparent business area is rather naive. The assumption that in the sex market *mala fide* entrepreneurs can easily be replaced by *bona fide* businessmen neglects the dynamics and modus operandi in this market. By definition, in the 'vice' industry a symbiotic relationship exists between legitimate and illegitimate activities.

According to Nelen and Huisman (2008) the contemporary situation in the sex industry in the Red Light District reflects an interesting paradox. On the one hand, this industry officially has been legalised since the legal ban on the exploitation of prostitution in the Netherlands was lifted in 2000. On the other hand, entrepreneurs in this sector still encounter serious difficulties in finding a regular bank that is willing to support them financially. Financial institutions keep their distance from the sex industry as they want to avoid being associated with 'vice'. Thus, according to the law, the exploitation of prostitution is a 'normal and regular' economic activity, but the sector still operates in a moral twilight zone. Due to this paradox, entrepreneurs in the sex industry (still) are highly dependent on informal financial institutions and arrangements. For a long time, Fat Charles supplied many colleagues in his branch with loans and, by doing so, operated as an *informal banker*. As a result, the vulnerability of the sector to becoming involved in money laundering operations has not diminished since the process of legalisation of the sex industry. Parts of the sex industry have gone 'underground' and the transparency of the sector has not improved. A counter-productive effect of the increasing external pressure of the local authorities may be that more entrepreneurs will start looking for informal solutions to their problems. They may for example sell their regular brothels, sex houses and sex shops and become active in the escort branch – parts of which are not regulated by law and are not properly monitored.

The administrative pressure on Fat Charles reflects another important change in crime control policy in Amsterdam. It is an open secret that during the period 1996–2007 the city authorities had negotiated with Fat Charles intensively on the most appropriate locations for his business activities. During the same period, representatives of the City of Amsterdam also engaged quite openly with the local chapter of the Hell's Angels. At the same time the public prosecution department tried to secure a judicial verdict that would make the organisation of the Hell's Angels illegal and, as a result, enable it to be dismantled. These developments indicate that the authorities no longer support the idea of 'regulated tolerance', i.e that they want to stay in touch with (groups) of people who may cause public nuisance. In contrast, the contemporary crime control ideology seems to be that these people should be banned from public life through all possible means.

According to the research of Huisman *et al.* (2005) an important causal assumption in the context of the administrative approach is that the improvement of administrative processes and the introduction of a multi-agency approach actually will decrease the power and impact of organised crime. Many policy-makers tend to subscribe to such a causal relationship, but no one is able or willing to specify the nature of it. A specific problem with the assumption is that it does not take the situational context in Amsterdam into consideration. In contrast to Italy and New York, racketeering activities are not a common feature of organised crime in the Netherlands. The vast majority of criminal activities are focused on illegal markets (drugs, vice). Few offenders are interested in economic and political power in the Netherlands. Here the ways in which public administration might be facilitating organised crime have to be reconsidered. Of course, in an *illegal* market the public administration by definition has no regulatory instruments. But when criminals, in the course of their activities in an illegal market or in the course of a money laundering operation, abuse public facilities, (local) governments may have some options for control (Huisman and Nelen 2007).

The Van Traa Project and the matrix of situational crime prevention

If we look at the developments with regard to the Van Traa Project from the perspective of the matrix of intervention techniques of Clarke and

Situational organised crime prevention in Amsterdam

Table 6.1 Intervention techniques within the framework of the Van Traa Project

Increase the effort	Increase the risks	Reduce the rewards	Reduce provocations	Remove excuses
Target harden Withdrawal of permits Purchase of real estate	*Extend guardianship* BIBOB bureau RIEC FIU	*Deny benefits* Confiscation of assets Fiscal measures	*Reconstruct area* Renovation Purchase of real estate Attract other businesses	*Alert conscience* Communication on entwinement between organised crime and certain branches
Deny access Facilities Areas	*Assist natural surveillance* Integral approach Criminological expertise *Reduce anonymity* Demand transparency (UBO)	*Disrupt markets* Withdrawal and denial of permits Purchase of real estate Closure of establishments Fiscal measures Investigation and prosecution *Identify property* Screening procedures		

Cornish (see Table 6.1), a first conclusion is that the emphasis in these projects is strongly on increasing the efforts, increasing the risks and reducing the rewards. Screening procedures and the purchase of real estate can be considered as forms of target hardening. The exclusion of entrepreneurs from specific branches or even areas – one of the conditions of the deal between the city authorities and Fat Charles is that the latter is no longer allowed to invest money in businesses in the Red Light District – suggests a denial of access. The establishment of the Van Traa team, BIBOB bureau, Financial Intelligence Unit (FIU) and Regional Intelligence and Expertise Centres (RIEC) has both extended guardianship and reduced anonymity (since in order to acquire a permit, one is obliged to fill in a form and supply background information to the local authorities). For crime analysis purposes, a team of criminologists has been requested to assist the local teams. At the same time, the police and fiscal authorities have developed a proceeds-of-crime approach in order to confiscate criminal assets, and more generally, deny the benefits of criminal activity.[4] Markets are being disrupted in a number of areas and property – the ultimate beneficial owner (UBO) of this property in particular – is being identified.

In contrast with the first three columns, the efforts that are being put into reducing provocations and removing excuses are rather limited. The contemporary reconstruction and revitalisation of the Red Light District, as well as the public relations strategies of the city administration to alert conscience and increase awareness, are the only measures that can be linked with interventions in the last two columns. In order to reduce provocations an interesting option would be to improve the opportunities for entrepreneurs in the sex industry to borrow money from regular financial institutions. As mentioned, banks are very reluctant to lend money to these kinds of enterprises. As a result, entrepreneurs in the sex industry have become increasingly dependent on *informal* bankers, like Fat Charles. If the local authorities could succeed in developing a system that would allow entrepreneurs to borrow money in a regular way, they would kill two birds with one stone. Undoubtedly, the transparency in the sector will increase, and the dependency on dubious financers will diminish.

The SBA Bureau: the screening and monitoring approach in containing organised crime

To a certain extent, the goals of the second pillar of the administrative approach – the SBA Bureau – resemble the central premise of both the BIBOB Act and the Van Traa Project. By screening the level of integrity of applicants in major tender procedures in large-scale infrastructural projects – construction, project development, etc. – the SBA Bureau is expected to contribute to a strengthened authority that wants to prevent criminal abuse of its services.

The screening and monitoring approach comprises the following consecutive stages:[5]

- All companies submitting a tender are required to complete a special questionnaire.
- The screening and analysis are conducted by a multidisciplinary team. The thrust of the recommendations is determined on the basis of this risk analysis.
- Screening is conducted within a six-week advisory period. This period starts as soon as the contracting department issues the instruction for an integrity check on a given company. The advice has to be based on information that can be reasonably collected and analysed within that period.
- Recommendations drafted by the manager of the SBA Bureau are made known to the relevant company, for information and possible rectification. The recommendations are then passed to the contracting department. The final decision is made by that department.

The SBA Bureau has access to different types of information. The first is supplied by the tendering companies that have to fill in the questionnaire issued via the SBA Bureau. The second type of information is freely available from Chambers of Commerce, the Land Registry, trade information bureaux, digital newsletters, newspapers and other publications. The third category is verification information, i.e. the declarations provided by the companies, which can be checked at the institute or body that issued them. The fourth type of information is classified, i.e. subject to the Police Records Act, the Judicial Records and Certificates of Good Behaviour Act, or the State Taxes Act (Van der Wielen 2002). However, research by Nelen and Ritzen (2008) reveals that the SBA Bureau hardly uses classified information.

Exclusion from tendering is the most extreme measure available. The risk of a claim for damages in the event of exclusion on the basis of the European Directive 2004/18/EC is considered to be small, as long as it is well grounded and the municipality has sufficient evidence.[6] Shortly after the introduction of the SBA Bureau, approximately one quarter of its recommendations suggested exclusion of companies from tendering, but this percentage has gradually decreased to 6 per cent in 2006. As an overview of the outcome of the activities of the SBA Bureau is lacking, it is not clear how many companies actually have been excluded by contracting departments of the City of Amsterdam (Nelen and Ritzen 2008).

The SBA Bureau has been officially operational since 2000, but some screening and monitoring activities date back to the beginning of the 1990s. One of the most striking examples of screening activities by the local administration in Amsterdam is related to the construction of the new North–South subway line. Although, due to a number of technical problems, the construction work is still in progress (according to the most recent calculations, this subway line will be operational in 2017!), the first blueprints for the project were drafted around 1990. Given the discussion at the time about infiltration by criminal organisations into *bona fide* companies and their efforts to get a grip on the governmental apparatus via tendering, a multidisciplinary project group was established in 1993, representing both the City Transport Department and the police. The tender procedures were audited, the backgrounds of all tendering parties were checked, and methods were developed to prevent cartel formation. Notably, the city made no secret of this project and it was discussed quite openly when the construction plans were presented in October 1994 (Fijnaut 2002).

This example underlines the fact that the original programme theory of the screening and monitoring approach suggested an association between organised crime and large-scale (criminal) investments in Dutch infrastructure. The general idea seemed to be that if criminal organisations could be excluded from public contracts, the investment of criminal capital and the infiltration of the legal economic sectors would to a large extent be hindered. However, as aforementioned, the assumption that criminal groups and networks are interested in generating economic and political power in the Netherlands has not been supported by empirical research. In contrast, the public image of entwinement between economic sectors and serious forms of crime is dominated by white-collar criminals and corporate criminals. For instance, a Parliamentary Inquiry on fraud in the Dutch construction industry in 2002 revealed a large number of irregularities and crimes occurring in this sector, including price fixing, double-entry bookkeeping, slush funds, tax fraud and corruption. However, these activities were not conducted by hard-core criminals or crime families, but by major corporations with an established position in the construction industry.[7] Another example of symbiotic relations between regular economic activities and crime can be found in the world of real estate. Although the empirical evidence is scarce, research in the property market suggests that this sector not only attracts 'adventurers' who invest illegitimate funds for money laundering purposes, but that the real estate sector is primarily an attractive playing field for white-collar criminals (Nelen 2008b).

Taking the Dutch context into consideration, it is not surprising that the SBA Bureau has slowly changed its priorities and activities. The key principles of the contemporary screening and monitoring approach are transparency and corporate stability. The central premise is that more insight in both the financial and corporate structure of an enterprise will prevent *mala fide* entrepreneurs from participating in tendering procedures. This assumption seems to be rather obvious at first hand, but the empirical evidence to demonstrate that screening and integrity testing in large-scale tender procedures actually has decreased the vulnerability of the public sector to criminal abuse is limited. Moreover, as the analysis of the SBA Bureau increasingly is directed at the assessment of the level of corporate stability, the screening and monitoring approach tends to drift away from its original mission, i.e assessing corporate integrity. The centrepiece of the screening activities has shifted from situational crime prevention to the containment of financial risks the city of Amsterdam might run by doing business with unstable and unreliable parties (Nelen and Ritzen 2008).

Another important finding of the research of Nelen and Ritzen (2008) is that the activities of the Van Traa Project, the Integrity Bureau and the SBA Bureau are not attuned to one another. There is neither formal nor informal communication, let alone consultation, between these agencies despite the fact that they all have specifically related tasks and target groups, and officially the three bureaux are part of one integral administrative approach. In this respect, some form of communication and cooperation was to be expected.

The SBA Bureau and the matrix of situational crime prevention

Table 6.2 shows that, similar to the Van Traa Project, the emphasis in the screening and monitoring approach is on intervention techniques in the two columns on the left. However, a major difference with the Van Traa Project is the lower number of intervention techniques and the absence of any techniques to reduce either the rewards or provocations or to remove excuses.

Table 6.2 Intervention techniques within the framework of the SBA Bureau

Increase the effort	*Increase the risks*	*Reduce the rewards*	*Reduce provocations*	*Remove excuses*
Target harden	Extend guardianship			
Screening procedures	SBA Bureau			
Deny access	Reduce anonymity			
Exclusion from tendering	Demand transparency			

The Integrity Bureau

The Integrity Bureau was officially established in February 2001, but from the mid 1990s onwards the Amsterdam city authorities had paid increasing attention to breaches of integrity by civil servants and public managers.[8] The objective of the Integrity Bureau is to develop and promote municipal integrity policy and to monitor it. This bureau also overviews and fine-tunes projects aimed at improving the integrity level of public officials.

The Bureau is an advisory body and its main activities can be described as:

- Prevention: charting risks and vulnerabilities, providing assistance by means of risk analyses and preventive investigations;
- Compliance: carrying out internal investigations when suspicions of a breach of integrity arise. During these investigations the Bureau can use those investigative powers that belong to the employer of the civil servant investigated;
- Judicial advice;
- Awareness: providing training courses – dilemma-training sessions – to all civil servants and managers. A code of conduct for all civil servants of the City of Amsterdam and the oath of office are the core written documents upon which the courses are based.

The Central Registration Office for breaches of integrity is a part of the Integrity Bureau. Here all the integrity-related situations are registered. Moreover, the Registration Office has a front desk which was set up for those who want to report an alleged breach of integrity. Reports can be made by anyone: civil servants, aldermen and civilians. Between 1996 and 2002 there were 286 cases reported to the Central Registration Office. The majority of these cases were not related to serious forms of crime, but to minor frauds, petty crimes and other small-scale irregularities (Nelen 2003).

Three assumptions form the backbone of the programme theory of the Integrity Bureau:

- The integrity of public officials is a necessary condition for successful implementation of the other two projects;
- The City of Amsterdam needs a specialised team for embedding integrity in the local organisation;
- More emphasis on integrity policy will decrease the vulnerability of the city administration to fraud and corruption.

The last assumption suggests that relatively high levels of fraud and corruption are evident in the Dutch capital but, again, empirical evidence in this respect is scarce. The empirical findings that do exist, along with the views of experts, confirm the impression that corruption is not a widespread phenomenon in Dutch politics and administration (Huberts and Nelen 2005). However, publications by Dutch journalists on a number of 'corruption' cases relating to close relationships between local public functionaries and businesses in the construction and real estate industry have revealed that policy-makers and politicians sometimes are receptive to corruption and collusion. The way in which entanglement between public officials and private interested parties seems to be taken for granted in the Netherlands may be a relevant factor in this respect (van den Heuvel 2005).[9]

With respect to organised crime, the case of a former member of the Amsterdam fire brigade attracted a lot of public attention some years ago. At the end of the 1990s, fireman Tonnie had close contacts with some notorious criminals and with some entrepreneurs in the Red Light District, including Fat Charles. Tonnie was accused of taking part in a major money laundering operation in which drugs money was channelled to Cyprus and finally invested in the sex industry in Amsterdam. Due to these allegations, Tonnie was fired by the city authorities. He became a major player in the Amsterdam property market until he was found dead in October 2006 near one of his premises. The official version is that Tonnie committed suicide, but it is rumoured that he was liquidated because of his knowledge of various money laundering operations.

The Tonnie case led to both an investigation by the Integrity Bureau and a criminal investigation by the police and the judicial authorities. The latter investigation focused on money laundering activities, rather than corruption or other breaches of integrity. In general, the number of criminal investigations into corruption in the Netherlands is rather low: 130 a year. This kind of investigation is most frequently conducted by the regular police and the National Police Internal Investigation Department (*Rijksrecherche*) – an independent investigative unit that is part of the Public Prosecution Service. Within the Public Prosecution Service, a National Public Prosecutor for Corruption has been appointed to coordinate the fight against corruption. One third of the investigations of corruption result in the prosecution of one of the primary suspects (Huberts and Nelen 2005).

The Integrity Bureau and the matrix of situational crime prevention

Before we discuss the matrix of situational crime prevention it must be stressed that the intervention techniques developed by the Integrity

Situational Prevention of Organised Crimes

Table 6.3 Intervention techniques within the framework of the Integrity Bureau

Increase the effort	Increase the risks	Reduce the rewards	Reduce provocations	Remove excuses
	Extend guardianship Integrity Bureau Central Registration Office	*Deny benefits* Civil claims Asset recovery		*Set rules* Code of conduct Oath Whistle-blowers' procedures
	Assist natural surveillance Risk assessment/ auditing Investigations	*Remove targets* Job rotation Suspension Dismissal Resignation		*Increase awareness* Dilemma training sessions
	External supervision National Public Prosecutor for Corruption			

Bureau of the City of Amsterdam differ in one major respect from those discussed earlier in relation to the Van Traa Project and the SBA Bureau: they are aimed at different target groups. The primary focus of situational crime prevention in relation to the Integrity Bureau is on the attitude and conduct of civil servants and public managers, while the Van Traa Project and the SBA Bureau try to decrease the opportunity structures for (alleged) criminal entrepreneurs.

Table 6.3 shows that the interventions of the Integrity Bureau boil down to three categories: increasing the risks for civil servants and public managers to breach integrity rules, reducing the rewards and removing excuses. The emphasis that is being put on the last category is rather exceptional, compared with the interventions within the framework of both the Van Traa Project and the SBA Bureau. This is hardly surprising given that it is much easier to set rules and increase awareness within an organisation than to influence the attitudes and behaviour of outsiders.

Conclusion

In contrast to some other contributions to this volume, the goal of this chapter was not to analyse crime scripts, opportunity structures and facilitators and use such an analysis to identify the most promising pinch-points. A 'reversed' perspective was chosen in scrutinising the practical application of situational crime prevention techniques that are already being used in the framework of the administrative approach in the City of Amsterdam. The programme theory of all three subprojects of this approach was additionally scrutinised from a situational crime prevention perspective.

It is clear that during the past 10 years, the authorities in Amsterdam have developed new and interesting administrative instruments to prevent organised (and corporate) crime and disrupt markets that may facilitate intertwining of legal and illegal activities. If we look at the various intervention techniques applied in Amsterdam using the situational crime prevention framework, it is obvious that the emphasis has been put on 'increasing the efforts', 'increasing the risks' and 'reducing the rewards'. The Integrity Bureau also has put some effort into 'removing excuses' by providing training sessions for civil servants and public managers and introducing new rules and regulations. Hardly any techniques can be found in the category 'reduce provocations'. The exception to the rule in this respect is the reconstruction of the Red Light Area that is – to a large extent – theoretically founded in the Broken Windows approach of Wilson and Kelling (1982). In order to extend the scope of this intervention strategy ('reduce provocations'), it is advisable to improve the opportunities for entrepreneurs in the sex industry to borrow money from regular financial institutions.

Despite the fact that the Van Traa Project, the Integrity Bureau and the SBA Bureau officially are considered to be interrelated, the three projects developed independently and are not geared to complementing one another. Thus, there is no integrated administrative approach in Amsterdam. Additionally, all projects have drifted away from their original *raison d'être*: preventing organised crime. The focus at the time of writing is on a broader range of irregularities. It may be that this net-widening is inevitable, given uncertainties over what is meant by organised crime in daily practice. Nevertheless, it is recommended that situational measures be tailored to the specific attributes of the particular type of organised crime being addressed and this is not necessarily now happening. A second relevant condition for successful implementation of any situational organised crime prevention technique is that it is based upon an empirically tested (or at least plausible) programme theory. Although the administrative approach in Amsterdam in many respects is innovative and promising, it cannot be denied that some assumptions that lie at the root of the approach are debatable, contradictory or have proven hard to implement in practice. As a result, it is far from clear that the approach is effective.

The only project so far that has been systematically evaluated is the Van Traa Project. However, the research group that conducted this evaluation study (Huisman *et al.* 2005) stressed the difficulties in assessing the outcome effectiveness of situational measures designed to prevent organised crime since it is problematic to establish causality between measure and effect. Reliable conclusions on causality require experimental research designs or statistical analysis. Since criminal entrepreneurs generally try to hide the illegal nature of their business, these methodological requirements cannot be met when evaluating the effects of measures on organised crime. It is hard, if not impossible, to isolate one specific project and to find empirical evidence of a causal relationship between a specific set of instruments used by the local authorities and the preventive effects of those instruments on organised crime. As a result, little is known empirically about patterns of displacement, diffusion of benefits, and adaptation. One of the challenges of the near future will be to develop evaluation designs that help us better to understand why and how specific situational crime prevention techniques have an impact in a specific local context.[10]

Notes

1 Nelen (2008a).
2 After the transaction with Fat Charles a number of other brothel-keepers had to close down their sex houses, due to the fact that the local authorities had withdrawn their permits. The most famous Dutch brothel, Yab Yum, was one of the brothels that was put out of business. This brothel allegedly was run by the notorious Amsterdam chapter of the Hell's Angels. The official manager of the brothel was considered to be their straw man.
3 Van de Bunt and van der Schoot (2003) took into account the roles of public administration, legal professions, official and informal financial services, and forged official documents. Nelen and Lankhorst (2008) concentrated on the facilitating role that legal professionals, lawyers and notaries public in particular play between criminal networks. Nelen et al. (2008) also focused from a situational crime prevention perspective on the crime inducing factors in the Dutch real estate sector. Besides the aforementioned studies that aimed at identifying facilitating circumstances and opportunities, some evaluation studies on situational crime prevention projects have been conducted. The emphasis in the latter studies was put on the question how these projects had been applied in daily practice and to what extent they can be regarded as an additional effective instrument to prevent and contain organised crime. Van der Schoot (2006) applied the theoretical framework on the Dutch anti-money laundering legislation, the Dutch Screening and Auditing Approach, and the aforementioned Van Traa Project in Amsterdam. Huisman et al. (2005) conducted a more in-depth evaluation study of the latter project.
4 Some authors, among others Nelen (2004) and Levi and Maguire (2004), have pointed out that, so far, these strategies have not been very successful.
5 For more detailed information, see Van der Wielen (2002).
6 According to article 45 of the 'Directive 2004/18/EC of the European Parliament and of the Council of 31 March 2004, on the coordination of procedures for the award of public works contracts, public supply contracts

and public service contracts', any candidate or tenderer who has been convicted (by final judgment) for either participation in a criminal organisation, corruption, fraud or money laundering, shall be excluded from participation in a public contract. Section 2 of the same article enumerates the grounds that can be used to exclude an economic operator from participation.
7 See Van den Heuvel (2005) for more information on the findings of this parliamentary inquiry.
8 The City of Amsterdam employs 22,000 civil servants for a population of about 800,000 (www.amsterdam.nl).
9 Collusion, defined as 'a secret agreement for fraudulent or deceitful purposes', was referred to as one of the key problems in the aforementioned report of a Parliamentary Inquiry into Irregularities in the Dutch construction industry (Parlementaire Enquête Commissie Bouwnijverheid 2003). The Commission distinguished three types of collusion. The first type refers to companies secretly engaging in antitrust conspiracies (i.e. price fixing). The second refers to preferential treatment of a number of companies at an organisational level by the public administration. The third meaning of collusion can be found at an individual level. According to the Commission, 'the frequent contacts between individual public servants and contractors had led to an increased risk of breaches of integrity' (Parlementaire Enquête Commissie Bouwnijverheid 2003: 270).
10 Kleemans et al. (2007) refer to a basic 'methodology' of mapping interventions and (theory-driven) 'browsing' for evidence in this respect. Such a methodology might provide us with more insight in relevant intervening mechanisms.

References

Bunt, H.G. van de, and Schoot, C. van der (eds) (2003) *Prevention of Organised Crime; a situational approach*. Den Haag: Boom Juridische uitgevers.
Cornish, D. and Clarke, R.V. (2003) 'Opportunities, precipitators and criminal decisions: A reply to Wortley's critique of situational crime prevention', in M. Smith and D. Cornish (eds), *Theory for Situational Crime Prevention*. New York: Criminal Justice Press.
Fijnaut, C.J.C.F. (ed.) (2002) *The administrative approach to (organized) crime in Amsterdam*. Amsterdam: Public Order and Safety Department.
Fijnaut, C., Bovenkerk, F., Bruinsma, G., Bunt, H.G. van de (1996) 'De georganiseerde criminaliteit in Nederland', in Enquêtecommissie Opsporingsmethoden: *Inzake opsporing: Bijlage XI: deelonderzoek IV*. Den Haag: Tweede Kamer 1995–1996, 24 072, nr. 20.
Heuvel, G. van den (2005) 'The Parliamentary Enquiry on fraud in the Dutch construction industry; collusion as concept between corruption and state-corporate crime', *Crime, Law and Social Change*, 44: 133–51.
Huberts, L.W.J.C and Nelen, J.M. (2005) *Corruptie in het Nederlandse Openbaar Bestuur; Omvang, Aard en Afdoening*. Utrecht: Lemma.
Huisman, W., Huikeshoven, M., Nelen, H., Bunt, H. van de, Struiksma, J. (2005) *Het Van Traa Project; evaluatie van de bestuurlijke aanpak van georganiseerde criminaliteit in Amsterdam*. Den Haag: Boom Juridische uitgevers.

Huisman, W. and Nelen, H. (2007) 'Gotham Unbound Dutch Style. The administrative approach to organized crime in Amsterdam', *Crime, Law and Social Change*, 48(3–5): 87–103.
Kleemans, E., Klein-Haarhuis, C., Leeuw, F., Ooyen-Houben, M. van (2007) 'Law enforcement interventions in the Netherlands: mapping interventions and "browsing" for evidence', *Evidence and Policy*, 3(4): 487–504.
Leeuw, F.L. (2003) 'Reconstructing program theories: methods available and problems to be solved', *American Journal of Evaluation*, 24(1): 5–20.
Levi, M. and Maguire, M. (2004) 'Reducing and preventing organized crime: An evidence-based critique', *Crime, Law and Social Change*, 41: 397–469.
Nelen, H. (2003) *Integriteit in publieke functies; het Centraal Registratiepunt Integriteitschendingen van de gemeente Amsterdam doorgelicht*. Den Haag: Boom Juridische uitgevers.
Nelen, H. (2004) 'Hit them where it hurts most; the proceeds-of-crime approach in the Netherlands', *Crime, Law and Social Change*, 41(5): 517–34.
Nelen, H. (2008a) *Evidence maze; het doolhof van het evaluatieonderzoek*. Maastricht: Universiteit Maastricht.
Nelen, H. (2008b) 'Real estate and serious forms of crime', *International Journal of Social Economics*, 35(10): 751–62.
Nelen, H., Luun, B. ter, Bruin, A. de (2008) *De omgeving van de Rijksgebouwendienst: integriteitsrisico's bij de koop en huur van vastgoed*. Maastricht/Amsterdam: Maastricht University/Vrije Universiteit Amsterdam.
Nelen, H. and Huisman, W. (2008) 'Breaking the power of organized crime? The administrative approach to organized crime in Amsterdam', in D. Siegel and H. Nelen (eds), *Organized crime: Culture, Markets and Policies*. New York: Springer, pp. 207–18.
Nelen, H. and Lankhorst, F. (2008) 'Facilitating organized crime: the role of lawyers and notaries', in D. Siegel and H. Nelen (eds), *Organized crime: Culture, Markets and Policies*. New York: Springer, pp. 127–42.
Nelen, H. and Ritzen, L. (2008) *Bureau SBA; verleden-heden-toekomst; een verkenning; advies aan de manager van het Bureau Screening en Bewakingaanpak van de gemeente Amsterdam*. Maastricht: Maastricht University.
Parlementaire Enquête Commissie Bouwnijverheid (2003) *De bouw uit de schaduw, eindrapport*. Den Haag: SDU.
Schoot, C.R.A. van der (2006). *Organized Crime Prevention in the Netherlands. Exposing the Effectiveness of Preventive Measures*. Den Haag: Boom Juridische uitgevers.
Wielen, L. van der (2002) 'The screening and auditing approach in combating crime', in C.J.F.C. Fijnaut (ed.), *The administrative approach to (organized) crime in Amsterdam*. Amsterdam: Public Order and Safety Department.
Wilson, J.Q. and Kelling, G. (1982) 'Broken Windows', *Atlantic Monthly*, 249(3): 29–38.

Chapter 7

Mortgage fraud and facilitating circumstances

Barbra van Gestel

Abstract

In the Netherlands, the degeneration of private dwellings in urban quarters often goes hand in hand with financial and economic crime. Mortgage fraud is a key feature in that kind of crime. Mortgage fraud is committed for various reasons; sometimes simply to help people get accommodation but at other times to generate illegal income by collecting rent for accommodation acquired fraudulently, for example, by renting it out to illegal immigrants or cannabis growers. Mortgage fraud can also be part of more complicated illegal operations, with the main purpose of making a lot of money in a short period of time. Moreover, mortgage fraud is sometimes used for tax evasion. In other words: mortgage fraud is a tool which can be used for several purposes. In light of the specific purpose of the mortgage fraud, this chapter describes the modus operandi of real estate traders and brokers. Based on that description, it will become clear which actors and situations – consciously or unintentionally – facilitate mortgage fraud in the Netherlands. In doing so the following facilitating conditions are distilled: the variable prices of real estate; a specific demand for accommodation; the limited information about property, income and applicants; civil-law notaries and secrecy; the commercial interests of facilitators and the absence of buyers ('paper' transactions). Based on these facilitating conditions, in the final section two general opportunity-reducing interventions are discussed, that may be taken in order to prevent mortgage fraud.

1. Introduction

In the Netherlands, the degeneration and dilapidation of private dwellings in urban quarters often go hand in hand with financial and economic crime. Mortgage fraud is a key feature of that kind of crime. Mortgage fraud occurs where a mortgage is obtained from a bank or building society for the purpose of buying a dwelling on the basis of misleading information. Although this type of fraud has many different guises, it is usually committed by using false documents, such as false pay slips and false employer's statements. Mortgage fraud is committed for various reasons; sometimes to help people get accommodation and other times to generate illegal income by collecting rent for accommodation acquired fraudulently, for example by renting it out to illegal immigrants or cannabis growers. Mortgage fraud can also be part of more complicated illegal schemes that aim to make large sums of money quickly. Moreover, mortgage fraud is sometimes used for tax evasion. In other words: mortgage fraud is a tool which can serve several purposes.

Previous research has found that practices associated with mortgage fraud have produced adverse effects on the quality of life and safety in some urban areas. Illegal subletting, overpopulation, the presence of cannabis plantations and the sale of premises in auctions (for the purpose of foreclosure) leave a negative imprint on a residential district (Carswell *et al.* 2009; Van Gestel 2008).

The chapter examines the modus operandi of suspects when they commit mortgage fraud. It explores which actors – consciously or unintentionally – are involved; the facilitating conditions (and social circumstances) which make mortgage fraud possible; the role played by facilitators; and, possible opportunity-reducing interventions. For this study, information was collected from 12 completed police investigations in the four largest cities in the Netherlands.

Initially the study was focused on cases where slum landlords played the leading role and where the degeneration of residential properties was the focal point. However, during the fieldwork the focus broadened and shifted in the direction of cases with a stronger financial and economic component, as this financial and economic crime appears to be characteristic of illegal activities in the housing sector, including in the cases in which problems related to degeneration gave rise to the criminal case. The focus was on investigations that were initiated by the police between 2000 and 2005, and completed investigations that the police had handed over to the Public Prosecution Service for further processing. After all, in such cases it is likely that the 'hard' material collected by the police is sufficient to proceed with criminal prosecution. Ultimately 12 large-scale, completed investigations in the four major cities were selected, which could be studied intensively: three cases in Amsterdam, three in Rotterdam, five in

The Hague and one in Utrecht. In this selection the focus was on variety in the investigations (city, types of parties, types of criminal behaviour). Incidentally, there were not all that many investigations to choose from. It became clear that by no means were dozens of investigations being conducted in this field; rather, there were just a few investigations per city.[1] For each selected investigation case study police officers and public prosecutors were interviewed and the police files were subsequently analysed. Based on the interviews and the information from the files, key information from each case has been summarised.

Section two provides a brief description of the suspects in the 12 cases examined. Section three describes the modus operandi in individual mortgage fraud cases; section four describes the modus operandi in organised mortgage fraud cases. Section five addresses the facilitating conditions that provide the opportunity structure for committing mortgage fraud. The last section (six) lists some opportunity-reducing measures.

2. Legal actors and illegal activities

In the 12 police files studied, a total of 211 suspects are involved, 24 of whom were 'prime suspects'. The number of suspects in each case varied between two and 41 individuals; the number of prime suspects varied from one to four per case. The 24 prime suspects acted as leaders and had an active, initiating role in organising the illegal activities. They were, so to speak, 'the brains' behind the illegal activities. In the 12 police files studied, almost all of the 24 prime suspects operated essentially from a legal position: most as traders who invest in real estate. These real estate traders (or 'property traders') buy properties with the intention of holding them for a (short) period of time. They then let them to tenants, hoping to sell the properties after a while for a profit. In addition, several prime suspects worked in finance and insurance business as consultants or mortgage brokers. Almost none of those suspects engaged exclusively in illegal deals and in an illegal market.

The link between illegal and legal is therefore primarily formed by the main suspects themselves. Their lawful professional position in the business community formed the basis from which illegal activities were developed. Their profession provided them with the opportunity to learn about illegal schemes through which extra financial gain could be realised. Through their profession, such people also have the opportunity to get to know people who are willing to help them in committing the fraud: mortgage brokers, estate agents/valuers and civil-law notaries.

3. Personal mortgage fraud

Owner-occupied property

Private individuals who wish to buy a property usually depend on the bank for its funding. Whether or not the bank is willing to lend them a large sum of money to buy that property depends on the nature of their employment and the salary of the prospective buyer. If a prospective buyer earns too little, is unemployed or has an occupational disability, s/he will have trouble finding a bank that is willing to take the risk and grant a mortgage. For people who nevertheless want to buy a property, this may be a reason to misrepresent their financial situation to the bank. They pretend that they earn more money, or they pretend that they have a permanent contract, whereas they in fact perhaps receive unemployment benefit, which may be 'topped up' with untaxed earnings. In other words, these suspects commit mortgage fraud because they want to buy a home and are unable to obtain the necessary funding due to insufficient legal means. This usually relates to low-priced and mid-priced housing. Most buyers intend to move into the property and live there.

Suspects come into contact with a 'mortgage broker' who agrees to obtain the necessary funding via relatives or acquaintances. This broker then forges documents, contacts a bank and acts as a mediator until the mortgage is granted. Sometimes an application is denied by a bank, because the forgery is immediately uncovered. If so, the broker will go to another bank. These mortgage brokers are the prime suspects in the criminal cases in which mortgage fraud was the vital element for people who wanted to buy their own house; they handled the fraudulent mortgage application for various people that came to them in a roundabout way. Case 1 provides an example of how people get in touch with the mortgage broker.[2]

Case 1

Irma is 32 years old, has four children and moved in with her parents after her divorce. For a while, she worked via a temping agency in carpet production facilities, but is now without a job due to health problems. She would love to have her own place to live with her children; she put her name down for rental accommodation, but has found out that there is a six-year waiting period. She discusses her problems with her in-laws, who recommend that she contact Mr Turan, the owner of an insurance agency. He can arrange a mortgage for her, and manages to take out a mortgage loan amounting to €195,000 euro in her name from the bank.

The key players in these cases act as administrative brokers, specialising in fraud involving financial institutions with false or falsified documents. The untaxed earnings of these key players consist of the fee (0.5 per cent to 2 per cent of the loan). Their illegal practices in the housing market are limited mainly to fixing documents for the purpose of obtaining a mortgage. Existing pay slips (of a former employer) and employer's statements are falsified by the mortgage broker or employment contracts are forged.

Mortgage repayment with black money?

The mortgage applicants in the above criminal cases, who obtained a mortgage on the basis of false documents, still have the same house a number of years after the application. Therefore, they did not buy the property to put it back on the market straight away, but committed mortgage fraud to get on to or to move up the housing ladder. They make the monthly mortgage payments, as agreed with the bank. But how do they manage to make those monthly payments? It is plausible that some are able to finance the mortgage payments from legal means, for example using income from unemployment or disability benefits. With low-priced homes, monthly mortgage payments are not much higher than the rent they would otherwise have to pay. Mortgage payments for a low-price home may even be less than the regular rent charged for housing in a city.

In the case of slightly more expensive houses, monthly mortgage payments are more likely to be paid with black money. In those cases, the expense of the mortgage payments is disproportionate to the legal earnings. The acquisition of the house and the associated mortgage fraud becomes a way of laundering money.

To obtain further insight into mortgage fraud for the purpose of money laundering, other police files were reviewed which only indirectly involved mortgage fraud. One police investigation concerned a man who generated income by dealing in counterfeit money and stolen designer-label clothing. Based on a forged employer's statement and forged pay slips, this man managed to acquire a property costing €300,000, in which he had been living for quite some time with his girlfriend and children. The monthly mortgage payments were paid with money earned from criminal activities. This was deposited into the bank account every month. In this case, a mortgage broker played an essential role in facilitating the fraud by forging the salary slips and the employer's statement. This broker helped people by forging documents for the purpose of mortgage fraud, on a large scale.

Another police investigation examined concerned a large-scale manufacturer of Ecstasy pills, who purchased a villa on the basis of forged pay slips and employer's statements. The man pretended that he earned a decent living by working for a real estate company, whereas in reality he made a living by synthesising drugs. The mortgage payments were made from criminal proceeds. The real estate firm where he allegedly was employed (according to the documentation) knowingly helped him with this illegal scheme: the business specialises in inventing fictitious jobs and forging employment contracts for mortgages, and also provides this service to people who make money from crime.

Illegal letting

Anyone who wants to buy a property to let it with a view to generating income can apply for a mortgage to acquire one. In the Netherlands, a bank will grant a loan amounting to about 70 per cent of the purchase price for a property to be let. The buyer will have to pay the difference between the purchase price and the money borrowed from the bank up front. If a purchaser lacks the required capital, they can misrepresent their financial situation to the bank in order to obtain full funding for the property. They will tell the bank that they intend to move into the property, whereas they in fact intend to let it. By doing so, they receive 100 per cent funding for the property. This form of fraud – misrepresentation on the use of the property – often goes hand in hand with the submission of forged documents regarding income and employer. In the police investigations studied here, at least, this form of fraud was usually committed by people who had no or insufficient income from regular employment and who did not have capital, but nevertheless wished to acquire a property to let. The mortgage payments were subsequently covered by the rental income.

This type of fraud is committed both on a large and a small scale. On a small scale, it is committed by private individuals who acquire a vacated apartment and let it at their own initiative. These people are not part of a larger illegal or criminal network. In order to obtain forged documents, they go to a broker whom they know to be willing to help with the fraudulent mortgage application (such as the brokers described in the preceding section). Usually, the properties are old, low-priced homes which, once owned by the mortgage applicant, are rented out to illegal immigrants, labour immigrants or cannabis growers. On a slightly larger scale, three individuals working together were found, forming a small-scale family network (Case 2):

> **Case 2**
> Within a couple of years, a father and his two sons acquired 10 low-priced, old and poorly maintained apartments, with the purpose of renting them out, in particular to temporary illegal labour immigrants from Eastern Europe and Africa. The father acquired four apartments, the sons four and two apartments respectively. The father coordinates the rental business, collects the rent and makes

> sure that the rental income is deposited in time into the various bank accounts, so that the mortgage payments can be made every month. The apartments are acquired via a mortgage broker who contacts a different financial institution for each mortgage, and tells the bank that the apartment is vacated and will be occupied by the owner. The broker forges employer's statements and pay slips.

In addition to individuals and small network frauds, mortgage fraud is also committed to make easy money in little time by buying and selling property. This is examined in the following section.

4. Organised mortgage fraud

Mortgage fraud for quick profit maximisation is committed in the context of wider illegal networks and forms part of larger-scale illegal schemes. This requires the involvement of a great number of actors, and real estate traders often take the lead in these cases. The financial profits exceed those of the cases described above, and that also applies to the financial loss sustained by both the banks and the other victims involved. Nevertheless, the schemes operate in roughly the same way as those described above (forged pay slips and employer's statements and pretending that the home will be for private use), but in these cases the fraud committed is part of a more complicated scheme rather than being a one-off event. There is another significant difference to the schemes discussed above, namely the use of 'straw men' as mortgage applicants and buyers of the property/properties. This section describes the way in which mortgage fraud is committed by large illegal networks, contributing to the quick money-making of real estate traders.

Real estate traders usually earn their money from the acquisition and sale of property. Profits can be increased within a short period of time by buying and quickly selling one and the same property. In itself, that method is totally lawful. The so-called ABC arrangement – in which A sells property to B, and B resells it to C – is permitted under the law, and even customary in the real estate sector (cf. Ferwerda *et al.* 2007; Keirse *et al.* 2010). The purchase and swift resale of properties, however, becomes unlawful where it depends on mortgage fraud. In almost all the police files where the prime suspects generated quick profits, mortgage fraud was an intrinsic part of doing so. To make a quick profit and be able to force up the price of a property, suspects have to find buyers who are willing to pay the relatively high price, and who are prepared to sign and pay quickly. The police files also show that suspected real estate traders apply several different strategies to find 'buyers' who meet this profile. In short, it amounts to the situation where the buyer is misled and given incorrect or incomplete information. That can be done in different ways.

Straw men as buyers

One of the strategies is to find someone who is prepared to buy the property 'on paper' against a small fee, but who has in fact nothing to do with the property or the mortgage payments. He does not care about the price of the property, because the purchase contract is merely signed as a formality. A source of employment is made up for this straw man, who usually has little income, with an existing business or a phoney business. Papers are forged, so that a mortgage application can be made. An advisor or mortgage broker who is involved in the illegal scheme provides the forged documents and the purchase contract. Once the application has been approved by the bank, the relevant civil-law notary transfers the borrowed money straight to the real estate trader, who thus gets the equity straight in hand. That way, a quick profit is made. The real estate trader actually remains the owner of the property, and he can subsequently generate income by letting it. He collects the rent – in cash – and remains invisible for the tax authorities. He becomes even less visible where an intermediary is used between the purchase of a property and its sale to a straw man, the so-called 'B' from the ABC arrangement. The police files examined show that real estate traders use such intermediaries to avoid having to pay corporate income tax on the money made by selling the property to the straw man. Case 3, part 1 illustrates this form of fraud for the purpose of quick profit-making. It also shows how the fraudulent practices in the property field are intrinsically linked to other forms of fraud and deception of financial institutions.

> **Case 3, part 1**
> Three men – a retailer (I), a bank employee (T) and the owner of an accounting office/owner of a bar (K) – jointly commit credit fraud on a large scale. They incorporate dozens of 'phoney businesses' and register them in the names of poverty-stricken acquaintances and relatives, who act as straw men. In the next stage, one of the prime suspects (K, who owns both an accounting office and a bar) starts trading in property and uses the phoney businesses and associated straw men. In his direct vicinity, he is on the lookout for people (employees, relatives) who are willing to buy a property that is to be resold shortly – usually on the same day – at a higher purchase price to a straw man. An accounting office brokering in mortgages provides the forged employer's statements and pay slips that are necessary for the mortgage application, and they make it look as if the straw man is employed by one of the phoney businesses.

> Prime suspect K sublets the properties purchased mostly to West African illegal immigrants and cannabis growers, but also to acquaintances and relatives. The rental proceeds are used to make the mortgage payments. Prime suspect K leads the whole process, is present at the notary's office whenever a sale or purchase transaction takes place and is assisted by a number of financial advisors. For the purchase and sale between B and C, he always uses the services of the same civil-law notary. The estate valuer's report drawn up for the benefit of C is every time from the same valuer, who always states that the property is intended for private use.

The police files examined here show that the straw men do not always know what it is exactly that they are cooperating in and are unable to see the long-term financial consequences of signing false documents. They have not been fully informed by the prime suspects; the prospect of a small fee is enough to have them quickly sign the papers as official 'buyers'. One straw man gave the following statement to the police: '[...] They sent a car round whenever they needed me to sign a document at the civil-law notary's, or at the Chamber of Commerce. Every time I did so, I got 50 euros. And then they took me back to my place.' In other criminal cases, straw men signed powers of attorney, with which the real estate traders could freely buy and sell properties in the names of these straw men, without them having to see the civil-law notary.

But what happens to the house once the mortgage has been granted and the profits have been made by the leaders of the network? That varies from one criminal case to the next, and even from one property transaction to the next. Sometimes, the deceived buyer sublets the property in order to be able to meet the monthly mortgage payments; at other times, the leader of the network manages and sublets the property. At yet other times, the straw man ends up in the role of sub-lessor or the mortgage payments are simply never made, which results in the bank foreclosing and selling the property in an auction. That situation, foreclosure, however, is a less obvious result of the mortgage fraud than often assumed in the relevant literature and policy documents. After the transaction, houses are often kept by members of the illegal network, to generate extra income and to be able to repay the mortgage (Case 3, part 2).

> **Case 3, part 2**
> Once the property is registered in the name of a straw man, T, prime suspect K (see Case 3, part 1) lets the house to a Nigerian illegal immigrant who works in a nearby call shop. After a few months, the Nigerian and K fall out with one another, the Nigerian stops paying

> the rent and moves out. Prime suspect K now contacts a person in the neighbourhood who acts as 'mortgage broker' and he lets the home to a man named Angel. However, Angel does not move into the house – he is already registered elsewhere – but he uses the house to grow cannabis. When the house is raided by the police one year later, Angel (which turns out to be a false name) denies that he is the tenant of the property. K tells T that the house is 'his problem' now and that he will have to figure out how to pay the mortgage. Pressured by K, T starts looking for a new tenant. In addition, he works overtime in K's bar so that he can repay the debts he owes the bank. Eventually, he and K fall out. He later gives the following statement to the police: 'It was a year ago that I saw K for the last time; I had a fight with him then. [...] I wanted money from him to clear my debts. I had to go to court, but he gave me nothing.'

A recurring element in the police files was the fact that the properties acquired through fraud are sublet illegally. That also shows us how various illegal practices of real estate traders and brokers in the field of property speculation start to mingle.

Illegal sub-letting

Deceiving banks and private individuals does not end because of the collaboration of other actors who have an interest in illegal subletting. Some of the actors are people who need accommodation without having any rights to or an appreciable chance of finding affordable accommodation, such as newcomers on the housing market, students, illegal immigrants or single-parent families that urgently need a place of their own. Others are people who want to hide from the authorities and for that reason like to remain untraceable, such as members of a criminal organisation who need (temporary) accommodation, or cannabis growers. The marginal or criminal position of various groups of people looking for accommodation enables the real estate trader to sublet property without the difficulties involved in keeping proper records of tenants and rental income.

At the same time, the prospectless and/or illegal status of people seeking accommodation creates the possibility of asking a relatively high rent for often rundown properties. If sub-lessees complain about the high rent or overdue maintenance, core members of the illegal network may have no problem with intimidating them because of their marginal position. Forms of intimidation used include making threats or destroying property. Physical violence is used rarely, but threatening to use violence against 'disobedient' sub-lessees was a recurring phenomenon in the police files examined here.

Recruiting people with a regular job

Real estate traders also follow other strategies in recruiting people to buy properties at a high price. In particular people with a regular job who want to benefit from the profits that can be realised in the property trade are recruited. They are misinformed by the fraudulent traders and persuaded to buy one or more properties as an 'investment'. Initially, these buyers willingly cooperate with the fraudulent real estate traders. They consent to the use of forged valuer's reports, which state that the house will be sold vacant, whereas it is in fact being let. By doing so they will get the highest possible mortgage loan and it allows them to acquire more than one property in their names. In the end, however, they will be fraud victims too as the property proves to be worth substantially less than the sum paid for it.

Citizens who join the prime suspects' illegal network as (temporary) buyers of property are mostly lured with the promise of money. Word about a quick and easy way of earning money reaches them via acquaintances, friends, relatives or colleagues. It becomes apparent from the criminal files examined here that 'recruiters' act on the instructions of the real estate traders within the illegal networks, recruiting people to buy properties from their direct acquaintances. The recruiters are often relatives, lovers, or individuals who already act as straw men and receive a so-called 'recruitment fee' for each new recruit.

Sometimes, they strategically target prospective buyers from a specific social group. In one kind of criminal case, for example, 'couples' are recruited to buy two homes. These couples are often police officers (or similar professionals) who inspire confidence among banks and other financial institutions. After all, one does not expect police officials – with a permanent contract and a fixed income – to break the law in order to get a mortgage. Recruiting people from generally respected circles is a way to dispel suspicion from financiers, a strategy applied by property dealers to minimise discovery of fraud.[3] Case 4 shows how police officials are persuaded to help with the illegal practices of the property traders.

Case 4
Sonja is the girlfriend of real estate trader H. She works for a casting agency. In that capacity, she regularly comes into contact with police officers who have a walk-on part in TV series. She recommends that the police officers see her boyfriend H, because he knows an easy way to get rich. It has to do with buying, letting and then selling properties. In the gym, Sonja also tries to persuade people to buy properties from her boyfriend H. For each person recruited, she is paid €1,000, and for each property sold she is paid over €2,000. Once the recruited police officers get in touch with property trader H, they

hear that they can buy a package of properties which they will be able to sell again within a few years' time, making very substantial profits. In the meantime, the properties will be let; in almost all cases, the properties already have tenants.

Real estate trader H works closely with his two brothers. The three of them lead the illegal network and they arrange everything concerning the transaction – the mortgage, the purchase agreement, the valuer's report, the conveyance at the civil-law notary – the only thing the police officers have to do is sign. Many police officers have personal loans taken out with the banks. Those loans are repaid in a lump sum by the brothers and subsequently the amounts are added to the purchase price of the properties. The officers have to claim to the bank and the civil-law notary that they will move into their properties, and therefore must keep silent about the fact that they are buying the properties for commercial purposes. Therefore, on the day of the conveyance they will go to a different bank and a different civil-law notary for each property. That way it is impossible for the financial institutions to verify whether the buyers have more properties registered in their names and whether they have any other loans outstanding. In addition, the full amount is borrowed for each property, and this amount is directly transferred to the bank account of one of the brothers' businesses. An estate valuer cooperates in the scheme and states in the surveyor's report that 'there are no signs indicating that a person other than the client will move into the premises', whereas several surveys are carried out on the same day for the same buyer. In the end, the properties prove to be worth far less than the amounts paid by the police officers, and they have problems making the mortgage payments. Between 2000 and 2007, the brothers sold approximately 300 properties under the scheme.

The buyers in the above case were not targeted just because they have a profession that inspires confidence; they were also easy prey because they had debts. This makes it impossible for them to buy a property legally (for investment or other purposes) in order to generate extra income and settle their debts. However, the promises made by the real estate traders – all debts settled and a quick profit realised – make it seem possible to get rich by investing in property.

In other police files too, it was apparent that people with a major outstanding loan from a bank or shop form a potential target group for real estate traders that operate illegally. Bars and restaurants also provide an opportunity for recruiting people. Many police files showed that the real estate traders are regular customers of specific bars or restaurants, where they get in touch with buyers and straw men among the clientele and staff. Sometimes, the place acquires the reputation of a 'meeting place', where members of the illegal network regularly get together. In some police files, this was an ordinary bar; in other cases it was an expensive and well-known restaurant where the leaders of the network showed off their luxurious lifestyles. One suspect straw man later told the police that he was impressed by those business people, who, as it turned out, were leaders in an illegal and fraudulent network: '[...] They wore smart suits, had their regular table in X; they had a lot of money and looked like successful businessmen.'

Buyers may be impressed by the social success that the real estate traders display. The luxurious lifestyle that they show off instils confidence in the buyers and persuades them to agree to the illegal practices. What is more, they agree to the purchase price of the properties on sale. Analysis of police files, along with the explanations given by public prosecutors and detectives concerned, create the impression of real estate traders who are respected in society, who use their rich, successful image to lure 'ordinary' people into opting for the road towards *easy money*.

Cooperation of other professional groups

The power of persuasion and the faith in the real estate traders is reinforced by the apparently respectable professionals involved in the transaction, such as financial advisors, mortgage brokers, estate agents/valuers and civil-law notaries. In actual fact, those professionals may be actively involved in the illegal organisation. The active and intentional collaboration of brokers has been described above. In the next section the cooperation of estate agents/valuers and civil-law notaries will be described.

Estate agents/valuers

The police files, in which buyers were deliberately deceived by real estate traders, explicitly revealed the intentional and culpable involvement of estate agents/valuers. Firstly, the surveyors' reports often contain incorrect information about the designated use and condition of the premises. The property is, for example, let at the time of the sale and is acquired as an investment, whereas the valuer's report states that the property has been vacated before conveyancing, and is designated for private use by the buyers. As a result, the buyer can obtain the maximum mortgage. Secondly, the intentional cooperation of the valuer becomes apparent from the fact that the survey report has been made on the instructions of the property dealer, whereas the surveyor's report invariably states the name of the buyer as the principal. Sometimes, buyers have had no contact with the valuer. Thirdly, it is sometimes found in an occasional second survey by those lending the money that the estimated value of the properties is significantly lower. In one case the active cooperation of the valuer surfaced during a police interview. During the interview, an estate agent/valuer stated that he knowingly cooperated in illegally pushing prices up under pressure from real estate traders, in order to deceive the parties acquiring those properties.

Civil-law notaries

After the estate agent/surveyor has rendered his services, the civil-law notary also has to give his consent to the fraudulent transactions. The civil-law notary is involved in the conveyance of the property as an 'unbiased expert', promoting the interests of all parties; as an unbiased expert, he has a duty of disclosure. That implies that he has to take an active role, in which he should be able to notice a rapid price increase and should draw the buyer's attention to that fact. In the case of obvious misgivings, he could also carry out a further investigation before lending his cooperation (Van de Bunt and Nelen 1995: 30; Ferwerda *et al.* 2007: 133).

The leaders of an illegal network use two different methods in order to secure the cooperation of civil-law notaries. In the first way, 'the evasion strategy', the network leaders knowingly visit several civil-law notaries on one day for illegal conveyancing. That way, they try to avoid a civil-law notary becoming suspicious. In that situation, it is quite possible that the civil-law notary is not aware of his facilitating role in the complicated illegal network. He cooperates without knowing it. The question here is whether he *could* have known that his services were abused for illegal purposes.

Second, there is 'the implantation strategy', whereby leaders of a network go to the same civil-law notary for each illegal transaction. In that situation, it is probable that the notary is knowingly involved in the illegal network, because the illegal nature of the transactions should be very obvious to him. An example would be when straw man acquires several properties in a very short period of time, he is always accompanied by a network leader, and each time he confirms that the property will be for private use. The illegal nature of a transaction should also be obvious to the civil-law notary if a real estate trader acquires several properties within a short period of time pursuant to a power of attorney granted by one and the same straw man, indicating each time that the properties will be for the private use of the buyer.

The police files also contained other clues indicating the intentional involvement of civil-law notaries; for example, where the profits of the sale of a property (according to the paperwork) accrue to the straw man, whereas the civil-law notary remits the profits directly to the bank account of the leader of the illegal network. Because of the right to refuse to give evidence, civil-law notaries can hide behind their obligation to observe secrecy and thus prevent inspection of files and accounts.

5. Facilitating conditions

Previous sections describe the modus operandi of the suspects. This section describes the facilitating conditions that provide the opportunities for illegal property trading.

The prices of real estate

Every property is by definition 'unique' (Nelen *et al.* 2008; Berkhout 2006). A consequence of that singularity is that there is no fixed price for property. There are no identical houses, as a result of which the value of a house is not automatically a given ('it is just what someone is willing to pay for it'). That singularity of property also makes it possible to manipulate property prices. As a result, the real estate sector gives illegally operating traders the opportunity to push prices up or down in ways that are unrelated to the real value of the property in question, which is not prohibited by law.

Demand for affordable accommodation

In many Dutch cities, there are waiting lists for affordable rental accommodation (for which housing allowances are granted). People looking for accommodation who want to be eligible for affordable accommodation must have a housing permit. There is a high demand for affordable accommodation among people with low incomes, who do not have a housing permit and are not (or not yet) eligible for such accommodation. Consider, for example, single-parent families, students and others entering the housing market. Apart from this group, there are legal/illegal labour migrants who need accommodation. Because of a shortage of Dutch unskilled labour in specific industries (for example the building and market gardening industries), there is a more or less permanent group of labour immigrants in the Netherlands, especially from Eastern Europe, who are looking for temporary accommodation. These labour immigrants – often residing illegally in the Netherlands – do not make high demands on the accommodation and usually settle for a 'place to sleep'. The demand for affordable accommodation creates a market for illegal subletting. The lack of affordable accommodation also makes people who look for accommodation willing to commit fraud.

Demand for anonymity

There is a demand for accommodation with no officially named tenants from people who want to reside in the Netherlands, without being visible to the authorities. This includes cannabis growers who need space for their plantations. It also includes individual members of criminal organisations who do not want to be registered at an official address and who want to have a place where they can live without registration, being protected from the authorities. These groups of people are prepared to pay large sums per month, so long as they can do so in cash, with black money. This is a form of money laundering. The judiciary refers to it as 'customary money laundering'.

Limited information about property, income and applicant

Banks and other mortgage lenders are limited in what they can do to check details of mortgage applicants with the Tax and Customs Administration or other government bodies, because of privacy regulations (personal data protection). This makes it easier for fraudsters to provide incorrect information on income, employment, and the use of the property for which a mortgage is applied. All organised mortgage fraud cases generally have one element in common: the information provided on the use and designated use of the property is incorrect. The valuer's report often states that the property has been vacated before conveyance and is intended for private use, whereas the official buyer has no intention whatsoever to move into the property. But banks have difficulty in checking this. A bank can ask a mortgagor to provide information on the use of the property, but does not have the power to access the property and verify this information. Nor do banks have the power to verify personal data with the 'municipal base administration' (the records of the Departments of Civil Affairs of municipalities, which contain data on the address where an individual is registered). The chance of the fraud being discovered is very low. In individual mortgage fraud cases, banks do have a possibility of noticing early signs of fraud, which will be discussed later.

Civil-law notaries and secrecy

The civil-law notary plays a key role in property transactions. After all, public notaries have special powers and privileges, such as the obligation to observe secrecy and the right to refuse to give evidence. If a civil-law notary goes to the court to obtain an order that the Public Prosecutions Department not be allowed to inspect his accounts, this could be detrimental for criminal investigation and for the image of the Public Prosecutions Department. Hence, police officers and public prosecutors will not readily start criminal investigations into the culpable involvement of civil-law notaries in criminal activities. Insight into cash flows concerning transactions by notaries therefore remains very limited.

Commercial interests of facilitators

Financial and legal professionals have a financial interest in cooperating (intentionally or otherwise) in the illegal practices of real estate traders. In the police files studied, the commercial aspect seems to prevail over professional ethics. Even if facilitators do not knowingly cooperate in those practices, and merely allow illegally operating real estate traders or brokers to 'use' them, they often have scope to carry out further investigations where they suspect fraud. The civil-law notary, for example, could notice as the 'independent expert' a conspicuous price increase and carry out further investigations if s/he had obvious misgivings, before deciding on cooperating in the conveyance. Yet, valuers, civil-law notaries, brokers and bank employees only carry out those checks in a limited way. With respect to banks, commercial interests also manifest themselves at two other points. Firstly, payment is possible with undeclared funds by making cash deposits every month. This is a matter of 'customary money laundering'. Financiers do not regard it as their duty to supervise the way in which the mortgage payments are made. That makes it possible to redeem the mortgage with unlawfully acquired capital. Secondly, it turns out that a bank does not immediately claim redemption of the mortgage once the fraud has been discovered. As long as the monthly payments are made, the bank does not incur any loss and the loan is not discontinued.

Absent buyers – 'paper' transactions

Transactions involving the acquisition of a property regularly take place without the official buyer being present in person. The whole process can be pursued without direct contact between the official buyer on the one hand, and the bank, valuer and/or civil-law notary on the other. This is particularly true for banks that grant more and more mortgages without directly meeting the mortgage applicants due to the growing number of mortgage brokers and insurance brokers. As a result, they no longer have a direct idea of the identity of the mortgage applicant. At the civil-law notary, too, it is not uncommon for someone to buy a property in the name of someone else by virtue of a power of attorney. The lack of direct contact between the official buyer and the service provider is in contravention of a 'know-your-customer' principle.

6. Opportunity-reducing interventions

Opportunity-reducing interventions could make mortgage fraud more difficult to commit, more risky and less excusable for real estate traders (e.g. Cornish and Clarke 2003; Clarke and Homel 1997). Based on the facilitating conditions that are discussed above, in this last section potential situational crime prevention measures will be formulated for reducing mortgage fraud. They will be limited to a brief discussion of two interlinked policy approaches. The first approach is focused on removing the excuses for the behaviour of real estate traders and their facilitators, the second on increasing the risks of being caught.

Remove the excuses by increasing the integrity of professional groups

The first approach to reducing mortgage fraud is to increase the integrity of professionals. As discussed above, for financial and legal professionals the commercial aspect seems to prevail over professional ethics. Greater awareness of fraud and of the responsibility of facilitators in that regard could contribute to professions being practised with more integrity. In addition, more supervision of the actions of facilitators could result in it becoming more customary for them to check out their clients, when in doubt. The 'know your customer' principle can be reinstated in the provision of services. This would make it more difficult for the facilitators involved to take a passive attitude and hide behind a 'lack of information'. As a result, a civil-law notary's obligation to observe secrecy and his right to refuse to give evidence may be reduced or curtailed. A regulatory body ought to be able to make a full inspection of the files of a civil-law notary, which would make it difficult for fraudulent real estate traders to hide behind the civil-law notary's records.[4] For the civil-law notary too, it would be more difficult to hide involvement (culpable or otherwise) with the need to observe secrecy. Financial service providers could identify individual mortgage fraud cases and the associated money laundering at an early stage by more carefully checking recurring cash deposits with which the monthly mortgage payments are made. If banks became more alert to the fact that the mortgage was redeemed with cash payments every month, they could also trace illegally operating administration intermediaries and affiliated criminal networks. In addition, banks can be required to withdraw a mortgage loan as soon as mortgage fraud has been identified. As a result of these measures, the excuses for a professional's involvement in criminal activities might possibly be decreased. This will lead to an increase in the risk of being caught.

Increase the risks by greater exchange of information

The second (interlinked) approach to reducing mortgage fraud focuses on the exchange of information. The section above describes how banks and professionals are limited in what they can do to check details of mortgage applicants. This makes it easy for fraudsters to provide incorrect information on income, employment and other relevant subjects. If it is easier to exchange information between different professionals and between professionals and other agencies (government or otherwise), the risks of being caught may be increased. For thorough investigations, and a better insight into the customer and the use of the property, professionals need to have access to relevant information. That information may, for example, come from the Land Registry, the Municipal Basis Administration or the Tax and Customs Administration. Access to databases of related agencies can increase the accuracy and completeness of the checks on a customer by facilitators and could have consequences for the risks of committing mortgage fraud.

Notes

1 For more information and an extensive explanation of the method used, see the WODC report *Vastgoed and fout*, van Gestel (2008).
2 To protect people from being recognised, fictitious names are used.
3 Other studies also reveal that leaders in fraud cases use people embedded in sociocultural networks as a form of cover (cf. van de Bunt and Nelen 1995: 102; Kleemans 2002).
4 A Dutch policy document is being drafted (2009).

References

Berkhout, T.M. (2006) 'Determinanten van eindwaarden en vastgoed verkend', *PropertyNL Research*, Quarterly 3.

Bunt, H.G. van de and Nelen, H. (1995) 'Eindrapport onderzoeksgroep Fijnaut. In Enquêtecommissie opsporingsmethoden', *Inzake Opsporing*, Bijlage X, Tweede Kamer der Staten-Generaal, 24072 nr. 19.

Carswell, A.T. and Bachtel, D.C. (2009) 'Mortgage fraud: A risk factor analysis of affected communities', *Crime, Law and Social Change*. Springer Science.

Clarke, R.V. and Homel, R. (1997) 'A revised classification of situational crime prevention techniques,' in S. Lab (ed.), *Crime prevention at a crossroads*. Cincinnati: Anderson Publishing Co., pp. 21–35.

Cornish, D. and Clarke, R. (2003) 'Opportunities, precipitators and criminal decisions: a reply to Wortley's critique of situational crime prevention', in M. Smith and D. Cornish (eds), *Theory for practice in situational crime prevention: Crime prevention studies*, Vol. 16. Monsey, NY: Criminal Justice Press, pp. 151–96.

Ferwerda, H., Staring, R., Vries Robbé, E. de, Bunt, J. van de (2007) *Mala fide activiteiten in de vastgoedsector: Een exploratief onderzoek naar aard, actoren en aanpak*. WODC, Ministerie van Justitie, Den Haag and Advies- en Onderzoeksgroep Beke, Arnhem/Erasmus Universiteit Rotterdam. Amsterdam: Uitgeverij SPW.

Gestel, B. van (2008) *Vastgoed & fout. Een analyse van twaalf strafrechtelijke opsporingsonderzoeken naar illegale en criminele praktijken in de woningsector*. Den Haag: Boom Juridische Uitgevers, Reeks Onderzoek en beleid, nr. 272.

Keirse, A.L.M., Oostrom, N.C. van, Schaub, M.Y., Barendse, C.M.J. and Steegmans, A.M. (2010) *Een evaluatieonderzoek naar de werking van de Wet koop onroerende zaken*. Utrecht: Molengraaff instituut voor privaatrecht (in print).

Kleemans, E.R., Brienen, M.E.I., Bunt, H.G. van de (2002) *Georganiseerdecriminaliteit in Nederland: Tweede rapportage op basis van de WODC-monitor*. Den Haag: Boom Juridische Uitgevers, Reeks Onderzoek en beleid, nr. 198.

Nelen, H., Luun, B. ter and Bruin, A. de (2008) *De omgeving van de Rijksgebouwendienst; integriteitsrisico's bij de koop en huur van vastgoed*. Maastricht/Amsterdam: Universiteit Maastricht/Vrije Universiteit.

Chapter 8

Infiltration of the public construction industry by Italian organised crime[1]

Ernesto U. Savona

Abstract

Using the script approach, this chapter analyses the different stages that characterise the infiltration of organised crime groups in the public construction industry. Three different Italian local contexts with a high presence of organised crime groups (Sicily, Calabria and Campania) are considered. Case studies based on data provided to the author by local judicial authorities are analysed using the script approach and following the dynamic of organised crime action: preparation, enabling conditions, target selection, the acts (of violence and corruption) or 'the doing', and the post-conditions or aftermath. The cases analysed through the script approach help in a micro-analysis of organised crime that draws on general knowledge on the topic deriving from the macro-analysis currently undertaken in the literature. Because to date this analysis has mainly produced crime control remedies, the author hopes that the micro-approach may help in developing more concrete situational crime prevention measures.

Introduction

Utilising the script approach means specifying a crime according to the steps followed by the criminal (Clarke and Cornish 2000). Employing this approach to analyse the infiltration by organised crime of the public construction industry requires addressing the following questions: (a) what is the added value of this approach in relation to the understanding of organised crime?, (b) what organised crime is being considered?, and (c) why is the focus on infiltration in the public construction industry?

There is a huge body of literature on organised crime. The approaches adopted are highly diverse and range from the stories of bosses to analysis of organisational structures. Also the methodologies used to assess the risk of organised crime differ considerably: from a bottom-up approach (Savona 2009) to a top-down one (Van Dijk 2008). All this knowledge, which derives from secondary and primary data, has considered the phenomenon more as an aggregate by setting it in relation to different environments, cultures and economic conditions. This attention to the aggregate phenomenon has been necessary in order to produce aggregate remedies in the form of international soft laws and national hard laws. The United Nations Convention on Transnational Organised Crime of 2000 and the myriad items of regional and national legislation addressing this phenomenon are oriented much more towards criminal sanctions and much less towards the reduction of crime opportunities.

Using the script approach has the merit of moving the understanding of organised crime from general typologies such as 'action on criminal markets' or 'infiltration in legitimate ones' to more precise actions explaining what these criminals do. Such knowledge is essential to prevent these crimes occurring in the first place (Levi and Maguire 2004). Situational crime prevention involves the development of techniques to prevent, constrain or disrupt criminal activity. These techniques use a variety of environmental manipulations to alter the risks, efforts and rewards of offending, and they are rapidly developing in number, range and sophistication (Cornish and Clarke 2001).

Intervention of this kind must fulfil two important requirements: (1) it must be crime-specific, and (2) it must analyse the details of crime commission in relation to specific crimes. Employing this approach involves defining the people and/or organisations that are preparing and/or 'doing' the crimes, and it must determine how to explain their action of infiltrating the public construction industry.

In regard to the definition of 'organised crime', this is more a mix of different concepts than a clear workable concept. This chapter considers the three criminal organisations typical of the South of Italy, mainly Sicily, Calabria and Campania: Camorra, N'drangheta and Mafia. These organisations have many differences in terms of history, structure and modus operandi.

The Sicilian Mafia, known as 'La Cosa Nostra', received close attention between 1970 and 1990 because it murdered more than 100 institutional figures: police officers, prosecutors, judges, local and national political leaders and journalists. At the end of the 1970s, the entry of the Sicilian Mafia into the international drugs business was one of the reasons for ferocious competition between two groups belonging to the same hierarchical structure: the old organisations and the newcomers. The latter were successful, and in the years 1980–1992 they achieved monopoly. Today, the Sicilian Mafia is a marginal actor in international criminal markets. Now more locally oriented, it has developed extortion and infiltration in the public construction industry as its core business. N'drangheta, which operates in Calabria, has received less attention than the Sicilian Mafia. It has committed very few important murders; it has kept silent about its transnational activities; and it has maintained total control over the territory. Hierarchically structured through families frequently reinforced by interfamily marriages, it has developed and maintained expertise in combining transnational activities (always through the migration path) with local ones. At this level, infiltration of the public construction industry is a means to launder and invest the proceeds from illicit activities, maintain control over the territory, and acquire legitimacy. The Camorra in Campania, beyond its historical origins, is today a label that covers numerous criminal groups competing against each other in drug trafficking and smuggling, extortion, and other kinds of criminal activity. This competition among groups has resulted in frequent internal killings of 'camorristi' belonging to opposing factions and occasionally in violence against external figures. These groups have control over portions of the territory and close links with the local political class. Infiltration in the public construction industry is part of their core business, as it is for N'drangheta and the Sicilian Mafia.

'Infiltration' denotes the capacity of criminal organisations to penetrate legitimate businesses and run them either alone or in cooperation with legitimate figures. The public construction industry is not the only sector infiltrated by organised criminals, but it is the one that they find attractive in Italy as elsewhere (Goldstock 1991). The construction industry combines the three production factors of all enterprises – raw materials, manpower and capital – which in the hands of organised crime facilitate the acquisition of economic and political benefits. Thus the production and distribution of concrete provides the means to control or influence competition with rival enterprises, to create job opportunities in areas of high unemployment and to launder the proceeds of crime through the mingling of 'dirty' and legitimate money. The criminal exploitation of these three factors produces power and influence at territorial level, and therefore control over votes for political elections that are exchanged for favours in promoting public construction projects whose beneficiaries are criminal enterprises. This generates a vicious circle that operates through the exchange of influence, corruption and violence (or threat of violence), organised crime, local economic and political power and local administrations.

Although there are no reliable data on the magnitude of this infiltration, or on the number of enterprises infiltrated by organised crime in Italy, the problem is recognised by the literature and by the Parliamentary Anti-Mafia Commission as most serious (e.g. Commissione Parlamentare Antimafia 2006a, 2006b). It is the bridge between criminal and legitimate activities which enables criminal proceeds to be invested. It strengthens control over the territory by distributing jobs and receiving consensus; and it pollutes the public administration and politics. Reduction of infiltration will therefore contribute to the transparency of political and administrative systems, and it will weaken the action of organised crime groups.

Framing the infiltration of organised crime in the public construction industry in a crime script analytical framework

While some work has been conducted in the area of criminal markets (Sarrica 2005; Morselli and Roy 2008; Levi 2008), few attempts have been made to explain the 'doing' of the infiltration of organised crime in legitimate businesses, and even fewer in the area of public construction. An important exception is the research conducted by Ronald Goldstock (1991) in the New York State of 1989, which assisted understanding of the processes by which La Cosa Nostra infiltrated New York's public construction market.

Two combined difficulties may explain this lack of research: firstly, the difficulty of finding relevant data on the specific actions committed by organised criminals; secondly, the cultural difficulty deriving from the aggregate paradigm of organised crime, which makes this concept a *passepartout* for the explanation of different phenomena in different contexts. To date, most research has been devoted to the macro-categories explaining organised crime without consideration of the micro behaviours that vary from one crime to another and from one criminal organisation to the other. While macro-analysis explains why organised crime uses corruption and violence, and the structural and cultural conditions for their use, the micro-analysis of individual criminal acts explains when, how, and where corruption and violence are used. This knowledge is essential for devising specific situational crime prevention remedies. For example, knowing that corruption is used to facilitate the infiltration of organised crime in the public construction industry may be the starting point for understanding how the Sicilian Mafia mediates among politicians, administrators and competing enterprises. If this behaviour is to be stopped, it is necessary to know the various processes and mechanisms involved in this mediation activity by the Sicilian Mafia, but in the awareness that other organisations in different contexts could use corruption in other ways.

A complete analysis of organised crime needs to 'zoom in', by which is meant combining macro- and micro-analysis. Macro-analysis has been conducted to date; now the micro-dimension needs to be developed, and this chapter is an exploratory attempt in this direction.

The data used here are drawn from three cases (one for each region and organised crime group) and they are representative of the types of infiltration by each group into the public construction industry. The theoretical approach used is an extension of the one employed by Cornish (1994), which would seem to fit with the complexity of organised crime actions and their dynamics. This can be described as the shift from the *protoscript* (Schank and Abelson 1977) consisting of the 'attractiveness of the public procurements to organised crime' for the three reasons previously explained, through the *script* consisting of the 'ways though which organised crime infiltrates the public procurements' to the *track* of 'infiltration by organised crime in the public construction industry'.

The following sections analyse three case studies dealing with the infiltration of organised criminal groups in the public (procurement) construction industry. The cases are as follows:

- *Case study 1* (Sicily) concerns the Sicilian Mafia's infiltration of the local public construction industry;
- *Case study 2* (Calabria) concerns infiltration by the N'drangheta of public procurements for the modernisation of the Salerno–Reggio Calabria motorway;
- *Case study 3* (Campania) concerns infiltration by the Camorra of the construction work on the prison of Santa Maria Capua Vetere.

The judicial decisions relate to criminal activities carried out in the late 1990s. Each of the decisions consists of approximately 1,000–1,500 pages describing criminal activities in detail, drawn from transcriptions of wiretaps and examinations of witnesses and justice collaborators.

The three cases are analysed using the script-theoretic approach in order to classify the content of the cases according to Cornish (1994). The script approach is based on a series of logical steps divided into five script scenes: preparation, enabling conditions (precondition), target selection (instrumental precondition), 'the doing', the post-conditions or aftermath. The preparation scene comprises the activities of organised criminal groups in agreeing among themselves on the infiltration. The second scene, enabling conditions (precondition), includes the activities of the organised crime groups in order to establish the conditions under which the crime in question can be committed (see, for example, Johnson *et al.* 1993). The target selection (instrumental precondition) and 'the doing' scenes refer to the actions (including individual crimes, such as corruption and/or violence, or a chain of actions resulting in the violation of administrative laws regulating public procurement) undertaken to infiltrate the public construction sector. Finally, the post-conditions or aftermath describe subsequent behaviours, which may include further crimes. As Felson puts it, 'in many cases, the aftermath to one crime becomes the precursor to the next' (Felson 2006: 42).

Collectively, these steps qualify the infiltration of organised crime in the public construction industry as a 'project' crime and as a 'complex' crime (Cornish and Clarke 2001). This means that specific criminal behaviour of this kind involves an *ad hoc* assembly of offenders with special skills to play their parts (see McIntosh 1971, 1975; Aliquò 2003). It also involves a considerable number, duration and location of script scenes as well as a large number of contributory crimes (such as corruption, fraud, false statements, extortion racketeering or cash flows) or violations of the administrative law regulating public procurement which have a contingent or necessary relation with the main criminal activity (i.e. infiltration of public procurements in public construction).

Case study 1: Sicily

THE *SIINO* METHOD

JUDICIAL ACTS/SOURCES: Tribunal of Catania, 13 April 2007, Firrarello + 19, n. 3815/02 + 2762/03 RG Trib.

INTRODUCTION

This case study deals with the so-called Siino method. Siino was the 'minister of public affairs' of the Sicilian Mafia and he was involved in the criminal administration of public procurements in the Sicilian public construction industry. The case reveals a complex network of individuals (mafiosi, white-collar workers, public officials, local and national politicians) all involved in the infiltration of public procedures. The mechanism created by Siino was designed to decide the winner of the selection before it took place. In this case, the infiltration was achieved on the basis of: (1) the imposition of subcontractors[2] and suppliers of services and goods on the contractor[3] and (2) the payment by the contractor and subcontractors of so-called 'messa apposto' (protection money).

THE SCRIPTS

PREPARATION/SELECTION OF THE TARGET

1. Define the 'sphere of influence'.
Families act on a territorial basis. The spheres of influence are historically defined and each family controls a given and well-defined territory. So that they can better organise and manage the division of the business of infiltrating public procurements, the families (Totò Riina) appoint a person in charge of managing the entire procedure:

namely Siino. He has contacts with the representatives of each family controlling a given geographical area. In fact, the public procedures are divided up according to the location where the works will take place, in accordance with the principle of territorial administration that has always been enforced within La Cosa Nostra.

2. Organise meetings: select co-offenders and identify the target.

Bosses of the families involved in the infiltration, administrators of businesses, white-collar workers (such as lawyers and accountants) and politicians meet in order to agree the division of the market and decide which entrepreneur(s) will become contractor/subcontractors in which public procurement procedure. Many entrepreneurs are available, but only one or a few of them are selected. Given the strong hierarchical basis of the decisions, entrepreneurs know that they need the protection and guarantees provided by the local Mafia families.

ENABLING CONDITIONS (PRECONDITION)

3. Set up new 'clean' businesses or structures such as temporary associations of companies which will act as contractors or subcontractors.

On the basis of the specifications of the public procurement, new businesses or temporary associations of companies are created with the support of white collar workers and professionals belonging to the public and private sector.

4. Provide the selected businesses or temporary association of companies which will act as contractor/subcontractors with formal requirements.

The businesses and temporary associations of companies selected are provided with all the legal and formal requirements. Local public officials as well as politicians are corrupted in order to obtain the documents.

5. Intensify relations (corruptive) with the enterprises.

The organisation and Siino or his men intensify relations with the enterprises in order to prepare the subsequent activities.

6. Intensify relations (corruptive) with the public official in charge of the procedure and other public officials.

The organisation and Siino or his men intensify relations with the public official in charge of the procedure and other public officials. The amount of the corruption is defined.

DOING

7. Identify the entrepreneurs.

By means of the relations established and the meeting previously organised, the future winner of the procedure is preselected.

8. Exclusion of the unwelcome entrepreneurs.
The Mafia families dissuade entrepreneurs from participating in the selection procedure or from reporting the facts to the police by means of intimidation and violence.

9. Design the bid – drawing up the tenders/proposals for the subcontract.
In addition to the above-mentioned violent activities, the public officials and politicians (national or local) agree with the families and the preselected winner on how a tailor-made bid should be prepared and assessed. The process is based on identification of specific constraints or exclusion clauses (e.g. economic and technical requirements imposed on participants), which will reduce the competition and 'eliminate' the competitors. They agree on the type of selection procedure (private treaty, public procurement, auction). On the basis of the procedure selected, they decide how to control the procedure more closely.

10. Award of the contract.
After the selection procedure, the bid is awarded to the preselected entrepreneur and the formal contract is stipulated.

11. Defining and awarding of the subcontracts and other contracts.
When organising the infiltration, the criminal actors also agree on the entrepreneurs and businesses which should be awarded subcontracts, or other contracts (e.g. supply of goods and services).

12. Imposition of employment.
The contractor and the subcontractors are asked by the families to employ local workers who belong to the criminal organisation or are close to it.

13. Imposition and payment of the extortion.
The contractor and the subcontractors agree with the organisation on payment of protection money. Extortion is enforced by means of intimidation and violence and other criminal acts (killings, shootings, arson attacks).

14. Create complicity with technicians and the persons in charge of the works.
Complicities are created with the technicians and the executive manager (i.e. the person in charge of execution of the works) in order to conceal the extortion transactions and to control the activities more closely.

15. Control of the work activities related to the contract execution.
Labour racketeering practices are used. Thanks to the help provided by trade unionists or by white collar workers and professionals, the organisation is able to control the works activities undertaken by the

contractor and subcontractors, manage unpleasant situations, control the workers.

AFTERMATH

16. Division of future public contracts regarding the works.
The families collaborate on sharing and controlling all future profitable works in the public construction industry.

17. Competitive relations among entrepreneurs for future public contracts.
Entrepreneurs, especially those excluded from the present contract, seek to prevail over the other businesses or companies in order to obtain contracts in the future. To this end, they cultivate relations with the executive manager and with the families.

Case study no 2: Calabria

WORKS FOR MODERNISATION OF THE SALERNO–REGGIO CALABRIA MOTORWAY

JUDICIAL ACTS/SOURCES: Tribunal of Reggio Calabria (GIP), Bellocco + 43, 2 July 2007.

INTRODUCTION

This case study deals with the infiltration by the N'drangheta of public procurements for modernisation of the Salerno–Reggio Calabria motorway. The criminal activities undertaken to infiltrate the public works are organised by means of specific agreements among the 'ndrine, the local businesses related to them, and politicians. The infiltration is carried out on the basis of: (1) the imposition of subcontractors and suppliers of services and goods on the contractor and (2) the payment by the contractor and subcontractors of protection money. Generally, the subcontractors, as well as the suppliers of services and goods, are businesses administered by the local Mafia groups.

THE SCRIPTS

PREPARATION/SELECTION OF THE TARGET

1. Define the 'sphere of influence'.
Families act on a territorial basis. The spheres of influence are historically defined and each family controls a given and well-defined territory. So that they can better organise and manage the division of the business of infiltrating public procurements for modernisation of the Salerno–Reggio Calabria motorway, the families create a 'direttivo provinciale' in order to take the most important decisions. The

N'drangheta has a strong and specific code of conduct consisting of precise rules, hierarchies and values. This code of conduct is enforced by means of violence and intimidation so as to protect economic interests and ensure the stability of relations, especially in the sector of public procurements.

2. Organise meetings: select co-offenders and identify the target.

Bosses of the families involved in the infiltration meet administrators of the businesses and white collar workers such as lawyers and accountants. The meetings are organised in the countryside and take place at night in order to protect fugitives; and sentries are stationed with special scanners able to intercept the radio conversations of the Carabinieri. The following issues are decided during these meetings:

- which entrepreneur(s) will become the subcontractor in which public procurement procedure. Many entrepreneurs are available, but only one or a few of them will be selected. The selection is based on the reliability of the entrepreneur, previous business concluded, and the relations that he/she has with public administrators and local and national politicians;
- how to organise the extortion racketeering activities. The extortion plan is defined with reference to the public procurement selected: which strategies, which entrepreneurs, how much to extort.

The results of the meeting and the decisions taken are always binding on all participants.

ENABLING CONDITIONS (PRE-CONDITION)

3. Set up new 'clean' businesses or temporary associations of companies which will act as subcontractors.

On the basis of the specifications of the public procurement, the entrepreneurs selected set up new businesses using figureheads (usually relatives such as daughters or brothers) and create temporary associations of companies. In other cases, local entrepreneurs related to the local families become members of big multinational groups or businesses set up in the north-west of the country.

4. Provide the selected businesses or temporary association of companies which will act as subcontractors with formal requirements.

All the selected businesses and temporary associations of companies are provided with all the legal and formal requirements (e.g. anti-Mafia documents, SOA certificates[4] or other compulsory documents). Local public officials as well as politicians are corrupted in order to obtain the documents.

5. Enable the selected businesses or temporary association of companies to control quarries and other locations (control of raw materials).

So that the selected businesses and temporary associations of companies can be made more competitive, they are assisted in finding quarries or sandpits close to the area involved in the construction works.

6. Intensify relations (corruptive) with the executive manager of the contractor firm.
The contractor firm has a person in charge at local level of organising the works and activities (executive manager). The families contact the executive manager and seek to create a bond with him. If he is not corruptible, or if the families are not able to 'cooperate' with him, they try to intimidate him or to have him replaced with a more corruptible manager.

7. Intensify relations (corruptive) with the public official in charge of the procedure and other public officials.
The members of the 'consortium' (clan + entrepreneurs) establish relations with the public official in charge of the procedure and other public officials involved in the public procurement procedure and seek to corrupt them with expensive watches and luxury cars.

DOING

8. Identify the entrepreneurs.
After the award of the contract, the executive manager, who is in touch with the local families, already knows which entrepreneurs are to be included in the subcontracts and is in contact with them.

9. Exclusion of unwelcome entrepreneurs.
Many entrepreneurs seek to obtain subcontracts or works from the contractor, but they do not find opportunities to do so. Hence they withdraw when they realise that the subcontractors have already been decided by the families. If they do not understand, acts of retaliation and intimidation are committed by the families. The subcontractors excluded rarely report these acts to the police because they know that if they do so, they will be definitively excluded and isolated.

10. Design the bid – drawing up the tenders/proposals for the subcontract.
The executive manager provides the entrepreneurs with all the information necessary to draw up a perfect winning proposal to be sent to the contractor in order to obtain the subcontract. He indicates the necessary documents and the professionals who can furnish them. Knowing the overall situation, he agrees with the entrepreneurs on the prices that make their tenders/proposals the most efficient. The entrepreneurs are able to offer better prices because they already control the quarries and the sandpits, and thus benefit from monopolistic positions.

11. Award of the contracts.
The executive manager vouches for the contractor to the 'protected' entrepreneurs and guides the selection procedure, which is performed by the contractor. After the procedure the entrepreneurs are awarded the subcontract.

12. Defining and awarding the subcontracts and other contracts.
Other entrepreneurs are selected by the clans. These entrepreneurs will conclude agreements on the purchase of goods (such as concrete or sand) or services with the subcontractors or with the contractor.

13. Imposition of employment.
The contractor and the subcontractors are asked by the families to employ local workers belonging to the criminal organisation or who are close to it.

14. Imposition and payment of the extortion.
The contractors, as well as the subcontractors, agree with the organisation on payment of the protection money. The amount of the extortion is usually around 2–3 per cent of the entire amount of the procurement. The extortive requests are enforced by means of intimidation and violence or other criminal acts (killings, shootings, arson attacks).

15. Create complicity with the contractor.
In order to conceal the payment of the extortion money, the contractor and the subcontractors commit cash flows. In addition, since the materials provided by the subcontractors and the suppliers are often of poor quality, the technicians of the contractors must establish fraud systems (i.e. false declarations on the amount of concrete used for the construction) in order to avoid problems with control procedures and quality checks.

16. Control of the work activities.
Labour racketeering practices are used. The work activities are controlled and managed by mediators (such as trade unionists). The mediator guarantees all the activities, controls the workers, settles disputes, and protects the *pax* of the construction site.

AFTERMATH

17. Division of future public contracts regarding the motorway.
The families collaborate in sharing and controlling future works regarding the Salerno–Reggio Calabria motorway and other profitable works in the public construction industry.

18. Competitive relations among entrepreneurs for future public contracts.
Entrepreneurs, especially those excluded from the present contract, seek to prevail over the other businesses or companies in order to

obtain future ones. To this end, they cultivate relations with the executive manager and with the families.

Case study no 3: Campania

THE CONSTRUCTION OF THE PRISON OF SANTA MARIA CAPUA VETERE

JUDICIAL ACTS/SOURCES: Tribunal of Napoli (GIP), 4 December 2003 (ord.), Belforte + 21 (RGGIP 32539/03).

INTRODUCTION

This case study deals with infiltration by the Camorra in the public procurement for construction of the prison of Santa Maria Capua Vetere. The criminal activities aimed at infiltrating public works in Campania are less organised than in the other regions owing to the fragmented structure of the Camorra. However, the infiltration is based on specific agreements among the Camorra groups, the local businesses related to them, and politicians. The infiltration is achieved on the basis of: (1) the imposition of subcontractors and suppliers of services and goods on the contractor and (2) the payment by the contractor and subcontractors of protection money.

THE SCRIPTS

PREPARATION/SELECTION OF THE TARGET

1. Define the 'sphere of influence'.
Clans act on a territorial basis, even if their spheres of influence are not as deeply rooted as in the other regions analysed by the study. The various clans organise and manage their own infiltration and protect their entrepreneurs, but there are conflicts among the clans or single members belonging to the organisation.

2. Organise reunions: select co-offenders and identify the target.
Bosses of the clan involved in the infiltration, administrators of the businesses, professionals (such as lawyers and accountants) and politicians meet in order to agree the division of the market and decide which entrepreneur(s) will become contractor/subcontractor in which public procurement procedure.

ENABLING CONDITIONS (PRECONDITION)

3. Set up new 'clean' businesses or structures such as temporary associations of companies which will act as contractors or subcontractors.
On the basis of the specifications of the public procurement, new businesses or temporary associations of companies are created with

the support of white collar workers belonging to the public and private sector (e.g. lawyers and notaries).

4. Provide the selected businesses or temporary association of companies which will act as contractor/subcontractors with formal requirements.
All the businesses and temporary associations of companies selected are provided with all the legal and formal requirements. Local public officials as well as politicians are corrupted in order to obtain the documents.

5. Intensify relations (corruptive) with the enterprises.
The organisation intensifies relations with the enterprises in order to prepare the infiltration activities. Usually, monopolistic positions are created in the earth movement and concrete sectors.

6. Intensify relations (corruptive) with the public officer in charge of the procedure and other public officials.
The organisation intensifies relations with the public official in charge of the procedure and other public officials, and 'captures' them by means of corruptive payments.

DOING

7. Identify the entrepreneurs.
Owing to the previous (violent) relations, after the award of the contract, the executive manager, who is in touch with the local families, already knows which entrepreneurs are to be included in the subcontracts and is in contact with them.

8. Exclusion of the unwelcome entrepreneurs.
Many entrepreneurs seek to obtain subcontracts or works from the contractor, but they do not find opportunities to do so. Hence they withdraw when they realise that the subcontractors have already been decided by the clans. If they do not understand, acts of retaliation and intimidation are committed by the families. The excluded subcontractors rarely report these acts to the police because they know if they do so, they will be definitively excluded and isolated.

9. Elaboration of the tenders/proposals for the subcontract.
Information for drawing up the proposal is given to the entrepreneurs. The entrepreneurs are able to offer better prices because they already control the quarries and the sandpits and benefit from monopolistic positions. The clan controls the selection: in fact the company that they control is the only one to submit an efficient bid for the subcontracts. All the other companies are obliged to submit extremely inefficient bids.

10. Award of the subcontracts.
The subcontracts are awarded by the executive manager, also bypassing the contractor.

11. Definition and awarding of other contract types.
Other entrepreneurs are selected by the clans. These entrepreneurs will conclude agreements for the purchase of goods (such as concrete or sand) or services with the subcontractors or with the contractor.

12. Imposition of employment.
The contractor is asked by the families to employ local workers belonging to the criminal organisation or who are close to it.

13. Imposition and payment of the extortion.
The contractors, as well as the subcontractors, agree with the organisation on the payment of protection money. The amount of the extortion is usually around 5 per cent of the entire amount of the procurement. Extortion is enforced by means of intimidation and violence and other criminal acts (killings, shootings, arson attacks).

14. Create complicity with the contractor.
In order to conceal the payment of the extortion money, the contractor and the subcontractors commit cash flows. In addition, since the materials provided by the subcontractors and the suppliers are often of poor quality, the technicians of the contractors must establish fraud systems to avoid problems with control procedures and quality checks.

15. Control of the work activities related to the contract execution.
The work activities as well as the extortion payment procedures are controlled and managed by mediators (such as trade unionists). The mediator guarantees all the activities, controls the workers, settles disputes, and protects the *pax* of the construction site.

AFTERMATH

16. Competitive relations among entrepreneurs and clans for future public contracts.
Entrepreneurs and clans, especially those excluded from the present contract, seek to prevail over the other businesses and clans in order to obtain future contracts. The process is highly competitive and involves clashes and violent acts.

Now that the activities carried out by the organised criminal groups in order to infiltrate public procurements have been described step by step, the following section considers the similarities and differences among infiltration processes. This will help in identifying the crime prevention measures that could be applied in order to reduce infiltration opportunities.

Similarities and differences among the three criminal organisations in the infiltration process

The three cases demonstrate similarities in the activities carried out by organised criminal groups when infiltrating the public construction industry in Italy. These may be replicated in different areas and by different criminal organisations. The similarities relate especially to the scripts concerning the 'enabling conditions – precondition' and the 'doing'. Differences emerge in the other scripts – 'preparation/selection of the target' and the 'aftermath' – and they are due to the different structures of the criminal organisations considered.

Similarities

Similarities in the activities undertaken by the groups can be distinguished through analysis of the case studies. So that these similarities can be linked with the public procurement process, they will be divided into three main areas representing the 'life' of a public procurement: design of the bid, execution of the result, and control of the results. This will help when devising crime prevention strategies, because the analysis will identify the vulnerabilities of the public procurement process.

1. Design of the bid and awarding procedures All the cases show that organisations act and organise the infiltration before the bidding procedure begins. In fact, they act before the design of the bid and the awarding procedures in order to:

- *control the businesses* that are to be the winners of the procedure (extortion);
- *control the raw materials* (e.g. concrete) needed when carrying out the work activities;
- *set up collusive/corruptive relations with white collars and professionals*, such as lawyers, accountants and notaries, who will act as facilitators in the setting up of new 'clean' businesses and the bypassing of legislative rules and obligations;
- *set up collusive/corruptive relations with public officials* in order to tailor the bids or to control the awarding procedure.

2. Execution of the works

- Organised crime groups exploit *criminal opportunities inadvertently created by the legislation*. In this case vulnerabilities are represented by: (a) subcontracting procedures and (b) agreements for the purchase of services and goods.

3. Control of the results

- Organised crime groups *set up collusive/corruptive relations with public officials and technicians* in order to avoid problems in contract execution and in quality checks and controls.

Differences

There are considerable differences among the infiltration processes identified by the three case studies. These differences are connected to the different organisational structures of the three criminal organisations: the Camorra is more flexible and competitive, while the N'drangheta and Mafia are more hierarchical and structured. Analysis of the case studies shows that the differences in organisational structures particularly shape the scripts regarding the 'preparation/selection of the target' and the 'aftermath'.

In fact, when the infiltration takes place in Campania the criminal actors (i.e. the clans of the Camorra) act competitively, which implies that although clans act on a territorial basis they often fight among themselves. When the construction industry is infiltrated in Calabria, the sphere of influence, as well as the public procurements to be controlled, are managed and defined in an authoritarian manner. For example, in the case of the works for modernisation of the Salerno–Reggio Calabria highway, a structure acting at provincial level (the 'direttivo provinciale') was created by the organisation in order to organise the criminal activities more efficiently and to reduce the risk of conflicts or disputes among the criminal families. The case of Sicily evidences a hierarchical and structured method to infiltrate public procurements whereby families attempt to mediate among themselves at the stage when the target is being prepared and selected, as well as the stage concerning the 'aftermath'.

Concluding remarks

What situational measures could be applied to reduce the opportunities for organised crime infiltration of the public construction industry in Italy? Considering that forthcoming legislation will invest 10 billion euros in this industry in the southern part of Italy alone, and that the speed of these investments will be increased, this discussion seems appropriate at least for its immediate policy implications.

Increasing the effort

The aim of infiltration of the public construction industry is to transport criminal enterprises into the legitimate world so that they can clean their assets and continue with investments using power. The infiltration starts in various voluntary ways (exchange of influence) or through corruption and violence, and usually in the form of a subcontracting enterprise which slowly becomes the main enterprise. Some solutions in the direction of increasing the effort have been proposed. One solution is controlling the subcontracting enterprises so that they are more permanent and less flexible. One way to do this is to require the main enterprise to declare the identities of the subcontracting enterprises that will be involved in the work during the phase of participation in the bid. This solution involves a trade-off between transparency and efficiency, because flexibility in the recruitment of subcontractors is a matter of efficiency. The result may be that, where enforced, strict regulations on identifying the subcontractors in the bidding process will increase the costs of the process as a whole.

Increasing the risk

Infiltration comes about through many different risk factors. A risk assessment model that uses these risk factors may help the authority in the surveillance of public procurement and the investigative police in monitoring the procurement system, alerting them when anomalies arise. This model should be updated with all the mechanisms used in the infiltration process, following the rule that the more risk factors are introduced, the more risk is assessed. The Italian Government in cooperation with Transcrime has developed a model called RISICO that alerts regulators and investigators to the risk of infiltration related to a single bid. This model has been constructed on different risk factors resulting from research carried out on the topic (Caneppele and Calderoni 2009).

Reducing the benefits

The benefits of infiltration are that it enables criminal organisations to invest money in legitimate investments, to strengthen their control over the territory through the protection of businesses and the distribution of jobs, and to exchange votes for favours from politicians while corrupting and/or using violence against administrators. The main solution is to favour competition among enterprises participating in the same bid. Criminals seek to limit this competition by perpetrating violence against potential competing enterprises and trying to gain monopoly over raw materials such as concrete. As in the above case of increasing effort, the solutions go in the direction of increasing the level of transparency, although this may increase costs in terms of efficiency. The temporary public ownership of raw materials, with their being made available to all those in need of them, could be a solution in areas where the organised crime exercises close control.

Changing opportunities

Opportunities are produced within a mix of procurement legislation (criminogenic) and context (the strong power/influence of the criminal organisation). Proofing of procurement legislation against crime is a way to reduce opportunities. 'Crime proofing' refers to a process that: a) aims at identifying the unintended criminal implications contained in existing legislation or proposed legislation; b) where possible, quantifies the risk of crime due to existing legislation or proposed legislation; c) having evaluated the crime risk within given existing legislation or proposed legislation, makes it possible to elaborate suggestions on how to mitigate it (Savona 2006; Dorn *et al.* 2008).

Reducing the excuses

In some of the regions with a high incidence of organised crime groups, a vicious circle operates between insecurity and development. Enterprises do not invest in these areas because of organised crime. This lack of investment generates unemployment, which is then easily controlled by organised crime to give jobs at low wages. The lack of investment reduces the amount of competition among enterprises and increases their control. One of the main excuses that favours the reduction of competition and protects local enterprises is the belief that this is the only way to keep employment within the territory. Explaining that this protection helps organised crime to infiltrate could serve to break this cycle. Recently, in territories where the presence of organised crime is intense, civil society movements and the press have tried to raise awareness of this vicious circle among the public and policy-makers. Public investment in the provision of greater education about lawful procedures has been solicited. Local enterprises have been asked to cooperate with the police in reporting cases of extortion, and many of them have done so. Also suggested is the blacklisting for the award of new contracts of enterprises involved with organised crime. This remedy could act as a disincentive for organised crime to infiltrate clean enterprises.

Many of the interventions suggested entail a trade-off between transparency and efficiency. This issue arises when evaluating the impact of situational crime prevention measures. The timing of the actions planned is crucial for minimising this trade-off. In particular situations, it might be worthwhile first to invest in greater transparency in the system so as to reduce the amount of organised crime, and then, in a second step, when the power of organised crime has been reduced, to act with more efficient interventions.

Notes

1 The author thanks Marco Zanella, PhD candidate on the International PhD Programme in Criminology at the Catholic University of Milan, for cooperation in discussing the script approach and framing the case studies used in this chapter (sections three, four and five).

2   By the term 'subcontractor' is meant a person or firm contracted by a main contractor or employer to carry out work or deliver services, labour or materials as part of a larger project.
3   By the term 'contractor' is meant a firm which undertakes works as part of a construction project by virtue of a contract with a public administration (client).
4   SOA certificates are quality certificates that, according to Italian legislation, are necessary to take part in public contract works and tenders.

References

Aliquò, V. (2003) *Mafia, appalti, processo penale. In attesa di nuove vie per la legalità*. FCSF: Aggiornamenti sociali.

Caneppele, S. and Calderoni, F. (2009) *La geografia criminale degli appalti*. Milano: F. Angeli.

Clarke, R. (1997) *Situational Crime Prevention: Successful Case Studies*. New York: Criminal Justice Press.

Clarke, R. and Cornish, D. (2000), 'Rational Choice', in R. Paternoster and R. Bachman (eds), *Explaining Crimes and Criminals: Essays in Contemporary Criminological Theory*. UK: Roxbury Publishing Company.

Commissione Parlamentare Antimafia – Commissione Parlamentare di inchiesta sul fenomeno della criminalità organizzata mafiosa o similare (2006a) *Relazione conclusiva*. Rome: Tomo I, Commissione Parlamentare Antimafia.

Commissione Parlamentare Antimafia – Commissione Parlamentare di inchiesta sul fenomeno della criminalità organizzata mafiosa o similare (2006b) *Relazione conclusiva*. Rome: Tomo II, Commissione Parlamentare Antimafia.

Cornish, D. (1994) 'The procedural analysis of offending and its relevance for situational prevention', in R.V. Clarke (ed.), *Crime Prevention Studies*, Vol. 3. New York: Criminal Justice Press.

Cornish, D. and Clarke, R.V. (2001) 'Analyzing organised crimes', in A.R. Piquero and S.G. Tibbetts (eds), *Rational Choice and Criminal Behaviour: Recent Research and Future Challenges*. Hamden: Garland Science.

Dorn, N., Levi, M. and White, S. (2008) 'Do European procurement rules generate or prevent crime?', *Journal of Financial Crime*, 15(3): 243–60.

Felson, M. (2006) *Crime and Nature*. London: SAGE Publications.

Goldstock, R. (1991) *Corruption and racketeering in the New York City construction industry*. New York: NYU Press.

Johnson, B.D., Natarajan, M. and Sanabria, H. (1993) 'Successful criminal careers: towards an ethnography within the rational choice perspective', in R.V. Clarke and M. Felson (eds), *Routine Activity and Rational Choice, Advances in Criminological Theory*, vol. 5. New Jersey: Transaction Press.

Levi, M. (2008) 'Organized fraud and organizing frauds', *Criminology and Criminal Justice*, 8(4): 389–419.

Levi, M. and Maguire, M. (2004) 'Reducing and preventing organised crime: An evidence-based critique', *Crime, Law and Social Change*, 41: 397–469.

McIntosh, M. (1971) 'Changes in the organisation of thieving', in S. Cohen (ed.), *Images of deviance*. Middlesex: Penguin.

McIntosh, M. (1975), *The Organisation of Crime*. UK: Macmillan.

Morselli, C. and Roy, J. (2008) 'Brokerage Qualifications in Ringing Operations', *Criminology*, 46(1): 71–98.

Sarrica, F. (2005) 'Smuggling of Migrants and Transnational Organized Crime', *Crossroads*, 5(3), text available at http://www.webasa.org.

Savona, E.U. (ed.) (2006) *European Journal on Criminal Policy and Research – Double Thematic Issue on: Proofing EU Legislation Against Crime*, 12: 3–4.

Savona, E.U. (ed.) (2009) *Organised Crime in the EU. A Methodology for Risk Assessment*. Rotterdam: Erasmus University School of Law.

Schank, R.C. and Abelson, R.P. (1977) *Scripts, Plans, Goals and Understanding. An Inquiry into Human Knowledge*. New Jersey: Erlbaum.

Van Dijk, J. (2008) *The World of Crime*. London: SAGE Publications.

Chapter 9

Situational prevention against unlawful influence from organised crime[1]

Lars Korsell and Johanna Skinnari

Abstract

Even if a more common practice is to avoid contact with the authorities, a characteristic of organised crime is the need to protect the criminal operation. One tool is to use unlawful influence, with the aim to influence an official, for example to refrain from acting or to reveal secret information. Another motive for using unlawful influence is to gain status within a criminal group. Unlawful influence consists of harassment, threats, violence, malicious damage and corruption. The presence of unlawful influence can also lead to self-censorship, which is triggered by the images of the motives and resources of organised crime. Unlawful influence is often exercised in certain types of situations and therefore situational crime prevention techniques are useful. Several such preventive measures are therefore suggested in this chapter. Violence and threats often arise in critical situations when feelings are aroused. Examples of such situations are when suspected persons are taken into custody or informed of negative decisions. This means that unlawful influence to a large degree occurs at work and the design of the workplace is important when formulating preventative measures. For instance, there should not be any items that may be used as a temporary weapon against the official. An effective preventative measure is to act correctly and invest effort in communication as cases are processed. When it comes to victims of crime and witnesses, the pressure from criminals and their associates is often exercised in or around the courtroom. One measure in reducing unlawful influence against victims of crime and witnesses is therefore to use separate entrances and waiting rooms in the courthouse. The chapter is based on several research projects conducted in Sweden.

Introduction

In November 2007, the door of the house of a prosecutor was blown up in the industrial town of Trollhättan in Sweden (Korsell 2008). The explosion was large, and the police classed the event as an attempted murder. The prosecutor was not at home when the bomb exploded. Perhaps she was at the Prosecution Authority, making final adjustments to a summons application against persons belonging to an outlaw motorcycle gang. The prosecutor is well known for her initiatives against such gangs and organised crime. The police are still investigating the case (January 2009), and suspicions are falling on members of a criminal gang.

This incident is both typical and unusual at the same time. It is unusual because of the force that was used, but typical when it comes to the suspected offender. Unlawful influence from organised crime in Sweden derives mainly from visible gangs such as outlaw motorcycle gangs and youth and suburban gangs (Brottsförebyggande rådet, the Swedish National Council for Crime Prevention (Brå) 2009: 7). In a Swedish context (and the Scandinavian countries more generally), organised crime is best described in a continuum from specialised networks to gangs, which stress a criminal identity and brotherhood (Larsson 2008; Korsell et al. 2008). Research suggests that the networks are more important than gangs when it comes to the criminal enterprise (Korsell et al. 2009). However, gang members can commit crimes with persons outside their own gang, such as people in specialised networks or other gangs.

It is not the first time that authority figures in Sweden have been subjected to spectacular attacks from organised crime and criminal gangs. Not long ago, the flat of another prosecutor was shot at. He, too, is known for taking on serious cases and has a high media profile. Indeed, several prosecutors, police officers and others in authority positions have been subject to threats and other forms of unlawful influence over the past few years (Brå 2005: 18, 2009: 7, 2009: 13). There is therefore awareness of the problem and more than one authority has introduced internal incident reporting systems. Some are also recruiting security managers and security officers (Brå 2009, 2009: 13).

Other events also point in the same direction, namely that persons with serious criminal records are trying to influence the authorities and their task of maintaining law and order. In connection with a spectacular robbery against the post office in Gothenburg last autumn, several cars were set on fire. One was even ignited outside the main police station, which can be seen as a demonstration of power from the point of view of the perpetrators. Gothenburg is the second largest city in Sweden and, already at the time of this event, was known for gang 'warfare' in the suburbs and occasional shootings in streets and open places. Earlier in the year, a parked police helicopter had also been fired upon at the airport.

Mainly as a result of these dramatic events, the unlawful influence of organised crime has also become an important criminal justice policy issue in Sweden (Ds 2008: 38). A contributing cause is also that during the past 10 years, a number of outlaw motorcycle gangs have been formed. Their increased visibility in the local communities (they wear leather waistcoats and other obvious symbols of gang membership) gives the impression that the number of such criminals is on the increase, and that the judicial system has not really caught on to the development (Wierup and Larsson 2007).

Significant for organised crime is its presumed capacity (Brå 2008: 8, 2009: 7). This has consequences for the way unlawful influence from such actors is interpreted. When a threat comes from a person who is connected to organised crime it is often assumed that a whole group or network is willing and able to carry out the threat. The gangs have a reputation for violence that is useful for all members, regardless of whether they have used violence or not (Brå 2009: 7; Wierup 2007). In Sweden this reputation is tied to the 'Nordic MC war' in the middle of the 1990s where several persons were killed (Wierup and Larsson 2007).

Within what is labelled politically as a 'mobilisation', great changes are now occurring within the organisation and budgets of authorities in order to address organised crime (Ds 2008: 38). Recently, the Swedish Security Service were given the special task of counteracting threats and other forms of unlawful influence from organised crime, not just against persons in authority, but also against elected representatives and journalists (Korsell 2008). This can be seen as a stage in the Security Service's role of safeguarding democracy by counteracting the powers that through unlawful influence strive to achieve inequality before the law, to influence the political system and to subvert free speech.

The Swedish National Council for Crime Prevention (Brå) has carried out a number of research projects on either unlawful influence or threats and violence against both persons in authority and victims of crime and witnesses (Brå 2005: 18; 2006: 5; 2007: 21; 2008: 8; 2009; 2009: 7; 2009: 13).[2] In several of these works, a number of situational crime prevention measures have been proposed. Although our research is focused on Swedish conditions, several of the results and proposed measures are applicable in other countries with a similar organised crime problem. More general measures are described in this chapter.

Unlawful influence

The concept of unlawful influence consists of harassment (subtle, not punishable incidents), threats, violence, malicious damage and corruption (bribes and other improper benefits and contacts), where the aim is to influence someone to act or to refrain from acting (Korsell et al. 2007). Not all threats, harassment etc. are examples of unlawful influence; there must be an intention to influence a decision, not just a will to express a threat. The different forms of influence will be described in more detail below. Unlawful influence may be directed at various persons in authority, but accomplices, witnesses and victims of crime can also be targeted to stop them from collaborating with the authorities (Brå 2008: 8).

A characteristic of organised crime is the need to protect the criminal operation (Brå 2007: 7; 2007: 4; 2008: 8; 2008: 24; 2006: 6). Even if the criminal activity is project-based, there is still a core of more or less active perpetrators who create the networks in which the criminal activity is carried out (Brå 2005: 11). It is primarily this continuity of criminal acts that makes unlawful influence a particularly important feature of criminality.

Furthermore, unlawful influence is often 'cost effective' since the punishments and financial losses that an intervention by the authorities, or an attack from other criminals incur can be relatively light compared with the gains of exercising unlawful influence (Brå 2008: 8; Korsell et al. 2009). This is true in particular when non-punishable harassment or hard-to-detect forms, such as corruption or extortion, are used.

Another motive for using unlawful influence, and in particular the more visible forms, is to gain status within a group. Using violence against police officers or accomplices who have contacted the authorities is one way of showing that you are serious in your commitment to the group (Brå 2008: 8; 2009: 7; Katz 1988). In this way, the group's reputation for violence is also reinforced. In particular people who are new to organised crime carry out violent acts, in order to establish themselves in the criminal environment, and at the same time to achieve other benefits in the form of passivity from representatives of the authorities and silence from accomplices.

The perpetrators have a need to acquire information about, for instance, police actions, what the police know and the level of Customs control at different border points (Brå 2005: 11; 2005: 18). Situations will also arise where perpetrators want those in authority to be active and to make decisions in a certain direction. This does not only impinge on people within the judicial system, but also on authorities with monitoring and control functions. Added to this is the interest in making persons with authority look the other way, exert controls on various investigations or in other ways remain passive.

Since unlawful influence is more than a regular threat or harassment, but has a more qualified aim, namely to influence someone's actions and decisions, it is not very common. Most people respect or at least accept the decisions of public officials.

When nearly 2,700 Swedish police officers responded to a questionnaire it was revealed that 7 per cent had been exposed to harassment, threats, violence and/or malicious damage where the aim was interpreted as an attempt to influence their work during an 18-month period (Brå 2009: 7). Customs officers and prosecutors are other groups of officials who face higher risks of influence from organised crime groups (Brå 2005: 18). For many other types of officials (judges, tax officials, coastguard officers etc.) the risks are lower (Korsell et al. 2009). There are no corresponding figures for victims and witnesses, but research suggests that they are not as much exposed as police and Customs officers in Sweden, especially those who do not belong to the criminal networks themselves (cf. Brå 2008: 8). However, by no means all persons connected to organised crime use unlawful influence. A more common practice is to avoid contact with the justice system and increase efforts to hide the criminal enterprises (Brå 2005: 11; 2007: 4; 2007: 7).

Our research suggests that some form of criminal group or network is behind about a quarter of the cases of unlawful influence, in the forms of harassment, threats, violence and malicious damage reported in a survey directed to public officials in regulatory and law enforcement agencies (Korsell et al. 2007). The corresponding figure for improper offers, i.e. a type of everyday corruption,[3] was one eighth. Individual influencers, who lack a connection to a criminal group, are in other words more common than organised crime.

The fact that one quarter of those exerting unlawful influence appear to belong to organised crime groups may be considered a disproportionately large share, given that these gangs and organisations consist of relatively few individuals in comparison with other categories in that survey, such as 'individual criminals', 'persons in desperate situations' or 'persons with mental disturbance', and all other individuals who may have a motive for exercising unlawful influence (Brå 2005: 18). It is clear therefore that unlawful influence is an important tool for organised crime; consequently, preventative measures should also be given priority, as they constitute an important cornerstone in a strategy against this kind of criminality, at the same level as prosecuting the actual crime itself (Korsell et al. 2008).

People connected with organised crime are also fairly active in bringing pressure to bear on accomplices or victims of crime and witnesses *within* the criminal network not to report crimes, provide information to the police, bear witness in court or in any other way collaborate with the authorities (Brå 2008: 8). However, it is very unusual for victims and witnesses of crimes *outside* the criminal environment to be targeted (Brå 2008: 8; see also Aromaa 2006; Fyfe and Sheptycki 2005; Graham 1985). It is thus somewhat of a myth that witnesses run the risk of being vulnerable to attempts to influence; a theme that is otherwise common in novels and films. However, mythology and people's own imagination lead to self-censorship. The imagined danger therefore affects the actual decisions that people make despite the lack of a substantial threat. In this way, self-censorship constitutes a greater obstacle to the authorities in trying to get information from victims of crime than their actual subjection to concrete attempts at influencing.

Self-censorship can be a problem

The presence of unlawful influence can entail self-censorship, which is triggered by images, threat assessments or figments of the imagination concerning the motives and resources of organised crime. With self-censorship, there is no sign that influencing actually has taken place; instead, it is constructed by someone who is frightened about being subjected to such pressure. If unlawful influence is not handled professionally by the authorities there is a risk that a fear of being exposed is spread among colleagues of those who have been targeted (Brå 2009: 7; 2005: 18). Cases where the management has failed to support or protect the exposed employee often quickly become known within the workplace.

Witnesses and victims of crime are particularly liable to self-censorship (Brå 2008: 8). There is also information that journalists and their editors may be susceptible to self-censorship (Korsell 2008; Månson 2007). Some news tip-offs and links are never followed up, and other articles are never written.

The fear of being subjected to the influence of organised crime leads some people to think that officials are not safe in their own homes, or that relatives of officials may suffer problems. This is reinforced by some unusual cases that receive a great deal of attention in the media. However, research shows that these fears are to a large extent unfounded. In most cases, unlawful influence occurs during work hours and in the workplace (Brå 2009: 7; 2009: 13; 2005: 18). It is also very rare for attempts at influence to be aimed directly at relatives (Brå 2008: 8; 2009: 13; 2009: 7).

Situational measures against unlawful influence will also help in reducing self-censorship. Especially visible measures can increase the legitimacy of the legal system and increase the feeling of security.

Versatile influencers

Organised crime is undoubtedly versatile in its choice of forms of influence, and uses everything from corruption to violence (Brå 2005: 18). It is a clear sign that the individuals involved in this type of criminality know what they are doing, and instrumentally use the form of influence that is assessed to provide the greatest effect. Unfortunately, this insight leads to an increase in the number of possible situations to be prevented.

At the same time organised crime groups should not be considered as a collection of actors with entirely identical interests. Depending on the position held in a criminal network, different advantages accrue to different types of unlawful influence. Those who are not so well established within the network can be labelled as *job seekers* and *project employees* (Brå 2009: 7). They want to get into a criminal project (such as a drug smuggling operation), or gain more secure 'employment'. One way for them to gain status within the group is by exercising clear and visible forms of unlawful influence, for example through malicious damage, direct threats and violence. Slightly more experienced are the full-time employees (Brå 2009: 7). They want to protect the criminal operation and consider themselves to have better knowledge about how to exert unlawful influence. For this reason, they mainly use harassment. The fourth category, project leaders, avoid direct handling of illegal goods, visible attempts at influencing and other criminal behaviour which increases the risk of detection. If they use influence, they like to use invisible forms, such as corruption and extortion. They might employ consultants, who belong to criminal gangs, and can be used by individual criminals outside the gang (Brå 2009: 7). Of course, people can change position both upwards and downwards, and they can act in direct opposition to their normal role as a result of being under the influence of alcohol or drugs, but the typology illustrates the sometimes conflicting interests that exist within a group. There may be individual members who want to be seen and win status, while others want to work in the shadows and avoid attracting the gaze of crime-fighting authorities.

Even if rationality is a central component in the choice of unlawful influence, one cannot ignore the fact that emotional and apparently irrational elements come into the picture. As already mentioned, there is sometimes a need to make an impression on others, while substance abuse and an aroused temper in an acute situation can sometimes get the upper hand (Brå 2008: 8; 2009: 7).

For local authorities it is important to have knowledge about the different individuals in a criminal network and to know which type they belong to. This will not only increase the feeling of security for public officials, but also make situational crime prevention measures more efficient (cf. Brå 2009: 7).

Harassment, threats, violence and malicious damage

This chapter will now continue with a closer look at the different forms of influence. First some results from the research will be described, to be followed by possible situational crime preventive measures.

Harassment

Harassment consists of deeds that are not always punishable and include 'markings' and implied threats (Brå 2008: 8). Much harassment is very subtle. During house searches, the police sometimes find documents that indicate that criminals chart the private lives of individual police officers or other officials (Brå 2009: 7; 2005: 18). This has been termed as 'marking'.

This term applies too where, for instance, a police officer encounters a person linked to organised crime a bit too often for it to be a coincidence. Looks and body language can also put pressure on people (Davis *et al.* 1990; Fyfe and McKay 2000; Verhovek 1996). When it comes to victims of crime and witnesses, this pressure is often exercised in or around the courtroom, although attempts to pressurise people also occur around the home – for example, motorcycles driving round outside someone's house, or persons linked to organised crime standing and staring at a private residence (Brå 2005: 18; Brå 2009: 7; 2008: 8; Graham 1985).

It is difficult for the authorities to do anything about repeated harassment, markings and implied threats using traditional criminal justice methods. Markings, looks and hints are distant from the 'smoking gun' needed as proof in a court. This is well known to the more established actors within organised crime who use these methods of harassment, an issue we shall return to.

At the same time, such acts are particularly stressful for the people exposed to them, because they allow free rein to the imagination. Who is behind this, what will happen, will it escalate? Even if harassment is seldom aimed directly at persons of authority or the relatives of victims of crime, perpetrators linked to organised crime often hint that they know things about relatives, and that nowhere is safe (see Brå 2008: 8; Brå 2009: 13; 2009: 7; Fyfe and McKay 2000). As with self-censorship, people tend easily to become victims of their own imagination, and the risk of this form of harassment turning into violence is often exaggerated (Brå 2008: 8; Calhoun and Weston 2009).

Threats, violence and malicious damage

In contrast to harassment, threats, violence and malicious damage are always punishable offences (Brå 2005: 18). This makes it easier for law enforcement agencies to do something about such events, in terms of preventing them (Brå 2009). Perpetrators can also be prosecuted in court.

Usually threats remain threats and are never realised (Brå 2008: 8; Fyfe and McKay 2000; Hadley 2006). From a legal point of view, threats can be labelled as unlawful threat or extortion. If a threat involves hindering somebody from contacting the authorities or bearing witness before a court, there is also the special crime termed 'interference in a judicial matter' (Brå 2008: 8).

Violence, like threats, often arises in critical situations when feelings are aroused (Brå 2005: 18; 2009; 2009: 7); for example, when suspected persons are taken into custody or informed of negative decisions. For police and Customs officers, this means that unlawful influence occurs to a large degree at work. Violence may also be planned, but this appears to be unusual (Brå 2009: 7; 2008: 8). However, in more established organised crime environments, self-control and the ability to control one's feelings are valued (Brå 2007: 7; Wästerfors 2007). This is one of several explanations why organised criminals show some reticence in using threats and violence. Studies of organised crime also show that within the criminal environment, loyalty and reliability are more highly valued than the propensity to become violent (Brå 2005: 11; 2007: 7; 2007: 4).

When a criminal group has established a reputation for violence, a look, gesture or word in passing can be enough to send the desired message. For outlaw motorcycle gangs, it can be enough to display a couple of leather waistcoats with colourful emblems on the back to cause people to suffer from sudden 'memory loss'. In order for the bad reputation to be maintained, someone linked to the group will have to display malicious damage or violence at regular intervals.

Contrary to threats and violence, malicious damage is frequently planned because equipment is often needed in order to damage property (Brå 2005: 18; 2008: 8). Some forms of malicious damage require significant preparation, as when explosives are involved. Reconnaissance and project planning may also be necessary, which further underlines the fact that malicious damage probably is one of the most highly planned forms of unlawful influence.

The damage may be aimed at the authority's property, but it is not unusual for it to be aimed at an official's home or private car (Brå 2009: 7; 2005: 18), which is a sign of the planned nature of malicious damage. When such damage is aimed at victims of crime or witnesses, they are affected in their capacity as private individuals (Brå 2008: 8; Davis *et al.* 1990; Fyfe and McKay 2000).

Situational crime prevention against harassment, threats, violence and malicious damage

In this section we shall discuss some situational measures to prevent harassment, threats, violence and malicious damage. They are discussed under the five overall classes of techniques of situational crime prevention (cf. Cornish and Clarke 2003), even if some measures are more suitable to prevent violence and others to prevent threats. In the following section resources to deal with corruption will also be discussed.

Increase the effort

As mentioned, unlawful influence may – through self-censorship – lead to a 'negative spread effect', where officials who have never been targeted become passive out of fear of violence. Through target hardening officials can be better prepared for, and more able to resist, influence. Many authorities have already made efforts to ensure that their offices are safe through traditional target hardening measures such as restricting access to areas, a reception area for visitors and special rooms for meetings with visitors. We argue that officials can better resist influence by 'intellectual' target hardening mechanisms. Management should show that they are aware of the problem (especially harassment) and that they are taking it seriously. For instance, with the help of action plans and well-anchored routines, the organisation can be prepared for situations of unlawful influence (Gill *et al.* 2002). First, staff must feel well prepared for future situations. If a situation then arises, and the workplace deals with what happened, this can create a 'positive spread effect' as the situation has been well managed. Good leadership, which shows that it takes care of the official subjected to influence and which musters the necessary resources, can, contrary to the perpetrator's intentions, strengthen cohesion within the authority. This will increase the effort for the perpetrator.

Another way to increase the effort is to control access to facilities. By asking all visitors for identification, anonymity in the authority's premises can be reduced. Pre-notification systems and visitors' badges are also methods to reduce anonymity. In court buildings there can be an increased use of security controls of visitors, such as access checkpoints and security gates (cf. Brå 2008: 8; 2009: 13; Department of Justice dir. 2008: 127).

Today in Sweden many witnesses and victims of crime feel that it is a strain to share a waiting room with the accused and his/her friends (Brå 2008: 8; see Hellströmer and By 2008). One of the most important measures in reducing unlawful influence against victims of crime and witnesses is therefore to use separate waiting rooms in the courthouse. That can deflect offenders. It may also reduce the risk of self-censorship, which is often linked to a fear of being subjected to attempted influence in the court building. Separate entrances can also be a means of reducing the risks of contact and thus possible influencing situations. This can also be applied to prosecutors, who often enter through the public entrances (Brå 2009: 13). Besides increasing the effort, separate entrances and waiting rooms may also reduce the risk for provocations.

In the courtroom itself, the witness stand can be positioned in such a way that the public has difficulty communicating with the witness, to avoid threatening gestures and facial expressions designed to influence the witness (Brå 2008: 8; see Fyfe 2001). Seats can also be reserved for the friends and relations of the victim, to ensure the public spaces are not filled with supporters of the accused.

As mentioned, unlawful influence takes place mostly when officials are working, and it is therefore natural that the design of the workplace is important when formulating preventative measures. For instance, there should not be any items that may, in a tense or volatile situation, be used as a weapon against the official (Brå 2009). Similarly, the furniture should be sufficiently heavy that items cannot be used as weapons. Officials should also have access to an exit door close by to enable them to leave the room quickly.

In step with unlawful influence having become a problem on the authorities' agendas, there is a risk that symbolic measures are taken in order to show activity in tackling it. Grilles and alarm hoops may be investments that can be seen and are noticed, impress the local trade unions and working environment committees and look good in the papers. However, against the often subtle threats made by organised crime which hint at the vulnerability of persons in authority in their private lives, such protective shells are unlikely to have much effect.

Increase the risks

Buildings can be equipped with alarms as a way to strengthen formal surveillance, but there are also tailored alarms that can be used by individual members of staff as a way of extended guardianship. Disturbance alarms, attack alarms and personal alarms are such systems, which can be used to increase the risk for the perpetrator of using, in particular, threats and violence. However, training is important in order for the alarms to have the intended effect, for instance in how the staff should react if an alarm goes off (Brå 2009).

The witness and victim support system, which to a great extent is provided on a charitable basis in Sweden, is also important to increase the feeling of security of the witness. Having a support person present could also be a way to extend guardianship.

Attempts at unlawful influence are not always reported internally within the authority, to managers or security staff (Brå 2005: 18; 2009: 13). Even fewer report to the police (Brå 2009: 7). By increasing both reports internally and to the police the risks for the perpetrator increase, and natural surveillance is assisted. Setting up a reporting system that includes both 'major' and 'minor' attempts at influencing, whether in the form of harassment, threats and violence or corruption, also has the side effect of providing the operation with a basis for risk analysis and assessment.

Camera surveillance has increasingly become a standard solution to increase the risk entailed in committing different types of crime (Brå 2009).

Reduce the rewards

Officials who are highly visible in the early stages of the judicial process are more likely to be subjected to unlawful influence (Brå 2005: 18). Prosecutors are a clear example of such officials, who are often identified in the media (Brå 2009: 13). It is always a named prosecutor who starts prosecutions, intensifies preliminary investigations, appeals to higher courts and in other ways embodies society's fight against crime. Police officers are more likely to be seen as members of a bureaucracy, where the individuals are perceived as cogs in the judicial machinery (Brå 2009: 7). Judges are more anonymous than prosecutors in the process and are too far along the judicial chain to influence the outcome of a trial (Brå 2009:

13). Highly exposed public officials, such as prosecutors, may sometimes need to be shielded. This can be achieved by their stepping aside while colleagues take over. If this were done regularly, the rewards of unlawful influence would decrease.

Concealing targets can also be attempted, for example by varying the daily routines of the potential victim, by redistributing cases between officials, and by withholding private information about them such as home addresses and the identities of former employers. Officials should not display objects, such as photographs, which may disclose information about private lives and family members (Brå 2009). One way of removing a target is to make it impossible for people outside the office to call an official directly. Instead all calls must pass through the operator. This is a way of preventing harassment and threats.

Witness protection programmes often aim to remove the target by temporarily or permanently moving a person whose life is in danger (Brå 2008: 8; Fyfe 2001). This can also include family members. Officials can also be protected from violence by being moved to a secure location (Brå 2009).

In order to deny the benefits that violence and malicious damage can confer in terms of a 'bad reputation' it is important that media reports of organised crime are responsible. In the county of Östergötland an action plan involving different local authorities and the media includes an agreement to give a less biased view of organised crime and a more realistic description of its resources and operations.

Reduce provocations

Research shows that long waiting times and reduced service increase the risk of harassment, threats and violence (Bowie 2002; Brå 2009). By showing that the operation is functioning efficiently, through good service and ready availability of staff, the frustration and stress that can lead to unlawful influence are reduced. One may think that organised criminals, compared with other influencers, are less likely to use influence as a result of provocations. Our research shows that this is not the case; in fact influence often occurs in situations where the criminal feels harassed, and they therefore often require a very professional attitude from the official (Brå 2009: 7; 2005: 18). Being involved in organised crime leads to a high level of stress and being treated with respect is especially important for such individuals.

An effective preventative measure is to act correctly and invest effort in communication as cases are processed (Brå 2009). An important feature of good communication is to explain that it is the authority and not the individual official who is acting, and why the authorities are acting as they are. In the event of a negative decision, the official must explain the circumstances on which the decision is based. It is then important to communicate clearly, calmly and factually, and that understandable language is used. The official must show that he or she understands the individual's circumstances.

Communication and approach are consequently important features in mastering the emotional conflict in a stressful situation that can lead to the official being subjected to unlawful influence. The perpetrators of organised crime should feel that they are respected as human beings, and that the authorities do not discriminate against individuals.

People in authority can encounter those with links to organised crime in a number of different situations. Situations where negative decisions are communicated or when controls of individuals and cars are 'sensitive', and sometimes the individuals feel that they are being unfairly treated (Brå 2009: 7). In order to avoid disputes it is therefore important not to give in to self-censorship, but at the same time to follow the rules exactly, and to behave in such a way that nobody loses face or feels dishonoured or insulted (Brå 2009: 7). For perpetrators with a criminal lifestyle, who are used to being confronted by persons in authority, it appears particularly important that everything is done in the right way and for officials to behave correctly.

Remove excuses

Harassment seldom comprises offences punishable by the criminal law, but research suggests that the police can do a lot to prevent it by setting rules (Brå 2009: 7). By contacting the offender and having a serious talk or by using resources to target the group that the offender belongs to, the police show that harassing officials or victims of crime and witnesses is taken very seriously. Attempts at securing illegal influence thus become counter-productive, while targeted officials feel supported by employers and colleagues (Brå 2009: 7).

Another preventive measure is to alert conscience. Offenders often do not know that unlawful influence directed against witnesses and victims of crime – interference in a judicial matter – is not only a separate crime, formally distinct from the original crime, but also one with a particularly high punishment tariff, often higher than the original crime itself (Brå 2008: 8). This lack of knowledge applies primarily to young offenders – 'jobseekers' – who wish to gain merit for a continued criminal career. Increased awareness of the crime of interference in a judicial matter should therefore have a certain preventive effect, although it should not be overestimated in relation to organised crime. As previously mentioned, it is knowledge of criminal law that often leads to implied threats and other subtleties being chosen instead of more overt forms of influence.

Corruption

Corruption is an insidious form of unlawful influence, and can start innocently with something minor, and then escalate (Brå 2007: 21).

Suddenly, matters cross the line from the inappropriate to the unlawful. In contrast to the target of previously mentioned forms of unlawful influence – harassment, threats, violence and malicious damage – the corrupted person can be blamed for greed, bad judgment or carelessness. This also makes it difficult to report the matter to superiors or the police. A threatened person is, by definition, a crime victim deserving sympathy. What understanding can a corrupt official expect?

According to the results of research on unlawful influence against public officials, the most common way to make the unlawful proposal is personally during a one-to-one meeting (Brå 2005: 18; 2009: 7). This is reasonable, as corruption presupposes discretion and this creates an opportunity structure for corruption. The typical situation is that only the bribe-giver and the bribe-taker are present. Unlawful proposals are made to officials who have controlling or monitoring tasks, and therefore are in the front line, often alone, and who have the opportunity both to act and to be passive (Korsell et al. 2007). It is therefore not unexpected that, among the professions included in the survey, Customs officials and police officers more often reported attempts to bribe them (Brå 2005: 18; cf. Brå 2009: 7). It is they who carry out their operations in the field and who regularly meet potential bribe-givers face to face.

Organised crime in Sweden is to a large extent concerned with smuggling, and thus individual Customs officials are a natural target for corruption. To some extent that is also true for police officers who possess information vital for the criminals. Organised crime in Sweden is also small-scale and project-based (Brå 2005: 11; 2007: 4; 2007: 7). The type of organised crime in the Nordic countries, presented briefly in the introduction to this chapter, means there is little need to bribe entire police forces (Johansen 1994, 1996, 2004).

Recruitment, rewards in arrears and relations

More subtle forms of corruption might concern old schoolfriends and acquaintances, who have ended up in different careers and who benefit from ties of friendship by exchanging 'favours'. The same could apply to people with a similar cultural and ethnic background. It seems that organised criminals are good at utilising such contacts (Brå 2007: 4). Old ties of friendship, of being able to give a helping hand and of feeling 'important' and 'needed', weigh more heavily in these situations than the financial benefits that are generally associated with corruption. If no clear financial inducements are involved, it might be less reprehensible for a police officer to suggest to an old friend that he or she 'lie low for a couple of days' as a result of planned drugs swoops in a particular area (see Brå 2007: 4; 2009: 7).

People connected to organised crime also invest resources in creating contacts. There are examples where Customs officials and people employed in packaging and logistics companies are considered useful 'assistants' to help facilitate smuggling of drugs (Brå 2005: 11). One strategy used is to find a 'tap' in an authority or a company (Brå 2005: 11). People with financial problems are a particular target.

The borderline between corruption and blackmail can also be wafer thin. Public officials who have succumbed to corruption can later be subjected to blackmail. Blackmail is also a form of influence often associated with organised crime (Marine 2006; Serio 1997).

Authorities such as the police are keen to build good relationships with people who have links to organised crime, in order to get information from them at a later stage (see Brå 2009: 7). Criminals can, in some cases, exploit this in their turn by making an official cross over the threshold from good relations to friendship corruption, where the information-giver ends up with useful information too. This means that both police officers and criminal persons try to 'corrupt' each other, an interplay that is necessary for the work of both actors.

Seen against the background of the deceptively creeping character of corruption, a number of situations can be described where the risk of corruption may exist. These are when contacts are made, by old acquaintances or unknown persons, which gradually encroach on the professional sphere. These contacts can be made in all sorts of circumstances.

Situational crime preventive measures against corruption

Preventing corruption from organised crime is mainly about increasing the risks and removing the excuses for the perpetrator.

Increase the risks

Both on the authority's premises and in the field, it is helpful if the authority can extend guardianship by having several people present, thus making it more difficult to subject an official to unlawful influence. Double handling is also a preventative method that makes corruption more difficult. This means that when negative decisions are given, or otherwise when there is risk of influence, there should also be two people present.

Natural surveillance can also be improved by supporting whistle-blowers. Often colleagues are in the best position for learning that all is not well, and adequate reporting systems should therefore be established (Brå 2007: 21). These systems can be anonymous in order to encourage whistle-blowers.

Anonymity is a risk factor for corruption among officials. Day-to-day documentation concerning important decisions and changes in decisions makes it possible to go back and investigate, and this increases the risk of discovery.

Remove excuses

It is easy to get into situations that may lead to corruption, and it may sometimes be difficult to draw the line between what is legal and what is not. To this can be added the border between what is appropriate and what is inappropriate. One way of affecting future corruptive situations is to set clear internal rules that 'translate' and operationalise abstract legislation (Brå 2007: 21). By anchoring guidelines through communicating them and maintaining a dialogue about what applies to the staff in a workplace, the preconditions for their being implemented are improved. This applies not least to the sensitive situations when police officers attempt to cultivate good relationships with criminals.

Lack of communication between different levels within an authority can lead to officials misunderstanding the rules about acceptable conduct. This in turn can open the door for prevarication that facilitates more or less unintentional forms of corruption. Introducing a clear division of responsibility and describing what is expected and required reduce the risk of officials becoming involved in corruption. Lack of communication and unclear rules can also exist at the management level, and managers and management should set a good example.

Conclusions

Unlawful influence is a central feature of organised crime (cf. Fijnaut *et al.* 1998). As unlawful influence is a way of hiding crimes and complicating investigations that deal with criminal groups and networks, preventive measures are very important when formulating strategies for counteracting organised crime. Therefore, measures against unlawful influence are not 'only' a question of preventing such influence but also a basic condition to effectively counteract organised crime. Although this chapter has dealt with findings from mainly Swedish research, it is certainly relevant for other countries, especially those that harbour the more network-based form of organised crime.

Some situational crime preventive measures have been discussed in this chapter and they are summarised in Table 9.1.

The research conducted at the Swedish National Council for Crime Prevention on unlawful influence shows that such influence seldom occurs randomly. In fact there are certain situations or meetings where there is a risk. Some members within the criminal networks are more likely to try to find opportunities for corruption, while others use direct threats or sometimes even violence. Finally public officials can through correct behaviour and professional communication, eliminate those situations where unlawful influence can occur, and instead create 'positive situations'.

Table 9.1 Preventive methods against unlawful influence from organised crime

Increase the effort	Increase the risks	Reduce the rewards	Reduce provocations	Remove excuses
'Intellectual' target harden mechanisms	Personal alarms	Increase the risk of discovery and reduce anonymity through pre-booking system, visitor badges, ID requirement and camera surveillance	Reduce provocations through effective management and good service	Act against harassment
Make it more difficult to influence witnesses and victims through having separate waiting rooms (perpetrators and their relatives separate), own entrance and witness stand not being directed towards the public	Support for witnesses and victims of crimes	Move officials and others who are threatened, have an operator take all calls from the public to protect official	Stimulate positive meetings through designing authority premises in such a way that they are perceived as welcoming	Counteract unlawful influence against witnesses and victims through informing, in particular, younger people that interference in a judicial matter is a particularly serious crime with a high punishment tariff
Make it more difficult to resort to violence by designing the workplace in a safe way	Make it more difficult to influence officials by identifying risk situations and introducing internal reporting systems	Make it more difficult to influence officials by varying their daily routines, redistributing cases between officials and making home addresses confidential	Reduce the risk of aroused feelings through good communication and respectful behaviour where decisions are notified clearly, calmly and factually	Prevent corruption through improved internal communications, introduction of clear division of responsibility and description of what is expected and required of officials

Continued

Situational Prevention of Organised Crimes

Table 9.1 Continued

Increase the effort	Increase the risks	Reduce the rewards	Reduce provocations	Remove excuses
Improve the control of access to facilities	Have two officials handling risky cases	Do not help to enhance the bad reputation of organised crime by reporting unusual cases, involving violence etc.		Reduce the risk of unintentional corruption by clarifying legislation through policies that are relevant to the operation, and make sure these are well anchored
	Increase the risk of discovery of corruption through documenting measures and decisions, introducing different types of controls and introducing systems with whistle-blowers			

As the research conducted is to a great extent based on questionnaires to a large number of public officials there is also a possibility to follow up crime preventive measures and see if they have affected the number of incidents or possibly even changed their structure. The knowledge thus gained makes situational crime prevention suitable for preventing unlawful influence from organised crime. The individual authorities could, through a proper internal incident reporting system, follow the development of unlawful influence and improve situational crime preventive measures. It is even better if authorities could share this knowledge and learn from each other because our research stresses that many authorities have a lot in common when it comes to situations and therefore how to avoid opportunities for unlawful influence.

Notes

1 The authors would like to thank researchers Patrik Baard, Isabel Schoultz and Johanna Hagstedt and legal assistant Saadia Aitattaleb for their comments on the script.
2 Extended English summaries of some of these reports are available on the website of Brå: www.bra.se. See the References list at the end of the chapter. The authors of these reports are Johanna Skinnari, Lars Korsell, Karolin Wallström, Patrik Baard, Sven Granath, Lotta Nilsson, Andreas Gårdlund, Monika Karlsson and Linda Weding.
3 For understandable reasons, it is not possible to ask people whether they have taken bribes; for this reason the question asked whether improper proposals had been made, not whether they had been accepted. The authors have drawn the conclusion that this is a reasonable measure of everyday corruption, i.e. it shows the type of proposals made in a relatively spontaneous form to officials (Brå 2005: 18).

References

Aromaa, K. (2006) 'European experiences in preventing organised crime: Field studies of best practices by a Council of Europe expert group', in K. Aromaa and T. Viljanen (eds), *International Key Issues in Crime Prevention and Criminal Justice. Papers in celebration of 25 years of HEUNI.* Helsinki: HEUNI, pp. 13–33.
Bowie, V. (2002) *Workplace Violence: A second look.* Paper presented at the Crime Prevention Conference. University of Western Sydney.
Brå (2005: 11) *Narkotikabrottslighetens organisationsmönster.* Stockholm: Brottsförebyggande rået.
Brå (2005: 18) *Otillåten påverkan riktad mot myndighetspersoner. Från trakasserier, hot och våld till amorös infiltration.* Stockholm: Brottsförebyggande rådet.
Brå (2006: 5) *Hot och våld mot kriminalvardens personal.* Stockholm: Brottsförebyggande radet. English summary: *Threats and violence against prison and probation service staff.*

Brå (2006: 6) *Häleri. Den organiserade brottslighetens möte med den lokala marknaden.* Stockholm: Brottsförebyggande rådet. English summary: *Receiving stolen goods. Where organized crime meets the legal market.*

Brå (2007: 4) *Vart tog alla pengarna vägen? En studie om narkotikabrottslighetens ekonomihantering.* Stockholm: Brottsförebyggande radet. English summary: *Where did all the money go? Summary of a study on the financial management of organized drug crime.*

Brå (2007: 7) *Narkotikadistributörer. En studie av grossisterna.* Stockholm: Brottsförebyggande rådet.

Brå (2007: 21) *Korruptionens struktur i Sverige, del 1: 'Den korrupte upphandlaren' och andra fall om mutor, bestickning och maktmissbruk.* Stockholm: Brottsförebyggande rådet.

Brå (2008: 8) *Otillåten påverkan mot brottsoffer och vittnen. Om ungdomsbrott, relationsvåld och organiserad brottslighet.* Stockholm: Brottsförebyggande rådet.

Brå (2008: 24) *Sexuell människohandel. En fråga om tillgång och efterfrågan.* Stockholm: Brottsförebyggande rådet.

Brå (2009) *Motverka otillaten påverkan. En handbok för myndigheter om att förebygga trakasserier, hot, våld och korruption* (2nd edn). Stockholm: Brottsförebyggande rådet.

Brå (2009: 7) *Polisens möte med den organiserade brottsligheten. En undersökning om otillåten påverkan.* Stockholm: Brottsförebyggande rådet. English summary: *Police encounters with organised crime. A research project about unlawful influence.*

Brå 2009: 13) *Otillåten påverkan mot åklagare och domare.* Stockholm: Brottsförebyggande rådet. English summary: *Unlawful influence on prosecutors and judges.*

Calhoun, F. and Weston, S. (2009) *Threat assessment and management strategies. Identifying the howlers and hunters.* London: CRC Press.

Cornish, D.B. and Clarke, R. (2003) 'Opportunities, precipitators and criminal decisions: A reply to Worthley's critique of situational crime prevention', *Crime Prevention Studies*, 16: 41–96.

Davis, R.C., Smith, B.E. and Henley, M. (1990) *Victim/Witness Intimidation in the Bronx Courts: How Common is it, and What are its Consequences?* New York: Victim Services Agency.

Department of Justice (dir. 2008: 127) *Säkerhetskontroll i domstol.* Directive for a committee.

Ds (2008: 38) *Nationell mobilisering mot den grova organiserade brottsligheten – överväganden och förslag.* Departementspromemoria from Department of Justice.

Fijnaut, C. et al. (1998) *Organized Crime in the Netherlands.* The Hague: Kluwer Law International.

Fyfe, N.R. (2001) *Protecting Intimidated Witnesses.* Hampshire: Ashgate Publishing Limited.

Fyfe, N.R. and McKay, H. (2000) 'Police protection of intimidated witnesses: A study of the Strathclyde police witness protection programme', *Policing and Society*, 10: 277–99.

Fyfe, N.R. and Sheptycki, J. (2005) *Facilitating witness co-operation in organised crime cases: an international review.* Home Office online report 27/05. London: Home Office.

Gill, M., Fisher, B. S. and Bowie, V. (2002) *Violence at Work. Causes, Patterns and Prevention.* Cullompton, UK: Willan Publishing.

Graham, M.H. (1985) *Witness Intimidation: The Law's Response.* Westport, Connecticut: Quorum Books.

Hadley, J. (2006) *Witness intimidation and protection practices: A front line view from Helsinki, consideration of Finnish police law, and review of research in the UK.* Finland: Polishögskolan.

Hellströmer, A. and By, U. (2008) *Hej, hoppas allt är ok. Att samtala med unga brottsoffer.* Stockholm: Jure.

Johansen, P.O. (1994) *Markedet som ikke ville dø. Forbudstiden og de illegale alkoholmarkedene i Norge og USA.* Oslo: Rusmiddeldirektoratet.

Johansen, P.O. (1996) *Nettverk i gråsonen. Et perspektiv på organisert kriminalitet.* Oslo: Ad Notam.

Johansen, P.O. (2004) *Den illegale spriten. Fra forbudstid til polstreik.* Oslo: Unipub.

Katz, J. (1988) *Seductions of Crime.* New York: Basic Books.

Korsell, L. (2007) 'Korruption – en fråga om ekonomisk och organiserad brottslighet?' *Nordisk Tidskrift for Kriminalvidenskab*, 94: 293–304.

Korsell, L. (2008) 'Hur organiserad är den organiserade brottsligheten?', in T. Alalehto and D. Larsson (eds), *Den ljusskygga ekonomin. Organiserad och ekonomisk brottslighet.* Umeå: Umeå Universitet, pp. 179–211.

Korsell, L., Skinnari, J. and Vesterhav, D. (2008) *Organiserad brottslighet. Vad vill vi bekämpa?* Paper. Stockholm: Brottsförebyggande rådet.

Korsell, L., Skinnari, J. and Vesterhav, D. (2009) *Organiserad brottslighet i Sverige.* Lund: Liber.

Korsell, L., Wallström, K. and Skinnari, J. (2007) 'Unlawful influence directed at public servants: from harassment, threats and violence to corruption', *European Journal of Crime, Criminal Law and Criminal Justice*, 335–58.

Larsson, P. (2008) *Organisert Kriminalitet.* Oslo: Pax.

Månson, H. (2007) *Hot mot journalister.* Styrelsen för psykologiskt försvar. Dnr SPF 288/06.

Marine, F.J. (2006) 'The effects of organized crime on legitimate businesses', *Journal of Financial Crime*, 13(2): 214–34.

Serio, J. (1997) 'Russian crime threatens foreign investment', *Crime and Justice International*, 13(3): 10–13.

Verhovek, S.H. (1996) 'Gang intimidation of witnesses is a growing problem', in D. Bender and B. Leone (eds), *From Gangs: Opposing Viewpoints.* St. Paul, Minneapolis: Greenhaven Press, pp. 77–81.

Wierup, L. (2007) 'Hot som affärsidé', in J. Hartelius (ed.), *Systemhotande brottslighet.* Stockholm: Bokförlaget Langenskiöld.

Wierup, L. and Larsson, M. (2007) *Svensk maffia. En kartläggning av de kriminella gängen.* Stockholm: Norstedts.

Wästerfors, D. (2007) *Fängelsebråk. Analyser av konflikter på anstalt.* Lund: Studentlitteratur.

Chapter 10

Organised crime and crime scripts: prospects for disruption

Graham Hancock and Gloria Laycock

Abstract

This chapter discusses the concept of crime scripts as a means of better understanding and thus preventing or disrupting organised crime. It briefly reminds readers of the characteristics of scripts and develops a framework within which they might be understood in the context of organised crime. It 'tests' the framework through interview material gathered from senior investigating officers in a major law enforcement agency and discusses the implications of this for future action against organised crime.

Introduction

Tackling organised crime is difficult. The extent to which it is 'organised' and the nature of the supposed hierarchical groups that conduct it have tended to dominate both academic and practitioner discourse. The focus of policing organised crime has thus, at the time of writing, been enforcement-oriented, with considerable effort being devoted to trying to understand the structure of organised crime groups (OCGs), to target the somewhat elusive leaders and to dismantle the supposed hierarchy.

Despite current responses, organised crime appears to be increasing and it has been estimated to cost the UK economy between £20 and £40 billion per annum (Home Office 2004). UK enforcement agencies are currently continuing with their arrest and prosecution policies while at the same time trying to expand the repertoire of police options to include more prevention and disruption. This chapter speaks to that development. We argue that prevention and disruption can be enhanced by looking at organised crime through the lens of crime scripts. In the next section we remind readers of this concept, first developed in relation to crime by Cornish (1994). We then outline a conceptual framework within which the analysis of organised crime scripts might usefully be considered and finally report the results of a series of interviews with senior investigating officers of a major UK law enforcement agency which try to tease out the usefulness of the framework.

Crime scripts and organised crime

Scripts arise from learned behaviour. As Nisbett and Ross (1980: 341) say, 'scripts generally are event sequences extended over time, and the relationships have a distinctly causal flavour, that is, early events in the sequence produce or at least enable the occurrence of later events'. This 'distinct causal flavour' is important if crime script analysis is to be developed as a useful methodology in working out ways to reduce organised crime. As an example consider the crime commission process for a mugging offence on the subway system. Table 10.1 (from Cornish 1994) shows the series of steps necessary to the commission of the offence, any one of which might be subject to intervention or disruption through the usual situational means.

Although offenders are adaptable, script analysis generally assumes the routinisation of criminal acts: that although each individual offence will have its unique characteristics, any one class of offending will have sufficient elements in common to allow the kinds of generalisation made by Cornish in Table 10.1, and thus facilitate the kind of preventive

Table 10.1 Robbery script

Script scenes/functions	Script actions
Preparation	Meet and agree on hunting ground
Entry	Entry into underground system
Precondition	Travel to hunting ground
Precondition	Waiting/circulating at hunting ground
Instrumental pre-condition	Selecting victim and circumstance
Instrumental initiation	Closing in/preparation
Instrumental actualisation	Striking at victim
Instrumental actualisation	Pressing home attack
Doing	Take money etc.
Post-condition	Escape from scene
Exit	Exit from system

Source: From Cornish 1994, after Leddo and Abelson 1986 and Ekblom 1991.

intervention that might be applied to the whole class of offending rather than treating each offence as an individual incident. Intervention would thus force large-scale offender adaptation that might otherwise not occur, and hopefully render offenders more vulnerable to detection. Alternatively they may be less prepared to take the risks inherent in some adaptive options, in which case the offences would be prevented. Script analysis is also underpinned by the process of rational choice as a decision-making tool.

Crime scripts are normally understood in terms of routine or low-level offending. Cornish and Clarke (2002) are an exception in discussing the potential of the crime script approach to organised crime specifically. Additionally, Tremblay and colleagues (Matifat and Tremblay 1997; Lacoste and Tremblay 2003) have applied these ideas to cheque card fraud (although they do not discuss the offending as a manifestation of organised crime, it is clear from their accounts that much of it could be so described). Their work offers the typically detailed analysis of the offending and shows that scripts for cheque/credit card fraud offences are clearly more complex than the one illustrated in Table 10.1. This chapter is closer in aspiration to that of Clarke and Cornish than to Tremblay *et al*. We are not embarking on a detailed analysis of crime scripts of organised criminals. Rather, we explore the potential utility of such an approach from the perspective of the law enforcement agencies tasked to deal with it. Crime scripts tend to be characterised as helpful to the crime prevention effort in broadening out the opportunities for prevention and disruption. In theory this is of course a persuasive possibility. What we hope to explore in this chapter is the extent to which these aspirations might be realisable in practice and some of the potential impediments.

We are not focusing on a specific organised crime type, although as it turns out many of the operations discussed later are in practice drug-related. We start from the observation that the generality of organised crime is likely to be more complex than, say, mugging, due to the number of different acts, actors, locations, the length of time of the offending process and the inclusion of sub-scripts such as the theft of cars and the acquisition of firearms (Naylor 2003). In some cases it is assumed that offenders utilise methods and tactics that have previously been found to be successful, for example means of moving commodities, dealing in goods that they know they can sell through methods they know work and disposing of funds in ways they know are unlikely to attract attention. In other cases, as Lacoste and Tremblay show, they combine their more routine offending practices with considerable innovation and creativity.

Additionally, organised crime groups (OCGs) and networks will not necessarily undertake one offence at a time. They may be involved in several simultaneously, each at a different stage of development but sometimes including common players, locations and equipment. Furthermore the yields from one crime may be used to fund further offending.

Applying the script approach to organised crime highlights this complexity, but also offers the potential for identifying points for intervention. It should enable us to develop our knowledge of what organised criminals use in terms of equipment and facilitators at what locations and to what effect. It will indicate some of the 'tools' or infrastructural requirements needed to complete the offence which might then be susceptible to preventive or disruptive interventions.

A particular difficulty that such an approach has in terms of organised crime is deciphering, in its more complex operating environment, what is uniquely an act in furtherance of a specific criminal offence, and what derives from the day-to-day management of criminal lifestyles which enables offenders to exploit criminal opportunities without breaking step. Attempting to tease out these differences through something like a script analysis offers potential. For example, behaviour which is known to feature as part of the crime commission process, such as travelling by car to the near continent for a very short trip, might form part of the police investigation and contribute vital evidence toward securing a conviction. But the vehicle used, which is unregistered, untaxed and uninsured as a matter of routine lifestyle choice by the offender and not established simply to facilitate the commission of the current offence, might be virtually ignored by the police whose focus is elsewhere. Subsequent offending by the individual concerned is supported by this and similar lifestyle choices.

In the next section we set out a potential method for conceptualising script analysis in relation to organised crime which we feel may clarify what law enforcement agencies need to do beyond their current emphasis on enforcement and the gathering of evidence to support prosecution, important though those processes are. This will enable us to shape strategic preventative and disruptive responses, force offenders to adapt (hopefully to their less preferred options) and minimise the possibility of displacing criminal activity.

The constituent parts of the organised crime script

We suggest that it is helpful to break organised crime scripts into three parallel processes as illustrated in Figure 10.1 on page 177 which shows the central column (labelled primary criminal act) as constituting the primary offence process (for example drug importation). This draws on and is supported by the other two columns – the criminal lifestyle and the participation in and further access to criminal networks, groups or individuals. The present focus of the majority of police investigations is on establishing the facts and evidence associated with the primary criminal act. The other two columns, although they may be noticed by investigators and indeed may be investigated to a limited extent, are often seen as marginal to the primary offence and are traditionally seldom pursued as a matter of course. As we hope to illustrate, paying greater attention to what might be seen as these necessary crime facilitators will increase the options for more permanent disruption of organised crimes. First a little more is said about how we see these three columns:

- The criminal lifestyle – the commission of organised criminal acts and involvement in criminal groups and networks are both dependent upon and facilitated by a lifestyle that may be regarded as inherently criminal in nature. The pursuit of anonymity and in particular the selection of which parts of the regulatory system to take part in are integral to the conduct of criminal business particularly in respect of moving and disposing of large quantities of cash. The use of stolen and unregistered vehicles, the use of false bank accounts and money laundering systems, the corruption of legitimate business and law enforcement officials are precipitators and constituent parts of the offending process but they both pre- and post-date it. These factors exist and are a lifestyle feature independently of any active offending process, and measures that seek to prevent and curtail them will ultimately hinder the undertaking of the primary criminal acts themselves.

- The organised crime group or network (OCG) – this is the identifiable criminal group, network or collection of individuals that is defined by its existence to conduct a criminal act. This 'group' may be either hierarchical or a loose network of peers, and in respect of the latter it is perhaps poorly characterised as a 'group' (which tends to assume more permanent features and a hierarchical structure). Groups may also work together as part of a larger and temporary network for a specific crime purpose. Of course the whole offending process from source to market (e.g. human trafficking, drug distribution) could in theory be undertaken by one group, but this would require a stable structure and a complex but identifiable chain of actions; it would also be more easily targeted by the police. Some aspects of the offending are, therefore, 'contracted out' to associated but largely pre-existing groups. This is akin to the conduct of legitimate business that seeks out suppliers, recruits transport specialists and identifies distributors or customers.

    We do not want to dwell too much on the definitions and distinctions here; we are taking a loose definition very much for the purposes of illustrating a point. Essentially, we wish to take as given that OCGs exist, or potentially exist (insofar as they can be readily constituted) independently of any particular offence. They also readily coalesce into more complex networks. Reactionary and enforcement-oriented responses often fail to recognise this.

- The primary criminal act/offence/enterprise – this is the crime(s) that is being undertaken, whether in isolation or part of a continuing pattern, in order to make money. The types of offences will vary but the crime process element describes the necessary behavioural steps to enact the crime. This is the central pillar of the scripting process but the offence is dependent upon the existence of groups and networks with the requisite skills, experience and tools and an ability to exploit opportunities as they arise. The actual process of offending can thus be seen as separate from but dependent upon these crime groups which recognise and exploit criminal opportunities.

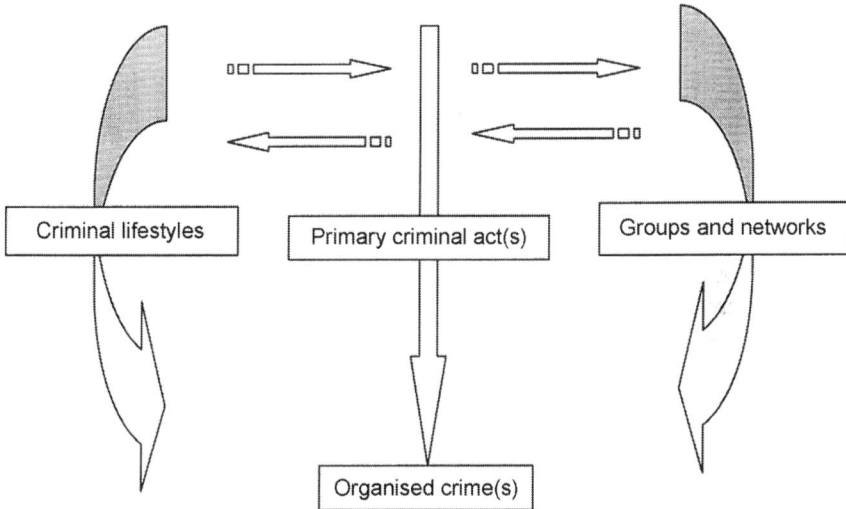

Figure 10.1 Representation of the constituent parts of organised crime

These three 'pillars' are illustrated in Figure 10.1, which together form the crime script.

Approaching the construction of scripts in this fashion allows for the formulation of responses that focus on the existence of the groups/ networks, the mechanics of the offence and the overarching lifestyle components. This may present three separate but interrelated streams of opportunity for preventative/disruptive effort. For example, targeting a lifestyle script, such as the purchase and use of an unregistered vehicle initially unlinked to a primary criminal act, would disrupt a later act of offending by reducing anonymity and affect interactions with other criminal groups in a network.

Exploring the utility of Figure 10.1

Senior Investigating Officers (SIOs) or case officers from a UK law enforcement agency were interviewed about law enforcement operations on which they were working with the intention of exploring the utility of this approach to scripts. These interviews were based on operations on which the officers had been or were currently working. The purpose was to explore the dynamics of organised crime and to find out to what extent the kind of analysis proposed above might hold promise in revealing additional preventive options. The operations were selected on the following basis:

1. Five offices of the law enforcement agency were chosen in the south of England considered to be typical of the other UK offices in terms of workload and size.
2. From these offices all operations that met the following criteria were examined:
   (a) The operation was substantially or wholly concluded.
   (b) The operation focused on serious or organised crime defined by the activities under investigation being considered at Level Three of the UK National Intelligence Model (NIM).
   (c) The criminality investigated was the work of an organised crime group or network, not purely acts of individuals, i.e. some organised element must have been present.

Eleven operations met these criteria. They almost exclusively involved drug trafficking groups which were also involved in money laundering as a by-product of their criminal activities. (This may limit scope for generalisation of the results to other forms of organised crime.)

Information was obtained from the accounts of the officers but it was expressed in terms of the 'prosecution case' and an apportionment of blame. Partly as a consequence there were some key items of information which would be desirable from a 'script' perspective, but which were unknown to the SIOs despite, in many cases, successful prosecutions being achieved. This missing information clearly did not unduly affect the overall prosecution of the offence, although a fuller, script-focused exercise would have probably led to more and more significant information relevant to the prosecution.

Additionally, it was noticeable that genuine non-enforcement-based preventative measures were only apparent on one operation studied, although encouragingly that was by the most senior and experienced of all the interviewees, and directed against the most established and entrenched organised crime group. Most interviewees referred to what they perceived as preventative methods which in truth were enforcement measures by another name, such as disruptive arrests. Although by no means a criticism of those interviewed, this underlines the enforcement-oriented nature of organised crime investigations or perhaps demonstrates the difficulty of combining covert policing with crime prevention measures. The approach explored here is not therefore one that is routinely undertaken by investigators.

We were interested in reviewing the various offences as understood by the SIOs and establishing whether there were common elements across the offences which would support the conceptualisation outlined in Figure 10.1. Specifically we sought to differentiate quite precisely between acts which were indicative of a criminal lifestyle, and those which were conducted purely for the commission of immediate offences. Twenty-four main offences were described by the SIOs. Money laundering offences were considered separately even if they were felt to be part of the disposal/movement or concealment of funds of the predicate offences.

Common components of the crime process

Processes common to all the crime scripts are summarised below:

Full-time employment

Underlining the possible economic motivation for organised crime and the applicability of rational choice approaches, it was noted that of the 87 individuals involved in the study, only 18 (21 per cent) were employed (including two full-time students) or had businesses that were believed to provide a legitimate income whether or not they were also used to launder proceeds or had been established using the proceeds of crime. In general terms opulent lifestyles were evident for a small number of individuals and these were heads, senior members of crime groups or their family members who were often used as a means of concealment of the proceeds of crime.

The involvement of various sub-groups

The vast majority of those involved in the movement of drugs were dependent on other crime groups at some stage of their offending process. Networks were clearly fluid and there was evidence of crime groups searching for others to partner or assist in the offending or simply to purchase the products.

Movement of commodities

In nine of the operations studied it was possible to assess the movements of commodities into and around the UK. In each of these cases legitimate hauliers moved the goods through identified ports either unknowingly (due to the corruption of the driver or other employee) or entirely knowingly. Complicity of the driver was the most common method and was a key enabling feature of drug trafficking in at least one operation examined. This operation also exposed a lack of security at some ports in the UK with the storage and collection of containers, which was also present in other of the operations studied. The need for transport specialists was often the reason for the recruitment of one OCG (specialising in transportation) by another.

Communication

This was principally conducted by prepay mobile phones which in the UK can be obtained without the requirement to provide subscriber details or a billing address. These phones were often used for specific criminal purposes and discarded afterwards. The extent of the use of prepay unregistered phones was more fully explored in operations A, B and H in order to quantify the general interviewees' claims that 90–99 per cent of the phones were prepay. These operations were chosen only on the basis of ease of access to data collected by the SIOs because it had been required for court proceedings. Table 10.2 summarises the findings and shows the high rate of use of prepay unregistered mobiles in the three cases. These demonstrated systematic, disciplined and tightly controlled use of mobile phones that was aimed principally at ensuring that the owner of the line was not identified.

Table 10.2 Breakdown of prepay mobile phone use for operations A, B and H

Operation	Number of mobile phone lines identified as significant	Number unregistered	Number registered	% of unregistered prepay mobile phone lines
A	44	38	6	86
B	6	5	1	83
H	33	29*	4	88
Total	83	72	11	87

*Includes one phone registered using false details.

The UK phone regulatory agency, OFCOM (2005) indicate that the percentage of prepay users in the general population is 67 per cent, well short of the 87 per cent shown in Table 10.2. There was also an indication of considerable use of telephone kiosks on many of the operations although this was difficult to establish consistently as it depended on surveillance operations or analysis of mobile phone bills. Where there was substantial telephone kiosk use such as operations A, B and H, international platform dialling cards were used which further confound any attempts to investigate call traffic. Finally, there was some evidence of the use of email for communication although this was not at all widespread.

There was thus no accurate means of identifying the true extent of the use of mobile technology as the medium of choice for communication in organised crime but it was clearly significant and it varied across offences. It was clear, however, that those involved in organised crime utilise non-traceable means of communication in order to maximise anonymity.

Bogus front companies

Front companies were a feature of a number of the operations either for the purpose of facilitating the criminal act or of laundering the proceeds. People with little or no employment history opened companies and purchased businesses. Entirely fictitious companies created to enable crime were a feature of four of the operations. There were also two other businesses which were trading but acted as a front for the offending. Some perfectly legitimate businesses were bought or established as a means of legitimising or laundering the proceeds of crime. One company was established nine months prior to the crime under investigation for the sole purpose of importing a number of bulk items to generate 'legitimacy'; it had no customers for these loads and never sought any.

The venue for business

Anonymity was ensured in the conduct of meetings, handover of commodities and day-to-day management of business, by the appropriate choice of location. While members of the same OCG would be prepared to meet in business premises and at home addresses this was not often the case for meetings between members of different groups. There was a wide and varied use of public places including car parks, restaurants, service stations, retail parks, hotels and railway stations. Safe houses were only identified in four of the operations. Two of these locations were only connectable to couriers, one was a business premises and one had been rented using false details. This aspect of the criminality presents the most difficulties as it represents explicitly the way organised criminals intertwine their activities with everyday life. Preventing the physical presence in a car park or cafe of persons who may exploit that location to discuss crime is even beyond the scope of Serious Crime Prevention Orders (SCPO)[1] and would raise serious ethical questions, as we shall discuss briefly later.

The division of labour

Risk management was clearly distinguishable in line with Dorn *et al.*'s (1998) strategic and tactical differentiation. The risky movement of cash and commodities was primarily but not exclusively the task of those lower in standing in the organisation. The greatest risk was associated with movement through the ports; anecdotal evidence from two interviewees suggests that such movements attract rewards of, for example, £1,000–£1,500 per kilo of heroin (in 2005) for a crime group providing transport facilities, but much smaller fees for individual co-opted or corrupted drivers. Only in three of the crime groups assessed (four were not able to be assessed) was tactical risk spread evenly across the OCG.

Disposal and concealment of funds

There was some evidence of coaching by senior members of crime groups in how best to conceal proceeds of crime. Cash was moved in a number of ways and it was evident that movements of large sums of money provided particular problems.[2] Corrupt money exchange/money service bureaux were a feature of two of the operations. By far the most prevalent means of utilising/disposing of the proceeds of crime was lifestyle including the purchase of jewellery, high-value vehicles and property inside and outside the UK. One interviewee described the disposal of funds by the crime group accordingly: 'They had bogus bank accounts, used a corrupt accountant, invested in property in five countries, bought nightclubs, an airline, expensive cars and had expensive lifestyles: I don't know what they did with the rest though.' The principal identified capital expenditures were, however, property, cars and semi-legitimate businesses. These purchases could all be undertaken without any need to justify the source of income. It was common for these properties or vehicles to be falsely registered, registered to businesses or registered in the name of third parties, particularly family members.

The disposal of funds was often not sophisticated, as in Operation H, where considerable amounts of the cash were passed through the bank accounts of family members in typical 'smurfing' fashion (small amounts and often) to avoid statutory disclosures. The amounts of cash generated differed enormously between the operations as reflected in the manner of disposal. There was a clear relationship between sophistication in the disposal of funds and the length of establishment of the crime group. It was clear, however, that once the groups started to generate more cash than could be spent day to day they needed to and in every case did seek to conceal the money by means as diverse as gambling in Holland and buying a cleaning business.

Use of unregistered vehicles

With the exception of Operation C the use of unregistered/falsely registered vehicles was prevalent throughout the operations examined and was again indicative of the desire for anonymity. Operation F recorded 12 vehicles that were vital to the offences, of which 10 were either unregistered or registered with false details, and a similar picture was evident on operation A which saw six of the nine relevant vehicles falsely registered or unregistered.

Stolen vehicles were also commonly used at the point of moving commodities, as were vehicles rented using false details or bearing 'in trade' registration plates (i.e. using temporary registration plates approved for use by motor dealers). These unauthorised or illegal vehicles were used not only to facilitate specific crimes but also on an everyday basis.

Use or threat of violence

Violence or the threat of violence was a feature of nine of the 11 operations. This involved the use of firearms or beatings, principally to enforce the payment of debts. It was considered a tactical option in response to an inter-group dispute rather than being a necessary and expected component of the offending process itself. It was thus more evident between OCGs than within them.

Use of legitimate business

Legitimate businesses were used or exploited either as facilitators of the crime event (such as haulage firms) or as a means of disposal of the proceeds of the crime through existing agents (such as accountants), or by purchasing or establishing new businesses. It was difficult to determine how far legitimate businesses and professionals were willing participants or innocent dupes. The use of legitimate businesses was considered key to the activities on all the operations as both an enabler and indeed a means of dealing with the cash generated from illegal activity.

Immigration status

The crime groups were overwhelmingly made up of British nationals with only 15 individuals (17 per cent) illegally resident in the UK. Although illegal residents featured in only a small number of operations, where they were present their status was believed to help preserve their anonymity. One asylum seeker found the offer of asylum less appealing after a charge for drug trafficking and absconded from bail, returning to the country of origin.

The nature of the groups

It was evident in examining the groups that they were small, tightly configured bodies that orbited around key personalities. These groups were held together by a bond of friendship often defined by nationality or family ties that was able to engender a sense of trust essential to the everyday conduct of business. The groups existed to some extent before, during and after the commission of the crime. What was distinctive about the members was an overwhelming commitment to crime. When asked about employment status of the crime group members three interviewees responded, 'criminal'. Relationships were fostered and maintained; trust developed and patterns of life followed for the purposes of committing crime. Only professionals, such as accountants, operated in the identifiably legitimate economy.

It is the crux of this chapter that such distinctive characteristics follow a pattern of purposive behaviour which by its very nature lends itself to a script process. Furthermore, each element of this behaviour, the criminal lifestyle, the crime process itself and the criminal groups and networks constitute three distinct and identifiable components that offer opportunities for preventative action that increases the risk to the offender.

Mapping the crime script

Having suggested the key constituents to the organised criminal process as shown in Figure 10.1 we can look to map this onto a scripted chart as in Table 10.3 below. The script is constructed as a sequential set of actions that feature as part of an offence consistent with drug or people trafficking. Column 1 details the stage of the crime from preparing for the offence to its completion. To that extent it follows the format of the example given in Table 10.1 above and is constructed around the actual offending process or those acts or elements that have a bearing on it. The key aspect of Table 10.3 is that it seeks to identify which of the three elements of the crime script as shown in Figure 10.1 are applicable to the progression of the offending cycle for a given organised criminal offence. So Table 10.3 differs from Table 10.1 in that it includes in the second column the identification of which of the three elements of the script processes the act described relates to; the elements of the primary criminal act, the networking or activity of groups or the criminal lifestyle. For instance networking with other crime groups is both a feature of the preparation stage of the criminal act and an element of the network script. The fourth column is for illustrative purposes only and suggests some of the possible preventive/disruptive activities that might ensue.

The approach shown in Table 10.3, and its application to our understanding of organised crime takes a bolder step than much of the current academic literature in seeking to articulate the processes associated with the commission of certain organised crimes by plotting the key stages of the offence. We can see that each of the three elements of the script plays a significant part in bringing about the successful conclusion of a criminal act. The three elements are interdependent; for the complexities of organised crime to be successfully completed all three need to exist in parallel.

What further complicates the construction of an integrated crime script is that certain acts feature at different stages according to need and for different reasons, such as obtaining false documentation. Such

Organised crime and crime scripts: prospects for disruption

Table 10.3 The integrated organised crime script

Function	Script category	Action	Preventative response
Preparation	Lifestyle Network	Formation/existence of an organised crime group	Association bans for those suspected/convicted of organised crime through imposition of SCPO
Entry	Crime Network	Interaction with other networks and groups to discuss opportunity	Imposition of travel bans post conviction and association bans based on intelligence not conviction (SCPO)
Precondition	Lifestyle Network	Maintenance of anonymity for group members due to illegal/undetermined residence in the UK	Introduction of ID cards Restricting access to prepay mobile phones Improving vehicle registration data
Instrumental precondition	Crime Network	Agreement to undertake criminal act	Restriction on access to prepay mobile phones
Instrumental initiation	Crime Lifestyle	Establishment of a bogus front company	Persons convicted of organised criminal offences to be banned from company ownership/directorship Tighter control of company formation Stricter adherence to AML regulations by solicitors
Instrumental actualisation	Crime Lifestyle Network	Arrange criminality through the use of mobile phones	Remove anonymity afforded by prepay mobile phones. All mobile phones to have registered subscriber and billing address
Instrumental actualisation	Crime Lifestyle Network	Movement of cash through corrupt money exchanges to pay for commodity	Vetting exchange staff Increased regulation or restriction on Money Service Bureaux
Doing	Crime	Movement of commodity into the UK utilising 'legitimate haulage firm'	Accreditation of companies entitled to take tractor units abroad. Accreditation of drivers. Introduction of bonded warehouse-style scheme for all goods
Doing	Crime Lifestyle	Movement of commodity within the UK using stolen/unregistered vehicle	Fuel purchase dependent on production of correct documentation

Continued

185

Table 10.3 Continued

Function	Script category	Action	Preventative response
Post condition	Crime Lifestyle Network	Movement of cash through bogus bank accounts	Banks withdrawing services under voluntary code to clients whose accounts raise suspicion. Persons convicted of money laundering or organised crime to declare conviction to bank. Financial reporting order restrictions
Post condition/exit	Crime Lifestyle	Disposal of funds through lavish lifestyles	Improved compliance with Money Laundering Regulations 2007 by the regulated sector, e.g. improved submission of suspicious activity reports (SARs). Financial reporting orders
Post condition/exit	Crime Networks	Complicity of accountants and lawyers in disposal of crime groups proceeds	Restriction on the type of transactions that pass through client accounts. External auditing. Suspicious activity regime
Exit	Crime Lifestyle	Disposal of funds through purchase of property	Compliance with AML Regulations and submission of SARs. Purchase of property dependent upon proof of taxable income
Exit	Crime Lifestyle	Disposal of funds through purchase and false registration of vehicles	HMRC notification for all vehicles. Tighter control on vehicle registration requirements. Fuel purchase controls, e.g. ID cards
Exit	Crime Lifestyle	Purchase of semi-/legitimate business to launder money through	Compliance with AML Regulations by legal representatives handling transactions. Cross-checking VAT records and tax revenues

Key: AML Anti-money laundering; HMRC Her Majesty's Revenue and Customs; SAR Suspicious Activity Report; SCPO Serious Crime Prevention Order.

documentation may for instance be obtained to enable certain lifestyle choices such as opening forged bank accounts during a well-established criminal career, but feature as one of the first steps to actually committing a crime such as renting a car in a false name to attend a planning meeting with other crime groups. These issues can be overcome by constructing the script around the criminal act as detailed by Cornish (1994) and illustrated at Table 10.3.

Discussion

We have sought to illustrate:

1. the extent to which the control of organised crime is currently enforcement laden;
2. the fact that there are pre-existing conditions which support organised criminality (lifestyle and knowledge of crime networks) and that although they are largely known to SIOs they are seldom explicitly explored any further than necessary to secure a conviction;
3. that there is merit in trying to 'partial out' these supporting mechanisms and to dismantle, disrupt or otherwise deal with them in ways intended to make organised crime more difficult; and
4. that it is helpful to approach this task as a form of script analysis – disentangling, or at least attempting to understand, the temporary, opportunity-driven characteristics that might facilitate the crime itself from the relationships and lifestyle features, which provide enduring conditions for the commission of the crime and are equally important but often ignored once a conviction is achieved.

Although dealing with organised crime remains enforcement oriented (for good reason) there are certainly signs that the law enforcement agencies are interested in broadening their response agenda. The current availability and use of SCPOs and Financial Reporting Orders[3] in the UK illustrates this, as does the greater use of powers to deport foreign nationals who intelligence indicates are involved in crime (although as with any such measure we may need to consider the possibility that deportation of foreign nationals actually enhances organised trafficking since it creates ideal conditions for individuals to establish or maintain contacts across borders).

More fundamentally we perhaps need to recognise that organised crime is as much dependent upon opportunity and its exploitation as the arguably more straightforward act of shoplifting. There may exist a greater need for the use of 'smoke and mirrors' in order to commit the more serious offence, but these steps are undoubtedly just elaborate extensions of risk-reducing measures found in other offending. Adopting a script approach to understanding organised crime presents an opportunity to take a substantial step forward in formulating context-specific preventative measures. Where organised crime differs is that it is more than a mechanical process of set cognitive steps and decisions. In order to undertake the acts and exploit the opportunity there need to be certain key factors in place, whether active or dormant, which manifest themselves in certain lifestyles and in the dynamics of certain groups. Without the ability to successfully dispose of large quantities of revenue, for example, there is no point in obtaining it in the first place. This chapter argues that such an approach to preventing and tackling organised crime does not currently exist, and there is a very real need to call time on primarily enforcement-oriented responses and seek to utilise a methodological approach that enables a better understanding of the context within which situational measures may be applied. Utilising the crime script approach offers an opportunity to break down the process of offending both horizontally in terms of its step-by-step actions and laterally by addressing its component parts, lifestyle and crime group, which have to date been approached by many as one entity. Organised crime is no less preventable than volume crime, it is just less understood, and thinking about it from a crime script perspective will, we argue, improve that understanding.

Attending to this broader agenda is not a trivial issue. First we need to be clear what it is necessary for officers to uncover in relation to offending to secure the needed conviction and what extra they may need to investigate to determine the lifestyle and network supports, and then how they may be disrupted. This process of identification and disruption requires different skills and a particular understanding of crime: an understanding sympathetic to the notion that crime can be controlled through situational means and needs to be considered in detail from that perspective; it also requires a commitment to prevention. There is therefore a training issue for law enforcement agencies and there are resource implications. Carrying out additional investigations and then acting upon the results will take time in a context of increased pressure to deliver convictions and then move on to the next case.

Secondly, although there was fluidity between the crime groups studied here, and their relationships were at times transient, there was also clear evidence of some stability in relationships. These trust and relationship characteristics were key facilitating elements to the commission of organised offending. Trust and risk may be seen as complementary relationships and yet despite the sizeable criminological attention that has been directed at the assessment of risk (O'Malley 1992) questions of trust have been largely ignored within the criminological literature. This is surprising as within the organised crime environment, trust releases people from the need for monitoring or checking that the desired activities have been carried out (Crawford 2002).

Preventing the association of members of identifiable crime groups addresses this issue of trust and would severely restrict the ability of the key people around whom these groups coalesce to undertake criminal activity of the kind seen. The introduction of serious crime prevention orders in the UK in 2007 makes it feasible now for associations to be limited for key identified individuals, although in practice this can be fraught with difficulties. Some of these relationships are familial and the ethics of prohibiting association between family members is problematic and could even be counter-productive in damaging social capital that might otherwise be used to encourage compliance with the law (Kennedy 2008). Basically we need to develop alternative methods to disrupt the trust on which the groups depend, and this perhaps calls for a greater understanding of its nature than we have at present.

Thirdly, the investigations studied in this research illustrated the extent to which offenders ensured that they retained their anonymity as a matter of lifestyle choice. The criminal lifestyle of offenders involved in organised crime is an enabling characteristic rather than a by-product or consequence. 'The major skill they have in common, over and above their special expertise, is that of keeping out of sight' (Mack 1972: 50). Criminal lifestyles and the style of interaction between individuals in crime groups and between networks is conducted in a manner that seeks to maximise anonymity and hence reduce the risks as and when criminal acts are undertaken and opportunity to offend exploited.

In maintaining anonymity offenders avoid vehicle regulation systems, fail to register their mobile phones and choose their banking arrangements with care. Similarly, almost every investigation identified that at some point the criminal took advantage of poor regulation over the movement of goods into and out of the UK and access to hauliers who were acting legitimately but within an inadequately regulated framework or were actively breaking the rules. Perhaps the biggest British crime prevention measure from an environmental design perspective is the English Channel, but such is the volume of all movements into and out of the country that applying appropriate measures is extremely difficult. Again this lack of regulation was a feature of the script approach at both ends of the criminal process, commodity in (in the cases discussed, drugs) and money out.

Tightening up the regulatory framework would not only make life more difficult for the organised offender, it would disrupt the activities of offenders in general. For example, the use of unregistered or falsely registered vehicles not only facilitates organised crime, it enables a wide range of other offences as well, for example by making possible the avoidance of traffic regulations and subsequent fine enforcement or driving bans and the non-payment of insurance. Unfortunately closing the loopholes that enable this anonymity to be maintained would not only make the lives of offenders more difficult but also impact on the largely law-abiding majority. Although it might be argued that 'policing is the task and responsibility not of the state or of a single specialist agency, but of everyone with an interest in preserving private property and personal security' (Garland 2002) there is a sense in which proposals that restrict an offender's access to prepay mobile phones, freedom to set up businesses, access to haulage services and movement of funds through the banking system are seen to disproportionately affect all our rights and freedoms. A judgment is needed as to when and indeed whether restriction on potential offenders impacts too heavily on the general public.

Furthermore, while it is perhaps arguable that, say, the UK vehicle licensing system needs to be tightened up in the interest of crime prevention, it is not within the gift of the police to do this. The central government department responsible for the regulation of vehicles is the Department of Transport and there is little appetite for a root-and-branch overhaul of a massive system involving up to 30 million vehicles on the grounds that it might make life more difficult for offenders. Similarly, one of the preventative responses in Table 10.3 is restriction of access to prepay mobile phones. These phones are provided by a range of suppliers in the mobile communications industry and the task of persuading them towards better regulation is not a simple matter. So although we might argue that systems need to be tighter in the interests of crime control, we have simultaneously to cope with the potential threat to all our rights (to prepay phones, cars, confidential banking arrangements) and the fact that the law enforcement agencies, although wishing to tighten regulations, are not competent to do so (Laycock 1996; Laycock and Webb 2000).

So, even if the implementation of some of the ideas listed in Table 10.3 might be difficult, we maintain that they need to be flushed out as options, and systematically considered. This process is facilitated by a script approach to organised crime as outlined here.

Notes

1 Serious Crime Prevention Orders were introduced in the Serious Crime Act 2007. They are intended to prevent and deter crime. They represent a civil order, the breach of which is a criminal offence, punishable by a maximum of five years' imprisonment. They can last for up to five years and can be placed on individuals, companies or other legal bodies.
2 This research was conducted prior to the introduction of the third EU Money Laundering directive in the form of the Money Laundering Regulations 2007, which further extended the anti money laundering regime and brought more businesses within the scope of the regulated sector.

3 Financial Reporting Orders were introduced in the Serious Organised Crime and Police Act 2005 (SOCPA) and are primarily intended to allow law enforcement to monitor convicted criminals' finances to ensure that they are not engaged in further criminal activity.

References

Cornish, D. (1994) 'The procedural analysis of offending and its relevance for situational prevention', in R.V. Clarke (ed.), *Crime Prevention Studies, Volume 3.* Monsey, NY: Criminal Justice Press.

Cornish, D. and Clarke, R.V (2002) 'Analyzing organised crimes', in A.R. Piquero and S.G. Tibbetts (eds), *Rational Choice and Criminal Behaviour: Recent research and future challenges*. Hamden: Garland Science.

Crawford, A. (2002) 'Situational crime prevention, urban governance and trust relations', in A. Von Hirsch, D. Garland and A. Wakefield (eds), *Ethical and Social Perspectives on Situational Crime Prevention*. Oxford: Hart Publishing.

Dorn, N., Oette, L. and White, S. (1998) 'Drugs importation and the bifurcation of risk', *British Journal of Criminology*, 38(4): 537–60.

Ekblom, P. (1991) 'Talking to offenders: Practical lessons from local crime prevention', in O. Nello (ed.), *Urban Crime: Statistical approaches and analyses*. International seminar held in Barcelona, Institut d' Estudis Metropolitans de Barcelona.

Ekblom, P. (1994) 'Proximal circumstances: A mechanism based classification of crime prevention', in R.V. Clarke (ed.), *Crime Prevention Studies, Volume 2.* Monsey, NY: Criminal Justice Press.

Garland, D. (2002) 'Ideas, institutions and situational crime prevention', in A. von Hirsch, D. Garland and A. Wakefield (eds), *Ethical and Social Perspectives on Situational Crime Prevention*. Oxford: Hart Publishing.

Granovetter, M.S. (1973) 'The strength of weak ties', *American Journal of Sociology*, 78(6): 1360–80

Home Office (2004) 'One Step Ahead: A 21st Century Strategy to Defeat Organised Crime', HMSO command 6167, March 2004.

Kennedy, David M. (2008) *Deterrence as Crime Prevention*. London and New York: Routledge.

Lacoste, J. and Tremblay, P. (2003) 'Crime innovation: a script analysis of check forgery', *Crime Prevention Studies*, 16: 171–98.

Laycock, G.K. (1996) 'Rights, roles and responsibilities in the prevention of crime', in T. Bennett (ed.), *Preventing Crime and Disorder – targeting strategies and responsibilities*. Cambridge: Cambridge University Press.

Laycock, G. and Webb, B. (2000) 'Making it all happen', in S. Ballintyne, K. Pease and V. McLaren (eds), *Secure Foundations: Key Issues in Crime Prevention, Crime Reduction and Community Safety*. London: IPPR.

Leddo, J. and Abelson, R.P. (1986) 'The nature of explanations', in J.A. Galambos, R.P. Abelson and J.B. Black (eds), *Knowledge Structures*. Hillsdale, NJ: Erlbaum.

Mack, John A. (1972) 'The able criminal', *British Journal of Criminology*, 12(1): 44–54.

Matifat, F. and Tremblay, P. (1997) 'Counterfeiting credit cards: displacement effects, suitable offenders and crime wave patterns', *British Journal of Criminology*, 37(2): 165–83.

Morrison, S. (2002) 'Approaching organised crime, where are we now and where are we going?', *Trends and Issues in Crime and Justice, no. 231*. Canberra, Australia: Australian Institute of Criminology.

National Audit Office (2005) *Report by the Comptroller and Auditor General. Reducing vehicle crime*. London: Home Office.

National Criminal Intelligence Service (2003) *United Kingdom Threat Assessment 2003*. London: NCIS.

Naylor, R.T. (2003) 'Towards a general theory of profit driven crime', *British Journal of Criminology*, 43: 81–101.

Nisbett, R.E. and Ross, L. (1980) *Human Inferences: Strategies and shortcomings of social judgement*. Englewood Cliffs, NJ: Prentice Hall.

OFCOM 2005. The Telecommunications Market 2005, 3 Telecommunications. Office of Telecommunications available at: http://www.ofcom.org.uk/research/cm/cm05/telecommunications.pdf

O'Malley, P. (1992) 'Risk, power and crime prevention', *Economy and Society*, 21: 252275

Pawson, R. and Tilley, N. (1997) *Realistic Evaluation*. London: SAGE Publications.

Schank, R.C. and Abelson, R.P. (1977) *Scripts, Plans, Goals and Understanding: An Inquiry into Human Knowledge*. Hillsdale, NJ: Erlbaum.

Serious Organised Crime Agency (2008) *The Suspicious Activity Regime Annual Report 2008*. London: HMSO.

Chapter 11

Policing mobile criminality: towards a situational crime prevention approach to organised crime

Stuart Kirby and Sue Penna

Abstract

This chapter considers how organised crime has been affected by changing patterns of geographical mobility. It reflects on the difficulty this brings for conventional law enforcement activity and illustrates the opportunities provided for situational crime prevention techniques. Conceptually, the chapter draws on the 'new mobilities paradigm' (Sheller and Urry 2006) to consider how social changes documented in this emergent social science field intersect with changes in the organisation of criminality – particularly evident in the organisation of mobile criminality – which have presented routine opportunities for organised, transnational crime. We examined this phenomenon through a small empirical study conducted in three English police forces between 2007–8. This study comprised an analysis of the organised crime investigations of a medium-sized force, supplemented by 11 interviews conducted with senior investigators in three police forces, attendance at seminars, and informal conversations with practitioners at different organisational levels and locations.

We propose that increased levels of mobile criminality are impacting significantly on the scope and variety of organised crime in England. In particular it is evident that, despite the attention paid to transnational policing in the organised crime literature, the burden of policing organised crime continues to fall upon local police forces where demand outstrips supply. In consequence, the necessity of a new paradigm for dealing with organised crime is critical. We argue here that a situational crime prevention approach, coupled with a further modification of that concept (which we refer to as situational crime disruption), is more effective, in terms of impact and cost.

Introduction

In this chapter we argue that increased mobility – the flow of people, goods, services and images across geographic borders – has been one of the most significant changes to contemporary society. Applying routine activity theory in this context suggests that new opportunities also present themselves for those involved in organised criminality. The policing of organised crime occurs in a complex structure of polycentric policy-making and national and international agencies (e.g. the United Nations Convention On Transnational Organized Crime and the Council of Europe Convention on Action against Trafficking in Human Beings). At a national level, in England and Wales during 2004 the National Intelligence Model (NIM) was introduced which aimed to provide policing with a systematic way to identify, collate, and action, intelligence relating to issues of crime and disorder. It also introduced a spatial distinction to policing with Level 1 at the local level, Level 2 at a force or county level (there are 43 forces of varying sizes and make-up) and Level 3 incorporating national and international investigations, involving agencies such as the Serious Organised Crime Agency (SOCA). Our discussion focuses on Level 2 policing because it has been clear from internal discussions within the Association of Chief Police Officers (ACPO) that dealing with organised criminality at that level is of particular concern (Her Majesty's Inspectorate of Constabulary (HMIC) 2006; 2009). Although it is commonly assumed that organised crime is dealt with by SOCA, the 2008/09 plan for the SOCA points out that it focuses on the higher end of organised criminality and is only able to target a small proportion of offenders and offences that have come to the agency's attention. Not only is there insufficient capacity but, as we show in this chapter, many instances of organised crime first come to light at local level, where the investigation is carried out by local police forces.

The discussion in this chapter originates from a small, two-part study we conducted. Initially we were provided with access to a police force in the north-west of England which polices a population of 1.4 million. We were provided with an overview of their proactive investigations of organised crime between 2007 and 2008. We supplemented this with 11 semi-structured interviews with senior officers both in this force and two other English police forces. One of these was a large urban force (approximately 6,000 staff), the other a smaller, more rural, police force (slightly under 3,000 staff). Each policed coastal areas and had both seaports and regional airports. We were also able to talk informally to detectives and attend internal seminars.

The research showed that the investigation of organised crime within English police forces is becoming more transnational in nature and more varied in the type of crime being investigated. While the extent and implications of the transnationalisation of crime has been extensively discussed (cf. Sheptycki 2000, 2002; Andreas and Nadelmann 2006), our interest is with the micro-level of a particular, dominant, mode of policing, the arrest-led paradigm. We argue that this model is becoming increasingly less effective when dealing with transnational organised crime because (a) there are too many offenders to pursue and arrest; and (b) there are increasing levels of complexity bringing corresponding increases in cost.

Thus we agree with Felson (cf. 2002, 2006) that the current dominant paradigm of arrest and enforcement is insufficiently sophisticated to combat these new challenges and we argue that a situational crime prevention approach could be used more effectively to disrupt and deter organised criminality. However, we propose that, rather than concentrate on the three areas often used to analyse the causes of volume crime – offender, target and location – it is the *crime process* which is central to understanding and tackling organised crime. In order to demonstrate these points the chapter is divided into three sections. The first section establishes the importance of mobility in generating new routine opportunities for organised criminality. The second section details the challenges facing law enforcement in the light of these new opportunities and explains why the dominant arrest-based paradigm of policing is unsuccessful in meeting these new challenges. The third and final section introduces situational crime disruption as a key aspect of the situational crime prevention approach, and provides a case study to illustrate how this can work in practice.

Mobility and organised crime

Defining organised crime is subject to well-documented difficulties (cf. Abadinsky 1985; Wright 2005; Albanese *et al.* 2003). Here, we characterise 'organised crime' as 'enterprise crime', a term that draws attention to the production and distribution of illegal goods and services (Naylor 1997), activities that require considerable skills in planning and organisation as well as extended networks of participants, and are organised in infinitely variable ways, as a pilot survey of 16 countries (United Nations 2002) and reports from policing agencies (SOCA 2007; Europol 2007) suggest. Since the 1990s there has been growing recognition that organised criminality has been developing complex, if unstable and impermanent, transnational networks, alliances and projects (Castells 1998). Acknowledging these points does not mean subscribing to a view of organised crime as global criminal cartels taking over the world (a view most pithily described by Naylor 2004: 1–3; 13–14), but does underscore the journeys made by goods and services sold in illegal markets, along with the range of actors involved in ensuring their passage from source to destination, which enables us to maintain a focus on the crime process.

The contextual referent for transnationalisation is most often 'globalisation', but in our view it is more helpful in understanding contemporary organised crime to draw on the study of mobility, a recent and fast-developing area. The 'new mobilities paradigm', initially promoted by sociologists (cf. Urry 2000, 2007), involves noting that while mobility is not a new phenomenon, the pace at which recent changes have occurred is unprecedented. Urry (2007: 4), in drawing attention to the immense scale of movement around the world, points out that in 1950 there were 25 million arrivals at international airports, whereas the prediction for 2010 is one billion. Research also reveals that whereas in 1950, Britons travelled an average of five miles a day, individuals now travel 30 miles, with the next generation being expected to travel 60 miles per day (Moynah and Worsley 2000). The Institute for Public Policy Research (2006) stated that 1:10 British citizens (5½ million) were now living abroad and this was balanced by an annual influx of 300,000 immigrants a year. Although the number of immigrants has since been contested, the Office for National Statistics (2007) assumes immigration will increase by a further 190,000 a year for the foreseeable future. This sort of mobility may be permanent, semi-permanent, or transitory and, as Urry (2007) points out, there are multiple aspects of mobilities and many contexts in which flows of people, goods, images and so on take place.

If we take mobility as a central category of analysis in the field of organised crime it is useful to consider Albanese's (2004, 2008) work which draws attention to the importance of opportunity factors in understanding organised crime behaviour and, in particular, locating changing opportunities in changes in social conditions, technologies and government policies. Examining the cases and scenarios outlined by Albanese and others highlights that opportunities to commit crime are often found in the usual rhythms of everyday life, as those writing in the field of situational crime prevention have demonstrated (cf. Cohen and Felson 1979; Felson 2002; Cornish and Clarke 2003). As mobility becomes a routine feature of everyday life, people generally travel further, and offenders are no exception. Mobility enables offenders to extend their reach both to discover more lucrative opportunities and to protect their anonymity (Canter 2003). Brantingham and Brantingham (1995) have established that crime clusters around nodes – those areas where individuals visit, work and spend leisure time – as well as concentrating around the pathways which connect such nodes. One of the unintended consequences of diminishing borders in the European Union and elsewhere is that natural opportunities for crime to be committed are provided. As new routine activities establish themselves not only is potential for new crime trends generated, but traditional practices and distinctions undergo substantial transformation (cf. Valier 2003; Aas 2007). Understanding changing 'crime-potential contexts' involves understanding criminal opportunities as processes, influenced by factors such as friendship networks, socio-economic conditions (Brantingham *et al.* 2005) and how cooperation between offenders is enacted (Felson 2006).

Such transformations are not straightforward. For example, although it is clear that migrants are susceptible to becoming victims of crime, it is also the case that some contribute to levels of crime in Britain in the same way that British nationals contribute to crime figures abroad. In the case of organised crime, Roger Gaspar (2001), Head of Intelligence at what was then the National Criminal Intelligence Service, told a BBC report on organised crime that:

> Organised crime bosses have embraced globalisation every bit as enthusiastically as the heads of legitimate international conglomerates. Which means Colombian, Italian, Chinese, Russian and Jamaican gangsters are doing business in London, Manchester, Glasgow and Belfast.

While the majority of organised crime groups in Britain are 'home grown', alliances and collaborations with offenders from other countries are now routine. In particular, their networks are becoming more fluid, extended and flexible (SOCA 2006: 2.1, 2.6; 2007; Europol 2007). A recent survey carried out by a UK newspaper, the *Daily Telegraph* (2007), under provisions in the Freedom of Information Act, alleges that one fifth of crimes committed in London are committed by foreign nationals from some 20 countries. Similarly HM Prison Service (2008) informs us that foreign nationals now represent 14 per cent of the overall prison population. As might be expected, these figures are embroiled in a set of disputed claims over involvement of foreign nationals in criminality. This is a contentious political issue as, with the enlargement of the EU, citizens of the 27 member states are free to travel and work within its borders and, indeed, sectors of the British economy rely heavily upon migrant workers (Anderson and Rogaly 2005; Anderson 2007). Not only that, but 'fortress Europe' with its ever-tightening immigration controls creates opportunities for those smuggling desperate immigrants from war- and famine-torn countries, for whom illegal entry becomes the only option. In discussing foreign nationals as offenders there is also the academic risk of contributing to moral panics over criminal aliens, for unfortunately the rhetoric of politicians (most recently described by Woodiwiss and Hobbs 2009) conflates various types and causes for mobility and collapses them into an alarmist 'discourse of threat'.

Despite these hazards besetting discussions of mobile criminality, it features as an increasing problem for police forces, as we show in the next section. Urry (*ibid.*) provides extensive data to demonstrate the pace and scale of contemporary mobility, supplying myriad examples. Some are of mobility which is disembodied, taking advantage of new opportunities created by the internet. As the 'wired' population expands (Urry cites calculations that by 2001 there were already one billion internet users worldwide) and becomes more comfortable in its ability to travel in cyberspace, offenders – both opportunistic and organised – exploit the potential of these opportunities to commit crime. The Association of British Insurers (2000: 29) aptly stated that:

> Developments in electronics, computing, biomedical sciences, chemicals and materials, communication and the Internet will produce a variety of goods, products and services both attractive to consumers and criminals. 'Information will be the raw material of the 21st Century' – creating a further crime market.

Recent studies of fraud have shown it to be at a record 10-year high with businesses, banks and individuals being susceptible (KPMG 2008). Most of this was phone/internet/mail order fraud where the credit or debit card was not present. The sum involved totalled £290.5m and the fraud was said to be mainly driven by criminals working outside Britain using stolen card details.

We therefore have a situation where mobility itself creates routine opportunities for all types of crime, a situation that has implications for policing. When we analysed the proactive investigations of a specialist police unit in one of the police forces we studied, comparing a three-month period in 2007 with a similar period in 2008 (N = 41), we found that international investigation was increasing. During 2007, 17 per cent of investigations were said to have an international connection, compared with 30 per cent in 2008. This was alongside the finding that the offences were increasing in variety. For example, during 2007 Class A drug trafficking (e.g. heroin, cocaine) was said to be the most common inquiry (67 per cent), followed by money laundering (17 per cent), and other isolated cases of: organised immigration crime; stolen vehicles or loads; and fraud. During 2008, the spread of cases was much wider. Class A drug trafficking only contributed to 39 per cent of all the cases, when it had previously accounted for a much larger proportion of police activity. This capacity was redirected to other priorities, such as stolen vehicles and loads (13 per cent), firearms (13 per cent), and money laundering (9 per cent). Other investigations included child sexual abuse, counterfeit goods, cannabis cultivation, fraud, and organised immigration crime (people trafficking). While these figures suggest that investigation of organised crime within this force is becoming more transnational in nature, presenting data in this fashion obscures some important observations. First, these categories do little to highlight the harm caused by such crimes. For example, one of the people trafficking cases related to a young woman who had been trafficked from Eastern Europe and had been sold from one 'owner' to another, being raped on multiple occasions. Second, a significant number of these transnational investigations involved multiple commodities (e.g. drugs and firearms) or involved a spread of offences (e.g. vehicle theft and money laundering); as Felson (2006: 15) points out, '... the growth of one type of crime very often feeds other types'.

The increasingly transnational dimension to crime was emphasised by a detective superintendent in this force when he told us that:

> Traditionally, criminals in our area traded with criminals from the bigger cities who in turn had the links with foreign nationals and the direct source of the product, usually drugs. However, we are now seeing direct links between 'our' criminals and criminals from around the world and in some cases direct into source countries, i.e. Colombia and West Africa. The advent of cheap flights has made foreign travel much easier and the opening up of Eastern Europe has also created new markets and here we have seen the first Polish organised crime group involved in guns and drugs, albeit working for major UK criminals from this region but based in Europe.

It was not only in this force that the increasing transnational dimension of organised criminality was emphasised. In subsequent interviews and conversations with other forces this characteristic emerged over and over as a source of considerable concern.

Consequences for the paradigm of arrest-based enforcement

Many aspects of the NIM have caught the interest of other law enforcement agencies around the world. However, implementation of the NIM, which has predominantly developed within a traditional arrest-based model of policing, is vulnerable on a number of criteria, to which we now turn.

There are too many organised criminals for law enforcement agencies to pursue and arrest

It is clear that organised crime groups can generally operate more flexibly and quickly than law enforcement agencies. For example, our study showed that in 2007 one Constabulary identified five cannabis factories located in its area, which were quick and inexpensive to set up as they often only required rented accommodation, a power supply and some knowledge of hydroponic cultivation. A year later the Constabulary had identified 42 separate factories, all operated by South Asian nationals. Interviews with detectives in other forces suggest this was a national phenomenon, with many more factories opening as soon as one was detected and shut down. A report published by Her Majesty's Inspectorate of Constabulary (HMIC 2006: 5) pointed out that ACPO (2004) (unpublished) had revealed that 'typically less than 6 per cent of over 1500 organised crime groups at force and regional level were targeted'.

Our interviews suggested this gap between demand and capability was becoming more acute. As one senior detective said:

> Since the report, there has been a greater appreciation of the growing threat of organised crime. As such we have seen increased resources coming into this area. This together with the fact that we are much better in terms of understanding what is happening shows us that there is a considerable amount of organised crime going on. Unfortunately we haven't got the resources to deal with it all, therefore we have to prioritise.

The problem is that despite ever-increasing formal transnational policing arrangements, Stelfox (2003: 119) points out that the burden of policing organised crime falls primarily on local police forces, and the increasing diversity and complexity of serious, mobile criminality brings with it different problems.

Increasing complexity and cost

Conceptually and practically organised crime has become more complex. As one detective chief superintendent explained:

> A few years ago the Force would concentrate its efforts on organised crime in the field of illicit drugs. We would have intelligence on which country the drug was being produced in, and its transportation routes both into the UK and locally. As such we would have intelligence on who was 'trafficking' the drugs and the 'pinch points' where seizure and arrest was more likely. Each of the agencies were clear where they fitted in, for instance Customs and the national squads would look for bigger importations and at a Force level we would look at smaller amounts coming in from regional traffickers. Now the picture has changed – the low-cost flights have opened it up both ways with more unpredictable importation routes and even our 'smaller fish' taking a chance and going abroad for a better deal.

Similarly the crime is more difficult to investigate with transnational offences generating complicated trails involving numerous people. As a detective superintendent put it:

> All of a sudden I was investigating an international people trafficking offence and tracking people and money halfway around the world. My team comprised people who the previous week had been investigating local offences such as burglary.

The investigation of serious and organised crime may also require local police officers to have familiarity with the geopolitics of far-flung regions. Glenny (2008) details how an apparently straightforward case of murder in Surrey led to the complex politics of Armenia and Chechnya, a politics embroiled in corruption and organised crime. Glenny (2008: 3) cites an officer involved in this case:

> We were suddenly dealing with crime and politics from a part of the world that, to be honest, none of us in the Metropolitan or Surrey police had ever heard of. We knew nothing about the wars, about the crime and about the politics – we were, frankly, all at sea.

The phenomena of failing states, government policies of liberalisation, the collapse of the Soviet Union, 'ethnic' wars in the Balkans and parts of Africa, and a host of other geopolitical developments have thrown up opportunities that have brought mobile and organised criminality to the attention of British police forces. There are, then, increasing levels of complexity at all stages of policing. A senior detective we interviewed in the smaller force, when discussing these problems, said that:

> This picture creates its own investigative challenges not only in terms of language and communication but also in managing the complex data sharing arrangements across boundaries, different jurisdictions and their specific requirements for evidence gathering and prosecution. Recovering evidence is complex and bureaucratic and in some cases foreign jurisdictions will not release evidence to be used in British courts. For example drugs or guns recovered in foreign jurisdictions but needed in court can be withheld.

What all the foreign–UK links create for transnational investigations is a plethora of complex issues involving multiple jurisdictions, and often ambiguity occurs in terms of who has operational priority and jurisdiction in a particular offence. Drug trafficking offences may incorporate a variety of actors, from the producer in Afghanistan or Colombia to the transporters, involving corrupt officials, smugglers, as well as the entrepreneurial offender who, rather than drive 50 miles to a local wholesaler, jumps onto a low-cost flight to buy a better quality product for a cheaper price, to the street dealer who further dilutes and distributes the product. The journey of that initial product may be varied, and that one agency could, or should have, jurisdiction in terms of investigation is not feasible. Therefore organised crime is continually subject to discussions about who should do what in terms of investigation.

When an investigation is reactive (i.e. a major crime has been committed and the culprits need to be brought to justice), ownership is clear. The Chief Constable in whose area the crime takes place is responsible and he or she would have suitably trained officers in place who are clear about the approach they will take. Unfortunately, this is not the case with proactive investigations, which form the vast majority of transnational organised crime police work. It is often difficult to establish which law enforcement unit should take responsibility for a particular organised crime group as the group transcends many force and international borders in both physical and cyber space.

We found that all three police forces had resource-intensive investigations which involved law enforcement agencies in other countries, covering investigations as diverse as: vehicle theft; drugs, firearms and people trafficking; fraud; money laundering and child exploitation. With complexity comes increased cost, which has been widely publicised both in terms of travel to investigate such issues as well as the massive increase in the cost for interpretation (ACPO 2008). Most significant are the total costs as each of the 43 police forces in England and Wales has to increase resources to map mobility across each of its borders. The relationship between transnationalisation, complexity and cost was echoed by all our interviewees, and elaborated on by the detective superintendent of the medium-sized force discussing an ongoing investigation:

> Mobile data and telecommunications play a significant part in this and the evidence gathering in this respect can be difficult and time consuming. For example in one current SOCU [Serious and Organised Crime Unit] case over 180,000 individual telephone calls have so far been analysed. Evidencing travel across boundaries, and complying with the CPIA [Criminal Procedures and Investigations Act 1996], in respect of foreign based unused material all provides a challenge. Not to be underestimated in this is the physical act of officers travelling to conduct these inquiries which is both time-consuming, expensive and attracts its own requirements via International Letters of Request.

In this quote the detective alluded to CPIA, the strict evidential requirements which require the prosecution to prove the case 'beyond all reasonable doubt' and in doing so to disclose to the defence any piece of information which may be relevant to them. This presents an incredible level of detail which when generated over transnational borders increases effort and cost.

Towards a conceptual model of situational crime prevention in organised crime

What we have found in our exploratory study is an environment where increased mobility has brought with it increased challenges to the investigation of organised crime. One government proposed response to the problems was to amalgamate police forces, thereby rationalising resources. However, this proposal ultimately failed and the thrust is now to engage in inter-force partnerships. Whether these agreements will be forged, or be operationally effective, remains to be seen and, in the short term, an expensive layer of regional resources has been introduced to hover above and across local police forces to maintain a strategic overview, thereby highlighting trends, threats and opportunities the local forces are not in a position to observe (e.g. Regional Intelligence, Asset Confiscation and Counter-Terrorism Units). However, we propose that there is a need for conceptual rather than structural changes. We suggest that the benefits of moving away from an exclusive arrest-based paradigm to one which also includes situational crime prevention are significant. The situational crime prevention approach has had increased popularity in the arena of volume crime (Clarke and Eck 2003) and, in recent years, this approach has been suggested as an effective means of tackling organised crime (cf. Cornish and Clarke 2002; Felson 2006). Ekblom (2003: 257) highlights the particularly challenging nature of organised crime and argues this 'has set the scene for an arms race between prevention and organised offenders, especially where social and technological change constantly creates new opportunities for offending ... new targets, environments, business models, tools and information sources'. Notably though, both he and Lewis (2007) agree that legislative and governmental solutions are significantly slow in adapting to evolving criminal patterns and it is often left to police forces to navigate international systems when investigating organised crime groups. This difficulty is exacerbated by the importance placed on enforcement of the criminal law as the most significant tool in the crime fighting armoury. Goldstein (1990) has argued that police forces, rather than thinking creatively about problem resolution, have over-relied on enforcement, a theme that has remained constant over the years (Read and Tilley 2000).

There are clear difficulties with only using enforcement as a tool to engage with organised crime. To arrest and convict an organised crime group within an English adversarial system requires evidence to show guilt beyond reasonable doubt, which requires significant resources, whereas a situational crime prevention approach has the potential to be extremely flexible in nature and can be applied to diverse types of crime. It can also be applied without specialist investigative training, which is a great advantage. The benefits of a situational crime approach are generally that: it is quicker to apply than other traditional investigative methods; it allows more organised crime groups to be tackled with the same level of resources; it is significantly less expensive than traditional methods; and there are fewer concerns regarding jurisdiction as practitioners can intervene when the opportunity crosses their area. We propose that tangible and immediate benefits can be gained by a more flexible and rapid response by law enforcement personnel.

However, the model of analysis for organised crime is different from that for volume crime. Rather than use the three areas of target, offender and location, which are often used in volume crime it is *the crime process* which is central to understanding and tackling the issue of organised crime. When analysing the process of a particular organised crime episode three questions are particularly critical:

- Where are the profits made? Although we acknowledge there are varied motivations (Naylor 2004; Hayward 2007) the common denominator for organised crime is generally financial profit.
- Who are the actors in the process? These may be offenders, victims and/or facilitators.
- Who are the stakeholders or guardians of the environment the crime takes place in?

Often organised criminality is reliant on the absence or the corruption of a system that is put in place to curtail abuse. For example, the offender may coordinate crime from a country they know they will not be extradited from. Similarly, as other chapters in this book show, offenders may engage in a criminal business they know is poorly regulated and in which they can commit their crime anonymously in relative safety. Additionally they may rely on areas of business they know are inherently corrupt and where the bribing of officials will be possible. The context of the particular environment is critical to understanding how the crime is taking place and most importantly how it can be disrupted or prevented. As Tilley (2005: 266) stated, 'crime is the intentional consequence of unintended opportunity' and it is critical to understand how the system or process unintentionally facilitates the crime. What we wish to emphasise here are the significant benefits that flow from *preventing* or *disrupting* organised criminality rather than pursuing it to arrest and criminal conviction.

This distinction between situational crime prevention and situational crime disruption is perhaps worthy of further discussion; in fact the terms of prevention and disruption are both currently used by law enforcement agencies in the UK. The term 'prevention' more aptly describes a means to tackle a single organised crime event (see the example of Morecambe Bay below). Such interventions change a process or environment in a sustainable manner. 'Disruption' is a more flexible, transitory and dynamic tactic which can be used more generally to make the environment hostile for the organised crime group. Without having sufficient intelligence to, for example, pinpoint a particular transport route or location for offending, this approach focuses on disrupting the offender's networks, lifestyle and routines. In this way the subject could have his/her assets seized, their reputation undermined or destroyed, and their means of operating otherwise damaged. Often preventing a criminogenic situation will have the effect of disrupting a network or process, as can be seen in relation to the counter-terrorism strategy and operational practice (cf. Clarke and Newman 2006 for a greater analysis of this subject). Although there are some obvious differences between organised criminality and terrorist activity (cf. Naylor 2004) there are also some similarities. The organisational structures can be similar (networked, fluid), the crimes are committed by motivated offenders, communications and actors traverse international borders, and both rely on others to supply facilitators to commit their crime. The predominant issue with counter-terrorist activity is to disrupt or deter the potential offender as (compared with drug trafficking or counterfeiting, for example) the risk of allowing the terrorist to achieve his/her objective is much greater. For example, the inability to intercept a consignment of heroin may have ramifications for the local price of the drug, but the inability to intercept a terrorist can result in mass fatalities and significant destruction. That is why much of the work conducted by the Security Services or the Special Branch rarely results in arrest or is visible to the public as disruption occurs further upstream in terms of the terrorist's objective. For government operatives the counter-terrorism paradigm revolves around the ability to understand the terrorists' system and actors they will be reliant on. The intervention then focuses on the removal of the facilitator (explosives, funding, chemical precursor, contacts). The point is that the policing of terrorism relies on understanding a process and either preventing it through changing processes or systems or disrupting the offender's networks and plans.

A situational crime prevention approach in a case involving people trafficking

What we aim to show now is how this approach has been used effectively following a high-profile case involving people trafficking. During February 2004, 23 illegally trafficked Chinese nationals, from the Fujian province, drowned while digging for cockles in Morecambe

Bay, Lancashire. The investigation that followed, to produce a seamless chain of evidence, was lengthy (about 18 months), costly, and conducted within the arrest-focused paradigm. At an international level this investigation involved interviews and the collation of evidence from business and government representatives within the People's Republic of China, as well as European cockle-processing plants and haulage companies. At a national level it involved the Department for Environment, Food, and Rural Affairs (DEFRA), the Department for Work and Pensions, and Immigration Service officials. At the local level the investigation involved the local authority, local landlords and local workers. These inquiries were difficult to accomplish due to diverse jurisdictions being involved, as well as problems of translation and cultural understanding. The case generated 1½ million pages of documentation (many of which were written in Mandarin, Spanish and French) and nearly 2,900 statements, 2,500 exhibits and over 20,000 calls were analysed for evidential purposes. Following a six-month trial three people (each supported by their own Queen's Counsel, barrister, solicitor and interpreter), collectively received 20 years in prison for manslaughter, conspiracy to pervert the course of justice, and immigration offences, with the presiding judge ordering their deportation on completion of their sentences (Lancashire Constabulary 2006). Although an overall cost for the investigation was never provided, the large-scale police investigation and subsequent court proceedings probably resulted in many millions of pounds being spent.

Despite this effort, the conditions for the occurrence of another such tragedy remained in place. This would be the case with most organised crime episodes as the environmental systems and frailties which the offender exploited remain in place while they are incarcerated, allowing another criminal entrepreneur to tackle the risks. Indeed, referring back to the critical factors we outlined earlier, three elements remained in place. First, the profits were still available as the 35 miles of coastline still contained substantial cockle beds. In 2003/4, abnormally mild winters had provided unusually high stocks, affording Morecambe international attention as cockle stocks elsewhere in the UK and Europe had fallen drastically. Sea Fisheries scientists calculated that 10,000 tonnes had been harvested from the Bay over the previous two years and considered it still contained millions of pounds worth of harvestable cockles. Prices had soared from around £200 a tonne four years earlier to £1,300 at the time the 23 Chinese workers died.

Second, the means to obtain the profits were still available. The process of harvesting cockles was simple so long as cheap labour was available. In this case the networks in the Fujian province were still open for recruitment and transportation. Profits were also enhanced because the illegal immigrants were willing to pay organised criminals up to £20,000 to enter the UK, this money being deducted weekly from derisory wages after working long shifts. Also, money was saved through accommodating them in cramped housing and spending little on safety equipment. Other criminal processes, such as the ability to launder any profits, also remained.

Third, the environment facilitated the offence on a number of levels. At a local level the vast shoreline provided anonymity to cocklers and their controllers, with numerous ways of accessing the sands and harvesting the cockles. Also the officials who controlled the environment locally had become lax in their enforcement of the protocols in place to govern safety and working practice. Analysis conducted in October 2004 showed the Sea Fisheries permit scheme contained scant applicant vetting procedures with only 160 permits being issued when it was estimated that over 800 individuals worked on the sands. In October 2004, there were 61 Chinese nationals working illegally on the sands, and it was estimated that 48 of them had fraudulently obtained permits. Further, the organised crime group that exploited these individuals had little interest in their safety and the Health and Safety Executive (HSE) and Marine Coastguard Agency (MCA) found that only 11 per cent of those working carried lifejackets, GPS (Global Positioning System) or flares. An average 100 vehicles carrying up to 400 cocklers visited the shoreline daily and of these 79 per cent were found to be unroadworthy, overloaded, or carrying multiple roof-riding passengers in a dangerous manner. As well as these transgressions the Department for Work and Pensions estimated 29 per cent of all cocklers were fraudulently claiming benefits, with HM Treasury losing £23,400 a week, equating to £1,216,800 between April 2003 and 2004 (Lancashire Constabulary 2006). Finally, coupled with the border controls being open to exploitation, the risk of apprehension and deportation within the UK was also limited. It appeared that immigration authorities had insufficient resources to detain and prosecute, and local experience suggested that, following identification as a potential illegal immigrant, individuals were released and asked to attend the immigration offices at a later date.

Having recognised that all the elements were still in place and fearing a further tragedy the Lancashire Constabulary decided on a situational preventative approach. All the stakeholders who were responsible for controlling this environment were identified and gathered together. These included the Department for Environment, Food, and Rural Affairs; the local Crime and Disorder Reduction Partnership; the Department for Work and Pensions; the Maritime and Coastguard Agency; the North West Chinese Council; the Health and Safety Executive; the Sea Fisheries Committee; Lancaster City Council; the Immigration Service; and English Nature. Following lengthy discussions numerous initiatives were put in place which could be aligned with the rational choice perspective outlined by Cornish and Clarke (1986) and which attempted to change the environment to increase the effort and risk to the organised criminals and reduce their reward (Cornish and Clarke 2003).

One of the critical issues to overcome was to reduce the anonymity of the organised crime group and the exploited workers. As Felson (2006) points out, concealment is critical for successful organised criminality. Ultimately this was done through the tightening of the permit scheme which was already in existence; however, the real innovation was the use of existing legitimate workers to assist in identifying illegal workers. Although legal workers were supportive of the authorities there had been no natural 'muster point' to brief and communicate legal, procedural and safety issues. After much reflection an expanse of foreshore affording safe access was identified and the local authority relaxed a local by-law to permit a catering caravan to park on the sands, which would also serve as a workforce welfare contact point. This informal point provided a focus for education and briefing and the owner consented to a prominent noticeboard being placed on the caravan with agency information on view. The cocklers liked the board, and introduced their own, which was agreed and used in tandem displaying vehicle and contact details of workers on the sands, tide times, cockle bed information, as well as agency details.

The benefits of this approach were diverse. The enhanced contact and communication allowed for better inter-agency working and detailed vetting procedures, resulting in 1,200 regulated workers being recorded on the new Fisheries permit scheme. As such more individuals started to work in the formal economy resulting in fraudulent benefit claims being reduced by 20 per cent, saving HM Treasury £828,000 in the first year. Revised procedures made it considerably more difficult for illegal immigrants to work in the industry, thus reducing the reward for organised criminal groups. Unroadworthy vehicle usage reduced by 84 per cent, with roof-riding eradicated. All workers started to carry personal life-saving equipment and lifeboat deployments to cocklers reduced from 34 in 2004 to one in 2005. The workforce went on to form their own shellfish association which convened weekly and self-polices standards on the sands (Lancashire Constabulary 2006).

All these initiatives stemmed from a situational prevention approach. However, while officers coordinated activity to prevent a further tragic event occurring at Morecambe Bay, wider disruptive activity was also taking place. Due to the resources devoted to the investigation detectives were able to uncover information concerning the wider process of people trafficking between China and the UK. This included information about the alleged actors, how the profits were being made, how money was being laundered, who the offenders associated with and how they spent their time. Although this information was insufficient to bring other offenders to trial, the fact that the officers shone a spotlight on these areas took away the anonymity of individuals and their ability to conceal themselves (Felson 2006). This meant the offenders were plying their illicit trade in a more hostile environment, with associates and facilitators becoming both suspicious and mindful that law enforcement attention might encroach onto their particular area of business. This disrupted the organised crime process and goes some way to explaining why the actors did not simply move their business to another area of England where cockles could be harvested.

Conclusion

We have shown here that increasing mobility has created more opportunity for organised criminality, and that the nature of this crime has become more complex due to its diversity and transnational nature. HMIC (2009) report that serious, organised crime is a £20-billion-a-year industry, with perhaps another £14m added by offences of fraud. Similarly, HMIC (2009: 1) point out that policing services in the UK consume a higher proportion of gross domestic product (GDP) than virtually any other Western democracy, including some 20 per cent more than the United States. We therefore contend it would make more financial sense to adopt the more problem-oriented approach contained in situational crime prevention strategies. Research which enhances our understanding of the organised crime process can assist practitioners in identifying opportunities which allow situational interventions to prevent and disrupt the crime process.

Organised crime, as we have tried to show here, is not a single event but consists of a chain of criminogenic events, committed by a diverse range of offenders, which may stretch across many countries and jurisdictions. Furthermore, each of these events relies on an environment which generates the opportunity to obtain illegal profit. By obtaining an overview of this dynamic process a more strategic analysis can be made allowing situational interventions to take place where the criminal process is at its most vulnerable. In our case study, for example, local law enforcement bodies could not change conditions (such as desperate poverty) within China which allow organised criminals to exploit economic migrants, nor could they change the lucrative European market for cockles in the hospitality industry. What law enforcement agencies were able to do was work with partner agencies to change the most vulnerable part of the criminal process from the perspective of the offender. In this case the response centred on reducing the anonymity of those allowed to work on the sands of Morecambe Bay. Of course the most effective response will vary according to the organised crime process and will always be highly context specific. It is for these reasons that we stress the importance of the paradigm shift from an arrest-focused perspective to one which is focused on situational disruption.

References

Aas, K.F. (2007) 'Analysing a World in Motion: Global flows meet "criminology of the other"', *Theoretical Criminology*, 11(2): 283–303.

Abadinsky, H. (1985) *Organised Crime*. Chicago: Nelson-Hall.

Albanese, J.S. (2004) *The Prediction and Control of Organised Crime, Trends in Organised Crime: A Risk Assessment Instrument for Targeting Law Enforcement Efforts*, Document No: 204370. US Department of Justice, available online at http://www.ncjrs.gov/pdffiles1/pr/204370.pdf.

Albanese, J.S. (2008) 'Risk Assessment in Organised Crime', *Journal of Contemporary Criminal Justice*, 24(3): 263–73.

Albanese, J.S., Das, D.K. and Verma, A. (2003) (eds) *Organised Crime. World Perspectives*. New Jersey: Prentice Hall.

Anderson, B. (2007) *Battles in Time: the Relation between Global and Labour Mobilities*. Centre on Migration, Policy and Society. Working Paper No. 55. University of Oxford.

Anderson, B. and Rogaly, B. (2005) *Forced Labour and Migration to the UK*. Study prepared by COMPAS in collaboration with the Trades Union Congress. Oxford and London.

Andreas, P. and Nadelmann, E. (2006) *Policing The Globe. Criminalization and Crime Control in International Relations*. New York: Oxford University Press.

Association of British Insurers (2000) *Future Crime Trends in the United Kingdom*, General Insurance Research Report no. 7. London: Association of British Insurers.

Association of Chief Police Officers (2008) *ACPO comment on migration and policing*. http://www.acpopolice.uk/press release.asp (accessed 16 April 2008).

Audit Commission (1993) *Helping with Enquiries: tackling crime effectively*. London: Audit Commission.

Brantingham, P.L. and Brantingham, P.J. (1995) 'Criminality of Place: Crime generators and crime attractors', *European Journal of Criminal Policy and Research*, 3: 5–26.

Brantingham, P.L., Brantingham, P.J. and Taylor, W. (2005) 'Situational Crime Prevention as a Key Component in Embedded Crime', *Canadian Journal of Criminology and Criminal Justice*, 47(2): 271–92.

Canter, D.V. (2003) *Mapping Murder: The Secrets of Geographical Profiling*. London: Virgin Books.

Castells, M. (1998) *The Information Age (iii). End of Millennium*. Oxford: Blackwell.

Clarke, R.V. and Eck, J. (2003) *Becoming a Problem-solving Crime Analyst – in 55 Steps*. London: Jill Dando Institute of Crime Science, UCL.

Clarke, R.V. and Newman, G.R. (2006) *Outsmarting the Terrorists*. Portsmouth, NH: Praeger Security International.

Cohen, L.E. and Felson, M. (1979) 'Social Change and Crime Rate Trends: A Routine Activity Approach', *American Sociological Review*, 44(4): 588–608.

Cornish, D. and Clarke, R.V. (1986) (eds) *The Reasoning Criminal; Rational Choice Perspectives on Offending*. New York, NY: Springer Verlag.

Cornish, D. and Clarke, R.V. (2002) 'Analyzing Organized Crimes', in A.R. Piquero and S.G. Tibbetts (eds), *Rational Choice and Criminal Behaviour: Recent Research and Future Challenges*. New York and London: Routledge.

Cornish, D. and Clarke, R.V. (2003) 'Opportunity, Precipitators and Criminal Decisions', in *Theory for Practice in Situational Crime Prevention*, Crime Prevention Studies, Vol. 16. Monsey, NY: Criminal Justice Press.

Daily Telegraph (2007) 'Foreigners commit fifth of crime in London', available online at http://www.telegraph.co.uk/foreigners-commit-fifth-of-crime-in-london, last accessed 9 December 2009.

Ekblom, P. (2003) 'Organised Crime and the Conjunction of Criminal Opportunity Framework', in A. Edwards and P. Gill (eds), *Transnational Organised Crime: Perspectives on Global Security*. London: Routledge.

Europol (2007) *OCTA. EU Organised Crime Threat Assessment 2007*. The Netherlands: Europol.

Felson, M. (2002) *Crime and Everyday Life* (3rd edn). CA: Pine Forge Press.

Felson, M. (2006) *The Ecosystem for Organised Crime*, HEUNI Paper No. 26. Helsinki: HEUNI (http://www.heuni.fi/uploads/2rreolo2h.pdf).

Gasper, R. (2001) *Organised Crime in the UK*. http://news.bbc.co.uk/hi/english/static/in_depth/uk/2001/life_of_crime/crime.stm (last accessed 6 July 2008).

Glenny, M. (2008) *McMafia*. London: The Bodley Head.

Goldstein, H. (1990) *Problem Oriented Policing*. New York: McGraw-Hill.

Hayward, K. (2007) 'Situational Crime Prevention and its Discontents: Rational Choice Theory versus the "Culture of Now"', *Social Policy & Administration*, 41(3): 232-50.

Her Majesty's Inspectorate of Constabulary (1997) *Inspection Report: the National Criminal Intelligence Service*. London: HMSO.

Her Majesty's Inspectorate of Constabulary (2006) *Closing the gap: A review of the 'fitness for purpose' of the current structure of policing in England and Wales*. http://crime reduction.homeoffice.gov.uk/policing (last accessed 30 March 2009).

Her Majesty's Inspectorate of Constabulary (2009) *Getting Together – a Better Deal for the Public through Joint Working*. London: HMSO.

HM Prison Service (2008) Perrie Lectures – 'Foreign nationals in prison and detention'. www.hmprisonservice.gov.uk/prisonservicejournal/index.asp., last accessed 9 December 2009.

KPMG (2008) *Fraud Barometer*, available from: http://www.accountancyage.com/accountancyage/news/22226 (last accessed 1 August 2008).

Lancashire Constabulary (2006) *When an industry's practices kill: Turning the tide, Operation Seaquest*, available from http://wwwpopcenter.org/conference/?presentations=2006 (last accessed 18 April 2009).

Lewis, C. (2007) 'International Structures and Transnational Crime', in T. Newburn, T. Williamson and A. Wright (eds), *Handbook of Criminal Investigation*. Cullompton, Devon: Willan Publishing.

Moynah, M. and Worsley, R. (2000) *Tomorrow*. London: A & C Black Publishers Ltd.

Naylor, R.T. (1997) 'Mafias, Myths and Markets: On the Theory and Practice of Enterprise Crime', *Transnational Organised Crime*, 3(3): 1–45.

Naylor, R.T (2004) *Wages of Crime. Black Markets, Illegal Finance, and The Underworld Economy* (revised edn). Ithaca and London: Cornell University Press.

Office for National Statistics (2007) *News release*. Available from: http://www.statistics.gov.uk/pdfdir/emig1107.pdf (accessed 15 July 2007).

Read, T. and Tilley, N. (2000) 'Not Rocket Science?', *Crime Reduction Research Series, Paper 6*. London: Home Office.

Sheller, M. and Urry, J. (2006) 'The New Mobilities Paradigm', *Environment and Planning A*, 38(2): 207–26.
Sheptycki, J. (2000) (ed.) *Issues in Transnational Policing*. London: Routledge.
Sheptycki, J. (2002) *In Search of Transnational Policing: Towards a Sociology of Global Policing*. Aldershot: Ashgate.
SOCA (2006) *The United Kingdom Threat Assessment of Serious Organised Crime 2006/07*. London: Serious Organised Crime Agency.
SOCA (2007) *The United Kingdom Threat Assessment of Serious Organised Crime 2008/09*. London: Serious Organised Crime Agency.
Sriskandarajah, D. and Drew, C. (2006) *Brits Abroad: Mapping the scale and nature of British emigration*. London: Institute for Public Policy Research.
Stelfox, P. (2003) 'Transnational Organised Crime: a Police Perspective', in A. Edwards and P. Gill, P. (eds), *Transnational Organised Crime: Perspectives on Global Security*. London: Routledge.
Tilley, N. (2005) *Handbook of Crime Prevention and Community Safety*. Cullompton, Devon: Willan Publishing.
United Nations (2002) *Results of a Pilot Survey of Forty Selected Organized Crime Groups in Sixteen Countries*, Global Programme against Organized Crime. Vienna: United Nations Office on Drugs and Crime.
Urry, J. (2000) *Sociology Beyond Societies: Mobilities for the Twenty First Century*. London: Routledge.
Urry, J. (2007) *Mobilities*. Cambridge: Polity Press.
Valier, C. (2003) 'Foreigners, Crime and Changing Mobilities', *British Journal of Criminology*, 43(1): 1–21.
Woodiwiss, M. and Hobbs, D. (2009) 'Organized Evil and the Atlantic Alliance', *British Journal of Criminology*, 49(1): 106–28.
Wright, A. (2005) *Organised Crime*. Cullompton, Devon: Willan Publishing.

Index

Aas, K.F. 197
Abadinsky, H. 195
Abelson, R.P. 134, 173
ACPO *see* Association of Chief Police Officers
adaptation 12, 13
administrative approach in Amsterdam 93–108
    Integrity Bureau 104–5
    overview 93–6, 106–7
    SBA Bureau 100–3
    Van Traa Project 96–100
Afghanistan 201
AIDS (acquired immune deficiency syndrome) 65
Albanese, J.S. 18, 195, 196
Albini, J.L. 18
Aliquò, V. 135
Amsterdam *see* administrative approach in Amsterdam
Anderson, B. 197
Andreas, P. 195
anonymity
    crime scripts 176, 181, 183, 189, 190
    mobile criminality 196, 208
    unlawful influence 160, 165
Armenia 201
Aromaa, K. 155
Association of British Insurers 198
Association of Chief Police Officers (ACPO) 194, 200, 202
asylum 29–31, 183
Automatic Licence Plate Recognition (ALPR) 89

banks
    crime scripts 182, 185, 189, 190
    cross-border crime 26, 27, 32
    mortgage fraud 113, 115, 120, 121, 123, 125–7

Van Traa Project 97, 100
Banwell, S. 63
Beccaria, C. 35–6
Beebe, J. 11
Belanger, M. 11
Belgium 20, 38, 44
benefits 207, 208
Berkhout, T.M. 124
Berlin 37, 39, 45, 49, 50, 52
BIBOB Act (Public Administration Probity Screening Act) 95, 96, 100
biometrics 75
blackmail 165
black market 36, 37, 38, 40, 41, 51
black money 115, 126
Blickman, T. 32
body language 158
body scans 24, 25
bootlegging 38
border controls
    contraband cigarettes 44–6
    cross-border crime 29, 31, 32
    mobile criminality 207
    unlawful influence 154
Bosnia-Herzegovina 67
Bouloukos, A. 5, 37
Bowers, K.J. 5
Bowie, V. 162
Brantingham, P.J. 196
Brantingham, P.L. 196, 197
Brazil 83
bribery 81–3, 85–7, 153, 164, 169
Brottsförebyggande radet (bra) (Swedish National Council for Crime Prevention) 152–7, 158–63, 164–6, 169
Brown, R. 7
Burma 82
Busch, H. 45
By, U. 160

213

Calabria 130–2, 134, 138–42, 146
Calderoni, F. 147
Calhoun, F. 158
Cambodia 83
Camorra 131, 132, 134, 142–4, 145–6
Campania 130–2, 134, 142–4, 146
Candea, S. 38
Caneppele, S. 147
cannabis
  mobile criminality 198, 199–200
  mortgage fraud 110, 111, 115, 118, 119, 124
Canter, D.V. 196
Carswell, A.T. 111
cars *see* vehicle licensing; vehicle theft
Castells, M. 195
CCTV (closed circuit television) 89
chain of custody 89, 90
Chechnya 201
child exploitation
  mobile criminality 198, 202
  sex trafficking 63, 64, 65, 66
  what is situational crime prevention? 5
China/Chinese criminals
  contraband cigarettes 38
  cross-border crime 21, 32
  Morecambe Bay case study 205–9
  organised timber theft 82, 83, 84
  sex trafficking 63–4, 66, 68–9, 71–2, 74–7
Chin, K. 65, 66, 68, 73
cigarettes *see* contraband cigarettes
CITES (Convention on International Trade in Endangered Species of Wild Flora and Fauna) 83
civil-law notaries 121, 123, 125, 126, 127
Clarke, R.V.
  administrative approach in Amsterdam 95, 98–100
  contraband cigarettes 36, 37, 40
  crime scripts 174
  cross-border crime 17
  Italian organised crime 130, 131, 135
  mortgage fraud 127
  organised timber theft 87, 89
  policing mobile criminality 196, 203, 205, 207
  sex trafficking 59–60, 61, 67
  terrorism xvii
  unlawful influence 159
  what is organised crime? 7, 8, 9
  what is situational crime prevention? 4, 5
cocaine 20, 23–6, 31, 198
cocklers 205–9
Cohen, L.E. 196

collusion 90, 109
Colombia 27, 197, 199, 201
Commissione Parlamentare Antimafia 133
Community Transit System 41, 51
construction industry
  administrative approach in Amsterdam 102, 108
  Italian organised crime 130–49
    case studies 135–44
    comparisons between the criminal organisations 145–6
    crime script analytical framework 133–5
    overview 130–3, 146–8
  sex trafficking 65
contraband cigarettes 35–54
  conceptual framework 36–7
  crime scripts 39–41
  crime prevention methods on other levels 50–2
  data 37
  illegal cigarette market in Western Europe 38–9
  open retail selling 48–50
  overview 35–6, 52–4
  small-scale smuggling 41–8
convergence settings 47, 54
Cornish, D.B.
  administrative approach in Amsterdam 95, 98–100
  contraband cigarettes 37, 39, 40
  crime scripts 173, 174, 185
  cross-border crime 17
  Italian organised crime 130, 131, 134, 135
  mortgage fraud 126
  policing mobile criminality 196, 203, 207
  sex trafficking 61
  unlawful influence 159
  what is situational crime prevention? 2, 4, 5, 8, 9
corruption
  administrative approach in Amsterdam 102, 105, 106
  cross-border crime 32
  definition 85
  organised timber theft 82, 83, 85–8, 90
  policing mobile criminality 201
  sex trafficking 64, 74
  unlawful influence 151, 153–7, 163–6, 167–9
La Cosa Nostra (Sicilian Mafia) 130–8, 145–6
Council of Europe Convention on Action Against Trafficking in Human Beings 194

Index

Council of the European Union 38, 52
counter-terrorism 203, 205
CPIA (Criminal Procedures Investigation Act) 202
Crawford, A. 189
credit card fraud 174, 198
Cressey, D. 8
'crime pattern theory' 2
crime process 195, 196, 204
crime proofing 148
crime scripts
   contraband cigarettes 37, 39–43, 49
   Italian organised crime in the public construction industry 130, 131, 133–4, 135–44
   organised crime and crime scripts 172–90
      common components of the crime process 179–84
      constituent parts of the organised crime script 175–7
      crime scripts and organised crime 173–5
      discussion 185–90
      exploring the utility 177–9
      mapping the crime script 184–5
      overview 172–3
      research and policy agenda 13
      what is situational crime prevention? 2, 9, 10
criminal lifestyle 175–7, 184, 186–7, 188, 189
Criminal Procedures Investigation Act (CPIA) 202
cross-border crime 17–32
   cocaine 23–6
   Ecstasy 20–3
   human smuggling 28–30
   money mules 26–8
   overview 17–18, 30–2
   research into organised crime 18–20
culture of tolerance 77–8, 79
Curaçao 24, 25, 26, 31
currency exchange 27–8
customary money laundering 125, 126
Customs
   contraband cigarettes 38, 41–4, 46, 48, 49, 51, 52
   organised timber theft 87
   unlawful influence 154, 155, 158, 164
Cyprus 105
Czech Republic 45

Daily Telegraph 197
Davis, R.C. 158, 159
death penalty 32

DEMAND report 65, 77
Demir, O. 67, 68, 70, 71, 72, 74, 76
Department for Environment, Food and Rural Affairs (DEFRA) 206, 207
Department for Work and Pensions 206, 207
Department of Justice 160
Department of Transport 190
de Poot, C.J. 22
diffusion of benefits 5, 12, 13
displacement 2, 5, 12, 13, 23
document forgery *see* forged documents
Dominican Republic 25
Doomernik, J.M.J. 29, 30
Dorn, N. 148, 181
drugs
   administrative approach in Amsterdam 94, 98, 106
   crime scripts 174, 177, 179, 182, 184
   cross-border crime
      cocaine 23–6
      Ecstasy 20–3
      money mules 27, 28
      overview 18, 30, 31
      research into organised crime 20
   Italian organised crime 132
   mortgage fraud 111, 112, 115–16
   policing mobile criminality 198–201, 205
   unlawful influence 157, 164, 165
   what is organised crime? 5, 12
Dutch Organised Crime Monitor 19, 20
'dyadic cartwheel networks' 63

Eck, J.E. 4, 37, 40, 203
Ecstasy (MDMA) 20–3, 30, 31, 114
Ekblom, P. 5, 39, 40, 41, 173, 203
Elvins, M. 6
Emergo Project 96, 97
Engbersen, G. 30
English Nature 207
enterprise crime 195
Environmental Investigation Agency 81, 82, 83, 84
estate agents 123–4
ethnographic research 10, 11
euro 27, 28
European Central Bank 28
European Commission 36
European Parliament 51
European Union
   contraband cigarettes 36, 38–9, 41, 43, 45, 51, 52
   cross-border crime 32
   policing mobile criminality 196, 197
   what is organised crime? 5

Europol 195, 197
excise duties 36–8, 41, 43, 51, 53
extortion
　Italian organised crime 137, 141, 144, 148
　unlawful influence 154, 157, 158

Faber, W. 25
facilitating conditions 8, 9, 125–6
false documents *see* forged documents
Farrell, G. 5
Fat Charles 93–8, 100, 105, 108
Felson, M.
　contraband cigarettes 47, 53
　cross-border crime 17, 25
　Italian organised crime 135
　policing mobile criminality 195, 196, 197, 199, 203, 208
　what is situational crime prevention? 5
Ferweda, H. 117, 124
Fijnaut, C. 18, 94, 102, 166
Financial Action Task Force (FATF) 32
Financial Reporting Orders 185, 191
Finckenauer, J. 18, 65
firearms 174, 183, 198, 199, 201, 202
forged documents
　crime scripts 184–5
　cross-border crime 22, 28–31
　mortgage fraud 112, 114–18
　organised crime 7
　organised timber theft 86
　sex trafficking 74, 75
formal surveillance 45, 46, 47, 49, 50, 161
France 38
fraud *see also* mortgage fraud
　administrative approach in Amsterdam 102, 104
　crime scripts 174
　organised timber theft 88, 90
　policing mobile criminality 198, 202, 208
Freedom of Information Act 197
front companies 181
funds, disposal and concealment of 182
Fyfe, N.R. 155, 158, 159, 160, 162

Gambetta, D. 18
Garland, D. 190
Gaspar, R. 197
Gast, W. 50
Germany 6, 36–9, 41–7, 52, 54
Gill, M. 160
glassblowers 22–3, 31
Glenny, M. 201
globalisation 196, 197
Goldstein, H. 203

Goldstock, R. 132, 133
Gorta, A. 82
Gothenberg 152
Graham, M.H. 155, 158
Green, P. 82
Guerette, R.T 5
guns *see* firearms

Hadley, J. 158
The Hague 113
harassment 151, 153–5, 157–8, 159–63, 167
harm reduction 12
Hato International Airport 24, 25
Hayward, K. 204
Health and Safety Executive (HSE) 207
Hell's Angels 98, 108
Hellströmer, A. 160
Her Majesty's Inspectorate of Constabulary (HMIC) 194, 200, 208
heroin 182, 198, 205
HM Customs and Excise *see* Customs
HMIC *see* Her Majesty's Inspectorate of Constabulary
HM Prison 197
HM Treasury 38, 208
Hobbs, D. 8, 197
Homel, R. 126
Home Office 172
Honduras 84
House of Commons 39, 44, 51, 52
Huberts, L.W.J.C. 105
Huisman, S. 23
Huisman, W. 95, 96, 97, 98, 107, 108
human rights 32
human smuggling 20, 28–30, 31, 61–4, 70
human trafficking
　administrative approach in Amsterdam 94
　crime scripts 184
　cross-border crime 28
　policing mobile criminality 198, 199, 201, 202, 205–9
　sex trafficking 61–4, 68, 70, 71, 77
　what is organised crime? 5

illegal immigrants
　contraband cigarettes 45
　crime scripts 183
　cross-border crime 28, 29, 30
　Morecambe Bay case study 205–9
　mortgage fraud 111, 112, 116, 119
illegal letting/subletting 116–17, 119, 120, 125
illegal logging 82, 83, 86

immigration
  contraband cigarettes 45
  crime scripts 183
  cross-border crime 28, 29, 30
  Morecambe Bay case study 205–9
  mortgage fraud 111, 112, 116, 119
  policing mobile criminality 196, 197, 198, 205–9
  sex trafficking 61, 62, 65, 69, 70
Immigration and Customs Enforcement (ICE) 61, 62
Immigration Service 206, 207
Indonesia 69, 82, 83, 84
Institute for Public Policy Research 196
Integrity Bureau 94, 96, 102, 103–5, 106
interference in a judicial matter 158, 163, 167
International Letters of Request 202
International Organisation for Migration (IOM) 63, 66, 71
internet 5, 39, 198
IOM *see* International Organisation for Migration
Iran 29
Irek, M. 42, 43, 45, 46, 47
Italian organised crime in the public construction industry 130–49
  case studies 135–44
    Camorra in Campania 142–4
    N'drangheta in Calabria 138–42
    Sicilian Mafia 135–8
  comparisons between the criminal organisations 145–6
  crime script analytical framework 133–5
  overview 130–3, 146–8

Jacobs, J.B. 18
Jahic, G. 62, 63, 66, 67, 70, 71, 74
Jakarta 69
Jamaica 64
Japan 64, 69
Jin Ling brand cigarettes 38, 52
Johansen, P.O. 164
'john schools' 78
Johnson, B.D. 134
Joossens, L. 36, 38, 40, 52
journalists 153, 156

Kaliningrad 38
Kampf, H.J. 51
Katz, J. 154
Keirse, A.L.M. 117
Kelling, G. 107

Kennedy, D. xvii, 189
Khatchadourian, R. 82, 84
kidnapping 63, 70, 71
Kleemans, E.
  administrative approach in Amsterdam 108
  cross-border crime 18, 19, 19–22, 28, 29, 30
  sex trafficking 76
Korps landelijke politiediensten (KPLD) 21
Korsell, L. 152, 153, 154, 155, 156, 164
KPMG 198
Kristof, N.D. 58, 59

Lacoste, J. 174
Lakhdar, C.B. 38
Lancashire Constabulary 206, 207, 208
Lancaster City Council 207
Lange, A.G. 74
Lankhorst, F. 108
large-scale smuggling 38
Larsson, M. 153
Larsson, P. 152
Laycock, G. 5, 190
Leddo, J. 173
Leeuw, F.L. 96
Levi, M. 7, 26, 108, 131, 133
Levin, M. 38
Lewis, C. 203
Liberia 84
Lüdi, J. 45
Luxembourg 44

Mack, J.A. 10, 189
Mafia 5, 6, 18, 130–8, 145–6
Magrath, W.B. 87, 89, 90
Maguire, M. 108, 131
Malaysia 69, 83, 84
malicious damage 151, 153–5, 157–63
Manson, H. 156
Marine Coastguard Agency (MCA) 207
Marine, F.J. 165
marking 157–8
marriage fraud 28, 29, 31
master-script 9, 10
Matifat, F. 174
McConnachie, K. 82
McIntosh, M. 8, 135
McKay, H. 158, 159
MDMA *see* Ecstasy
media 76, 77, 156, 161, 162
migrant workers *see* immigration
Ministerie van Justitie 24
mobile phones 180, 189, 190
mobility 193–209

consequences for arrest-based
  enforcement 199–203
 mobility and organised crime 195–9
 Morecambe Bay case study 205–9
 overview 193–5, 208–9
 towards a conceptual model of
  situational crime prevention 203–5
Moldova 70
money laundering
 administrative approach in Amsterdam
  93, 94, 95, 97, 98, 105
 crime scripts 177, 178, 190
 cross-border crime 26–8, 31
 mortgage fraud 115, 126, 127, 128
 policing mobile criminality 198, 199, 202
 what is organised crime? 7, 12
money mules 26–8, 31
Morecambe Bay human trafficking case
  study 205–9
Morselli, C. 133
mortgage fraud 111–29
 absent buyers: 'paper' transactions 127
 facilitating conditions 125–7
 legal actors and illegal activities 113
 opportunity-reducing interventions 127–9
 organised mortgage fraud 117–24
 overview 111–13
 personal mortgage fraud 114–17
motorcycle gangs 152, 153, 159
Moynah, M. 196

Nadelmann, E. 195
Natarajan, M. 5, 7, 11, 59–60
National Criminal Intelligence Service 197
National Institute of Justice (NIJ) 65
National Intelligence Model (NIM) 177, 194, 199
natural surveillance 46, 47, 49, 50, 161, 165
Naylor, R.T. 174, 195, 196, 204, 205
N'drangheta 131, 132, 134, 138–42, 145–6
negative spread effect 159
Nelen, H.
 administrative approach in Amsterdam
  95–8, 101, 103, 105, 108, 109
 mortgage fraud 124, 125, 129
Nelen, J.M. 104, 105
Neske, M. 29, 30
The Netherlands
 administrative approach in Amsterdam
  93–108
  Integrity Bureau 104–5
  overview 93–6, 106–7
  SBA Bureau 100–3
  Van Traa Project 96–100

contraband cigarettes 38, 52
cross-border crime
 cocaine 23–6
 Ecstasy 20–3
 human smuggling 28–30
 money mules 26–8
 overview 17–18, 30–2
 research into organised crime 18–20
mortgage fraud 111–29
 absent buyers: 'paper' transactions 127
 facilitating conditions 125–7
 legal actors and illegal activities 113
 opportunity-reducing interventions 127–9
 organised mortgage fraud 117–24
 overview 111–13
 personal mortgage fraud 114–17
 sex trafficking 64
Netherlands Antilles 24, 25, 32
networks
 crime scripts 174–7, 184, 186–7, 188
 policing mobile criminality 195, 197, 205
 unlawful influence 152, 153
Newell, J. 84
Newman, G. xvii, 17, 205
new mobilities paradigm 193, 196
New York 98, 133
Nisbett, R.E. 173
Nordic MC war 153
North West Chinese Council 207

O'Brien, K.A. 52
Oder River 44, 45
OFCOM 180
Office for National Statistics 196
officials, unlawful influence on
 corruption 164, 165, 166
 harassment, threats, violence and
  malicious damage 159, 160, 162, 163
 overview 152–6, 167, 168
O'Malley, P. 188
Openbaar Ministerie Nederlandse Antillen 25
opportunity structures 8, 9, 10, 13
organised crime
 administrative approach in Amsterdam
  96, 98, 100–3, 105, 107, 108
 cross-border crime 17–32
  cocaine 23–6
  Ecstasy 20–3
  human smuggling 28–30
  money mules 26–8
  overview 17–18, 30–2
  research into organised crime 18–20

Index

definitions 5–6, 195
how does situational crime prevention see organised crime? 7–10
how should organised crime be studied for situational crime prevention? 10–12
Italian organised crime in the public construction industry 130–49
  case studies 135–44
  comparisons between the criminal organisations 145–6
  crime script analytical framework 133–5
  overview 130–3, 146–8
organised crime and crime scripts 172–90
  common components of the crime process 179–84
  constituent parts of the organised crime script 175–7
  crime scripts and organised crime 173–5
  discussion 185–90
  exploring the utility 177–9
  mapping the crime script 184–5
  overview 172–3
organised timber theft 81–91
policing mobile criminality 193–209
  consequences for arrest-based enforcement 199–203
  mobility and organised crime 195–9
  Morecambe Bay human trafficking case study 205–9
  overview 193–5, 208–9
  towards a conceptual model of situational crime prevention 203–5
research and policy agenda 12–13
sex trafficking 59–60, 71–2, 73, 75, 78
situational prevention against unlawful influence from organised crime 151–69
  corruption 163–6
  harassment, threats, violence and malicious damage 157–63
  overview 151–3, 166–9
  unlawful influence 153–7
what is organised crime? 5–7
what is situational crime prevention? 5
organised immigration crime *see* human trafficking
organised mortgage fraud 117–24
  civil-law notaries 124
  estate agents/valuers 123–4
  illegal subletting 120
  overview 117–18
  recruiting people with a regular job 121–2
  straw men as buyers 118–20
organised timber theft 81–91
  the corruption issue 85–6
  fundamentals 84–5
  overview 81–3, 90–1
  significance for organised crime 84
  situational prevention of timber theft 89–90
  specific analysis of the timbering process 87–8
  varieties of corruption 86–7
Östergötland 162

paedophila 65
Paoli, L. 18
Papua New Guinea 83, 84
Parlementare Enquête Commissie Bouwnijverheid 108
Parliamentary Anti-Mafia Commission 133
passports 29, 72, 74, 75
people trafficking *see* human trafficking
personal mortgage fraud 114–17
Peru 84
Peters, E. 18
Philip Morris 50
Phillips, R. 63
plea bargaining 20
PMK (piperonylmethylketone) 21, 30
Poland 42–7, 49, 50, 54, 199
police
  mobile criminality
    consequences for arrest-based enforcement 199–203
    mobility and organised crime 195–8
    Morecambe Bay case study 205–9
    overview 193–5, 208–9
    towards a conceptual model 203–5
  situational prevention against unlawful influence 154–5, 157–8, 161, 163–4, 166
ports 32, 179–80, 181
positive spread effect 160
powers of attorney 119
prepay mobile phones 180, 190
primary criminal act 175, 176–7, 184, 186–7
Primorsk Krai, Russia 84
prisons 134, 142–4, 197
Project Emergo 96, 97
prosecutors 152, 155, 160, 161, 162
prostitution
  administrative approach in Amsterdam 95, 97
  sex trafficking

219

background and context 59–65
implications for situational crime prevention 73–9
mining some data 65–7
overview 58–9
results 67–73
protoscript 134
Prutean, S. 45
public construction industry
Italian organised crime 130–49
case studies 135–44
comparisons between the criminal organisations 145–6
crime script analytical framework 133–5
overview 130–3, 146–8
Pye-Smith, C. 84

racketeering 18, 98
rational choice theory
crime scripts 174
policing mobile criminality 207
sex trafficking 59, 61, 64, 65, 73
what is situational crime prevention? 1–2, 12
Raw, M. 36, 40, 52
Read, T. 203
real estate sector 102, 108, 113, 117–19, 121–3, 125–8
record keeping 10, 13
Red Light District, Amsterdam 93–5, 97, 98, 100, 105, 107
refugees 30
Regional Intelligence 203
research 10–13, 18–20
Reuter, P. 18, 26
RILO (Regional Intelligence Liaison Office for Western Europe) 38
RISICO 147
risk 188
Ritzen, L. 101, 103
Rogaly, B. 197
Rogoff, K. 27
Ross, L. 173
Rotterdam 32, 113
routine activity theory 2, 17, 30, 36, 53, 194, 197
Roy, J. 133
Runkel, W. 45
Russia 38, 83, 84

SAGE First Offender Prostitute Program 78
Salerno–Reggio Calabria motorway 134, 138–42, 146

Santa Maria Capua Vetere prison 134, 142–4
Sarrica, F. 133
Savona, E.U. 131, 148
SBA (Bureau for Screening and Auditing), Amsterdam 94, 96, 100–3, 106, 107
scanners 52, 53
Schank, R.C. 134
Schengen countries 25, 46
Schiphol Airport 24, 25, 27, 31, 32
Schloenhardt, A. 83
Schmeichen, M. 63
Schulz, G. 47
SCP *see* situational crime prevention
SCPOs *see* Serious Crime Prevention Orders
scripts *see* crime scripts
Sea Fisheries 206, 207, 208
security controls 152, 160, 205
self-censorship 151, 155, 156, 158–60, 163
Serio, J. 165
Serious Crime Act (2007) 190
Serious Crime Prevention Orders (SCPOs) 181, 185, 190
Serious Organised Crime Agency (SOCA) 6, 12, 194, 195, 197
Serious Organised Crime and Police Act (2005) (SOCPA) 191
sex industry
administrative approach in Amsterdam 95, 96, 97, 100, 105, 107
sex trafficking 58–62, 64–6, 75, 77
sex tourism 64, 78
sex trafficking 58–79
administrative approach in Amsterdam 94
background and context 59–65
implications for situational crime prevention 73–9
mining some data 65–7
overview 58–9
results 67–73
Shared Hope International 65
Sheller, M. 193
Sheptycki, J. 155, 195
Shively, M. 78
Sicilian Mafia 130–8, 145–6
Siino method 135–8
Singapore 65, 68, 69
situational crime disruption 194, 204–5
situational crime prevention (SCP)
administrative approach in Amsterdam 93–108
Integrity Bureau 104–5
overview 93–6, 107–8
SBA Bureau 100–3

Index

Van Traa Project 96–100
cross-border crime 17–32
  cocaine 23–6
  Ecstasy 20–3
  human smuggling 28–30
  money mules 26–8
  overview 17–18, 30–2
  research into organised crime 18–20
definition xvii, 204–5
how does situational crime prevention see organised crime? 7–10
how should organised crime be studied for situational crime prevention? 10–12
organised crime and crime scripts 172–90
  common components of the crime process 179–84
  constituent parts of the organised crime script 175–7
  crime scripts and organised crime 173–5
  discussion 185–90
  exploring the utility 177–9
  mapping the crime script 184–5
  overview 172–3
policing mobile criminality 193–209
  consequences for arrest-based enforcement 199–203
  mobility and organised crime 195–9
  Morecambe Bay human trafficking case study 205–9
  overview 193–5, 208–9
  towards a conceptual model of situational crime prevention 203–5
research and policy agenda 12–13
sex trafficking 59, 62, 64, 73–9
techniques 3–4
unlawful influence from organised crime 151–69
  corruption 163–6
  harassment, threats, violence and malicious damage 157–63
  overview 151–3, 166–9
  unlawful influence 153–7
what is situational crime prevention? 1–5
Skeldon, R. 63
smart shops 94
Smits, E.M. 23
smuggling
  contraband cigarettes 35, 36, 38, 41–8, 51–4
  cross-border crime 18, 20, 21, 28–30, 31
  human smuggling 20, 28–30, 31, 61–4, 70
  sex trafficking 61–4, 70

unlawful influence 164, 165
sniffer dogs 52, 53
SOCA *see* Serious Organised Crime Agency
Soudijn, M.R.J. 20, 21, 28
'Soviet fallacy' 32
Special Branch 205
Staring, R.H.J.M. 20
Stelfox, P. 8, 200
Steyer, C.-D. 45, 46
stolen vehicles trafficking 8–11, 60, 183, 198
'straw men' 117, 118–20, 121, 122, 124
Suifenke, China 84
Suriname 32
surveillance 19, 20, 45–50, 53, 161
Sweden
  corruption 163–6
  harassment, threats, violence and malicious damage 157–63
  unlawful influence from organised crime 151–7
Swedish National Council for Crime Prevention (bra) *see* Brottsförebyggande radet

Taiwan 69, 72–3, 75, 82
taxes
  contraband cigarettes 36, 38, 43, 44, 46, 50, 51
  cross-border crime 18
  mortgage fraud 111, 112
techniques of situational crime prevention
  administrative approach in Amsterdam 95, 98–100, 103, 107
  contraband cigarettes 37
  unlawful influence 159–63, 165–8
  what is situational crime prevention? 2–4
telephones 180, 189, 190, 202
tendering 100, 101
terrorism 5, 17, 18, 205
Thailand 72
threats 151–5, 157–63, 166, 167, 183
Tilley, N. 39, 41, 203, 204
timber theft *see* organised timber theft
TIR (Transport International Routier) 51
tobacco industry 50
Tonnie 105
trafficking *see* drugs; human trafficking; sex trafficking
Transcrime 147
transit crime 18
transnational crime 193, 195, 196, 198–203
Transparency International 85
Tremblay, P. 174
trust 188

221

Turkey 67, 68, 70, 71, 74, 76

United Nations 61–2, 195
United Nations Convention on Transnational Organised Crime 131, 194
United Nations Office on Drugs and Crime (UNODC) 21, 24, 25
unlawful influence from organised crime 151–69
   corruption 163–6
   harassment, threats, violence and malicious damage 157–63
   overview 151–3, 166–9
   unlawful influence 153–7
UNODC *see* United Nations Office on Drugs and Crime
unregistered vehicles 182–3, 189
Urry, J. 193, 196, 198
Utrecht 113

Valier, C. 197
van de Bunt, H.
   administrative approach in Amsterdam 108
   cross-border crime 19, 20, 29
   mortgage fraud 124, 129
   sex trafficking 75
   what is situational crime prevention? 5
van den Heuvel, G. 105, 109
Vander Beken, T. 38, 53
van der Boom, J. 30
Vandergert, P. 84
van der Hoek, M.P. 43
van der Leun, J.P. 30
van der Schoot, C.
   administrative approach in Amsterdam 95, 96, 108
   cross-border crime 20, 29
   sex trafficking 75, 77
   what is situational crime prevention? 5
van der Wielen, L. 101, 108
van de Voort, M. 52
van Dijck, M. 38
Van Dijk, J. 131
van Duyne, P.C. 6, 52
van Gestel, B. 112, 129
Van Traa Project, Amsterdam 93–5, 96–100, 103, 106–9

vehicle licensing 89, 182–3, 189, 190
vehicle theft
   crime scripts 174, 183
   policing mobile criminality 198, 199, 202
   sex trafficking 60
   what is situational crime prevention? 5, 8–11
Venezuela 32
Verhovek, S.H. 158
vice crimes 60, 97, 98
victims of crime
   policing mobile criminality 197
   sex trafficking 60–3, 69–71
   unlawful influence from organised crime 151, 153–6, 158–61, 163, 167
Vietnam/Vietnamese criminals 42, 46, 47, 48, 82
violence 151, 153–7, 158–63, 166–8, 183
visas 28, 29, 30, 31, 72, 74
von Lampe, K. 36, 37, 39, 41, 47, 48, 53

Ward, T. 82
Waring, E.J. 18
Wästerfors, D. 159
Webb, B. 190
welfare state 28, 29, 30
West Africa 199
Weston, S. 158
whistle-blowers 165
White, R. 82
'white van trade' 44
Wierup, L. 153
Wilson, J.Q. 107
wiretapping 19, 20
witnesses 151, 153–6, 158–63, 167
Witt, A. 45
WODC (Research and Documentation Centre of the Ministry of Justice, Netherlands) 19, 20
Woodiwiss, M. 197
World Bank 24, 25, 81, 90
Worsley, R. 196
Wright, A. 195

Yab Yum 108

Zhang, S.X. 28, 63